CW00536140

FREEDOM
IN THE AIR

FREEDOM IN THE AIR

A Czech Flyer and his Aircrew Dog

by

Hamish Ross

Pen & Sword
AVIATION

First published in 2007 and reprinted in this format in 2015 by
PEN & SWORD AVIATION
An imprint of
Pen & Sword Books Ltd
47 Church Street
Barnsley, South Yorkshire
S70 2AS

ISBN 978 1 47383 436 1

A CIP catalogue record for this book is
available from the British Library

Typeset in Palatino by
Phoenix Typesetting, Auldgirth, Dumfriesshire

Printed and bound in England
By CPI Group (UK) Ltd, Croydon, CR0 4YY

Pen & Sword Books Ltd incorporates the Imprints of Aviation, Atlas,
Family History, Fiction, Maritime, Military, Discovery, Politics, History,
Archaeology, Select, Wharncliffe Local History, Wharncliffe True Crime,
Military Classics, Wharncliffe Transport, Leo Cooper, The Praetorian Press,
Remember When, Seaforth Publishing and Frontline Publishing

For a complete list of Pen & Sword titles please contact
PEN & SWORD BOOKS LIMITED
47 Church Street, Barnsley, South Yorkshire, S70 2AS, England
E-mail: enquiries@pen-and-sword.co.uk
Website: www.pen-and-sword.co.uk

Contents

Foreword by Jaroslav Beránek,
Military History Institute, Prague   vii
Acknowledgements   x

PART I   **1**
Master Aircrew   3
Young Democracy   9
Another Flag   23

PART II   **33**
Rebirth of an Air Force   35
Night Bombing   46
Training School   66
Bridge of Sand   78

PART III   **89**
Laurels and Ashes   91
Path into Exile   112
Antis DM   132
The Road Not Taken   148

PART IV   **159**
A Memoir   161
Gentleman of the Dusk   182
Distant Landfall   198

Notes   206
Bibliography   217
Index   221

Foreword

During WWII more than three and a half thousand Czechoslovak airmen served with the RAF. More than five hundred were killed. Each of them could make an excellent subject for a novel.

The life of Václav Robert Bozděch, that Hamish Ross depicts in his book, is in many ways similar to that of most of his comrades.

After the Munich Agreement escape to Poland and then to France, after her fall another escape, to Britain, to a camp in Cholmondeley. Here, in the grounds of Cholmondeley Park on 7th July 1940 the Czechoslovak Forces in Britain were formed.

Not only in Cholmondeley but also in many other parts of Cheshire local people still remember the cheerful and brave 'boys'.

"The memory of those Czech and Slovak soldiers and airmen has lived with us all the time. Although the number of the contemporaries is now rapidly declining, the heart-felt attitude towards the memory and their country has survived and the feeling is being shared by the second and even the third generation," says Robert Robertson, a member of the Parish Council. "People of Cholmondeley were doing for us all they could. Nobody could complain about us either. We would also do for them all we could," adds František Kaplan from the Association of Czechoslovak Legionaries, Cholmondeley Branch.

Czechoslovak airmen as well as soldiers of the Czechoslovak Army fighting in France, who managed to leave after her fall, were stationed at Cholmondeley. All together there were 3,500 of them. They formed the core of future Czechoslovak squadrons serving in the RAF as well as the Czechoslovak Brigade.

During the following war years 3,563 Czechs and Slovaks served with 4 Czechoslovak squadrons, which were an integral part of the RAF and other mixed ones as well. A further 5,623 soldiers served in the Czechoslovak Brigade.

Czechoslovak airmen represented, after the Commonwealth nations, the second largest national contribution (after the Poles) to the Allied Forces during the Battle of Britain. There were 88 Czechoslovak pilots who took part in the Battle and 8 of them lost their lives.

Only a few people realise that the Ace of Aces of the Battle of Britain was a Czech pilot. His name was Sgt Josef František. During a short period of only six weeks he managed to shoot down 17 enemy aircraft.

To some extent the words written in the pamphlet 'There's Freedom in the Air' published during the war apply also to Václav Bozděch.

"In peace we talk of war; in the middle of war we begin to talk of peace. The plans for peace are often grandiose, vague and illusory. But in the presence of thousands of young foreign airmen in Great Britain we have a fact from which a new international understanding, idealistic yet free from antipathetic ideologies, might grow to benefit the world. These men have lived in Britain and, while fighting for their own countries, have fought for Britain and the ideals, which will live while Britain lives.

We on our side must never forget this. (. . .) They, too, on their side, will never forget. Living in Britain, these men have seen our life. They have been into British homes, have become familiar with British customs. They have married British girls. Already some of them have families. The roots of Central Europe reach out and take new life in the English Midlands, in Edinburgh and London, in the mountains of Scotland and Wales, in the blitzed cities."

After Cholmondeley, Bozděch joined the RAF. Never ending flights with No. 311 Czechoslovak Bomber Squadron followed. After the end of the war in Europe, he returned to the liberated homeland. For Václav Bozděch though, the hard won peace was very short lived. In February 1948 came the communist coup in Czechoslovakia and yet again a dramatic escape across the borders and eventually he returned to Britain, which had become his second homeland.

The book 'Freedom in the Air: A Czech Flyer and his Aircrew Dog' reveals also another extraordinary story – that of Bozděch's faithful four-legged friend, the Alsatian with the name of Antis. This brave flying partner, who was already celebrated during the war and written about in the British Press, saved the life of Bozděch during their escape from Czechoslovakia. In 1949 his life-long bravery was recognised and as the first 'non-British' dog he was awarded the PDSA Dickin Medal.

Unlike many other similar publications Hamish Ross does not cover only the war years of Václav Bozděch. He follows his life through to the end. And in the last chapter he even briefly explains the events in Czechoslovakia and the Czech Republic after the fall of communism in November 1989.

At the very end of his book Hamish Ross describes the first meeting of Bozděch's son Jan, who had to remain in Czechoslovakia after 1948, and his 'English' half-sister Magdalena, which took place as late as in 2004! One would not invent a better example of the absurdity of the 20th century.

Ross's book is also valuable for its historical excursions, which put events into their rightful context. I have to mention as well his painstaking work with numerous archive materials and his use of interviews with the few living of Bozděch's contemporaries.

There are already many books about Czechoslovak airmen serving with the RAF published in Czech and even in English. One may say why write yet another one, since there is no more to be said. But thinking on these lines would be a great mistake.

Winston Churchill, the grandson of the famous British Prime Minister, a few years ago told me how his grandfather stressed the importance of studying history. "Only when you know where you are coming from may you have the chance to know where you are going to." In other words, a nation which is not aware of its history has no future.

I believe that this book by Hamish Ross is going to be yet another piece of the mosaic not only of the history, but also of the future of both our nations.

Jaroslav Beránek
Military History Institute, Prague

Prague, May 2006

Acknowledgements

T his work would not have been feasible without the co-operation of Maureen Bozděch who gave me access to her husband's papers, tapes and manuscript. I am most appreciative of her support and her patience with my frequent questions. Arnošt Polak, Secretary of the Free Czechoslovak Air Force Association, was a key link throughout the research with respondents both in the UK and the Czech Republic and I gratefully acknowledge his help. I am also indebted to Jaroslav Beránek of the Military History Institute in Prague for writing the Foreword to this book.

Interviews played a part in the research and my thanks are extended to: Magdalena Jarvis, Robert Bozděch, Jan Bozděch, Jiři Malik, Bunty Fialka, Iveta Irvingová, Arnošt Polak, Pamela Schutzmann and Tom Oddie for giving me their time and permission to use copyright material. I also wish to thank Pavel Vančata for his interest and excellent help; and Zdeněk Hurt, author of *Czechs in the RAF*, for his willingness to share information from his own research.

I would like to thank Stephanie Howell, Local Studies Department Cardiff Central Library; Edwina Burridge, Reference Librarian Inverness Library and her colleague Sue Skelton; Penny Ritchie Calder, Head of Exhibitions, and Emma Crocker, Curator Photographic Archive Imperial War Museum; Abbey Fox for research in the USA; and staff of the Air Historical Branch (RAF). I also want to include my thanks to Donnie Macleod for recollections of No. 311 Squadron in Tain, Richard Beith for written material and Alan Brown for early guidance; and I want to record my thanks to Willie McKechnie and his colleagues at the Photographic Unit of the University of Glasgow, and to Neil Planner who transferred 1950s' ¼ inch tapes to cassette.

I specially want to thank Ilona Klemm, Department of Slavonic

Studies at the University of Glasgow for translations from the Czech.

Milan Kundera kindly gave his permission to quote from his novels *Life is Elsewhere*, published by Faber and Faber, and *The Book of Laughter and Forgetting*, published by Knopf Inc. Extracts from the following works appear by permission of the publishers: *Fair Stood the Wind for France* by H. E. Bates, Longman, 1971; Edwin Muir's Collected Poems, Faber and Faber, and Oxford University Press, 1979; Antoine de Saint-Exupéry's *Flight to Arras*, Penguin, 1995; Alistair Cooke's *Letter from America 1946-2004*, Penguin, 2004.

Part I

CHAPTER ONE

Master Aircrew

As flies to wanton boys, are we to the gods;
They kill us for their sport.

William Shakespeare, *King Lear*

Newspapers in Britain, during the Second World War, carried photographs of a Czech airman standing beside his handsome Alsatian dog, called Antis. However, it was the dog that was the subject of the accompanying articles; for equipped with a specially adapted oxygen mask, he accompanied his master on operational sorties over enemy territory with No. 311 (Czechoslovak) Squadron of Bomber Command. The newspaper coverage was a distraction from disappointing war news, and it appealed to the public. The phrase 'dog of war' often appeared in the headline; the dog's prowess was written about in magazines and was reported by the BBC; and the war dog tag remained over the decades; it was even repeated when the Alsatian's Dickin Medal, the so-called 'Animal VC', was auctioned by Sotheby's almost half a century later. But little was written about the airman; indeed in recent time, more was known about him in the Czech Republic than in the UK, although he spent the greater part of his life in Britain, and served for eighteen years in the RAF. In part, it was his own doing: he sought anonymity in the UK because of the postwar political situation in Central Europe, where his family still lived. Yet Darryl F. Zanuck, the head of Production at Twentieth Century

Fox, wanted to make a film about the airman and Antis, and sent representatives to meet him at RAF Lyneham,[1] then went himself to meet him to discuss the project. It was not until after the fall of communism that the story of Václav Robert Bozděch could be researched and told.

That story certainly encompasses the extraordinarily strong bonding between the airman and his dog. With the passage of time, this episode in Bozděch's life seems all the more incredible, yet it is true: a dog of great loyalty, courage and intelligence, lying along-side his master's feet in the gun turret of a Wellington bomber, on operation after operation during the bombing campaign of 1941, sensing and sharing the men's fear of the flak and the night fighters; he was wounded twice by enemy fire, and ultimately, in recognition of his bravery, he had the ribbon of the Dickin Medal (the 'Animal VC') attached to his collar by Field Marshall Wavell. Of course, the dog's operational sorties were completely at variance with RAF regulations. But then the circumstances were unique. It all happened at a time when Britain's position was still precarious; the United States had not yet entered the war; and Bomber Command was the only force capable of hitting the enemy heart-land. It was a time too when aircrews had strong superstitions about what brought good luck in a campaign where losses were high; and then there was the verve and panache of the Czech crew, highly motivated men, their country already under the jackboot, accepting the Alsatian as one of the combat team.

However, the story has deeper levels. It spans the final years of the Austro-Hungarian Empire to the fall of communism, and arises out of the history and politics of Central Europe in the 1930s and 1940s; it is set in the context of the airmen and their belief in what they were fighting for, and the grave injustice that they subsequently suffered at the hands of a Stalinist regime for having served their country in the west; and it does not reach resolution until the end of the twentieth century. Bozděch's story tells of one man's response to the powerful external forces that can break the individual; it tells of resisting, and of the acceptance of loss; it is redolent of loyalty and endurance, for which his canine comrade-in-arms is a powerful symbol.

Like other Czechoslovak career servicemen who fled their country in 1939 in the hope of taking up arms to free it, after it fell under Nazi rule, Bozděch had first to sign the five-year contract of the French Foreign Legion and was transported to the Middle East.

Then when war was declared, he transferred to the French Air Force and served with it during 1939/40; and it was during this period that he acquired the dog that would be his companion for thirteen years. After the fall of France, he made his way to England, breached Britain's strict quarantine laws by smuggling the dog ashore, and rejoined the Czechoslovak Air Force, which was incorporated into the RAF. He served for five years in Fighter, Bomber, Training and Coastal Commands, and was decorated with the Czechoslovak Medal of Valour and the War Cross.

Political manoeuvring among the Allies over the liberation of the occupied territories as the war moved into its final stages foreshadowed the uneasy restoration of democracy in the homeland: the West's disinclination to trespass into the Soviet sphere of influence, as the Red Army and General Patton's army both converged on the country's borders during the Prague Uprising, turned out to be a strategic error.

At the end of the war, after numerous delays, the Czechoslovak Squadrons made a triumphant return to Prague, but found that their defence of democracy had also come at a high price for their families during the Occupation, if the Gestapo discovered that relatives were serving with the Allies. Some learned that their family had perished in the death camps. In Bozděch's case, his mother had been sent to an internment camp in Moravia.[2] She had survived but her health was seriously impaired.

He became a staff captain in the Air Force, working in the Defence Ministry; and he was friendly with the country's Foreign Minister Jan Masaryk, who was godfather to his son. He wrote several books and a radio script about the air force in the Second World War; and to his writing he brought a depth of experience, but he also had support from well-placed sources. He was given permission for one book to quote from the transcripts of speeches by President Beneš,[3] and in another he was allowed to reproduce letters from the wife of the President.[4] Two weeks after the communist coup in 1948, the body of Jan Masaryk was found amid suspicious circumstances in the courtyard of the Ministry. Bozděch later wrote that the two had met three days before Masaryk's death, and Masaryk had told him that he knew the airman was on a purge list.[5] No public inquiry into Masaryk's death took place; it was put out that it was suicide. Bozděch conferred with his commanding officer[6] and others he trusted; various pairing options for escape were considered, before he made his attempt. It was a bold attempt, carried out from the Defence Ministry on a working day; he had to leave his wife and infant son, but he took Antis with him on the perilous border crossing.

Two months followed in refugee camps in West Germany before he was able to rejoin the RAF; and he went from staff captain to aircraftsman in one move, for while the British Air Ministry waived nationality regulations to allow former members of the Czecho-slovak squadrons back into the service, its policy was to put them at the lowest rank to begin with. Bozděch's next step was back into aircrew at an Advanced Air Training School. Antis became a celebrity with the award of the Dickin Medal. The ceremony appeared on newsreels and in the press, but Bozděch kept well out of the limelight. Officialdom now looked indulgently on that irregular crewing of a Wellington bomber in No. 311 Squadron all those years before: Antis became squadron mascot, and Bozděch was not posted overseas during the remaining years he had the dog. They made their last flight together, on a troop dropping exercise; it was a nostalgic short trip in a Dakota over East Wretham, the airfield from which No. 311 Squadron had flown when it was in Bomber Command. Aged almost fourteen years, all but three of which were spent on air force stations, Antis died, and was buried in the Animal Cemetery at Ilford.

Bozděch had already been arraigned in his absence by the High Military Prosecutor in Prague for treason, conspiring against the state and desertion.[7] The regime would not allow the families of émigrés to be reunited; and the partner remaining in the homeland was pressured to petition for divorce. Now flying with Transport Command, Bozděch found ways of circumventing the regime's practice of intercepting incoming mail from marked émigrés like himself by writing under assumed names from third world countries.

While he was stationed at RAF Lyneham, in between flying on Transport Command's world routes, and serving in the Suez campaign, he devoted his free time and his energies to writing the manuscript of a book on his life with his dog. The outcome was impressive: the film rights of his story were bought by Twentieth Century Fox, and he had a meeting with Darryl F. Zanuck who was going to produce a film version. In 1962, Bozděch left the RAF. Civilian life was spent quietly with his second family in Devon; he became a successful small entrepreneur; and he carried out research into his old wartime squadron. He was never allowed a visa to return to his homeland, even although he appealed to the Czechoslovak Ambassador in London.[8] He died of cancer in 1980.

However, the story does not end with his death. Resolution of its elements could only come about after the fall of communism; and with the restoration of democracy, came restitution for those who had suffered at the hands of the regime, or had fled to avoid being persecuted. Posthumously Bozděch was advanced to the rank of colonel in the Czechoslovak Air Force; two of his books, banned for decades, were republished. Following a forensic expert's investigation into the death of Foreign Minister Jan Masaryk in the courtyard of the Ministry all those years earlier, the Czech police opened the case, then formally concluded that Masaryk had indeed been murdered. Bozděch's families in the UK and the Czech Republic finally met. And as a result, his story can now be told.

A range of sources exists, both in the Czech Republic and the United Kingdom. The Military Archive in Prague is particularly useful because it tracks an airman's career during the pre-war years, wartime (for the Czechoslovak Squadrons remained in their own country's air force at the same time as they were part of the RAF) and the postwar period. Because he was the subject of security investigation, the Archive of the Ministry of Interior of the Czech Republic contains very detailed records on Bozděch. In the United Kingdom there are the RAF operational record books for No. 311 (Czechoslovak) Squadron, which are contained in the National Archives; and information has also been obtained from the Air Historical Branch of the RAF, the Royal Air Force Personnel Management Agency and the Free Czechoslovak Air Force Association. In addition, the research is supported with transcripts of interviews with a number of Bozděch's contemporaries, as well as his family in the UK, and in the Czech Republic.

Maureen Bozděch has given access to her late husband's manuscript, papers and tapes; and these offer the deepest insights into the man. His papers show that he was penetrating in discernment and tenacious in arguing about principle. He was both a maverick and yet he was service-minded. The rank that he held for some time in the mid 1950s was appositely titled Master Aircrew: he was a very capable individual. In some respects he was typically Czech: undemonstrative, self-effacing, but he would survive and he could adapt to whatever situation he found himself in – whether it was as a staff officer in the corridors of power in the Defence Ministry in Prague, or in the NCOs' mess of a Royal Air Force station. But he was a troubled man too, ruminating silently over the suffering he had brought to his family, both during the war and under the communist regime.

Translations from the Czech of extracts from his book *Gentlemen of the Dusk* add a dimension to the war years. His English language manuscript, which he titled *Antis VC*, adds texture to the research: it supplements the operational record books of No. 311 Squadron; it deals with areas not covered by official documentation; and while Bozděch concealed more than he revealed in the section on his escape from Prague, he developed the frontier crossing by night in April into a taut and well structured account. Above all, both the manuscript and the tapes reveal the strength of his attachment to Antis.

He would not have seen himself in a heroic mould; but then he was a representative of a cohort of his compatriots, few of whom would have considered themselves in that mould. For they were not adventurers; they fought for freedom, and later suffered for it, through persecution or exile. So Bozděch's story is not bound by time or place; its elements: defending ideals, the primacy of survival, the enforced separation of families, the role of Antis in his life – a variation on that ancient association between man and dog – give rise to themes that are timeless.

CHAPTER TWO

Young Democracy

Bliss was it in that dawn to be alive,
But to be young was very heaven!
William Wordsworth, *The Prelude* (1850)

At the time Václav Bozděch was born in western Bohemia in 1912, his parents were subjects of Emperor Franz Joseph, dynastic head of the Austro-Hungarian Empire; but by the time he was in his first year of primary school, they were citizens of the democratic Republic of Czechoslovakia, under the leadership of its liberator-president Tomaš Masaryk.

The Czech lands of Bohemia, Moravia and Silesia had been part of the amorphous Austro-Hungarian Empire for centuries, and German took ascendancy over the Czech language. But the nineteenth century saw a remarkable resurgence of Czech culture, to such an extent indeed, that by the first decade of the twentieth century the Czech lands amounted to a nation without a state.[1] From those lands there emerged a number of potential political leaders – not from an existing ruling class, but intellectuals born of peasant stock – like Professor Tomaš Masaryk, who, in 1900 had helped found the Czech People's Party, and Dr Edvard Beneš, who both played key roles in bringing the state into being. The Great War was the catalyst that brought about the political and military activity on the part of Czechs and Slovaks, which secured their statehood.

When that war came Masaryk left Prague and based himself in

London, and Beneš went to Paris; for if statehood were to be re-established to their people, it would have to be as a result of the overthrow of the empire of which they were a part, and so alliances had to be sought with the Allies. Throughout the war years these two worked tirelessly to influence opinion among the Allies. Masaryk impressed as a philosopher-statesman; Beneš was an insightful negotiator; and both of them were internationally minded. Masaryk travelled to Britain, the United States and Russia; Beneš focused on the European capitals.

However, they did not come empty-handed to the negotiating table: Czech and Slovak volunteers in the Allied countries were prepared to be mobilised; in some cases entire Czech regiments of the Austrian-Hungarian armies turned themselves over to the Allied forces, offering to fight alongside them. Tenaciously, Masaryk, Beneš and others negotiated for the establishment of units of their countrymen within the Allied armies; and they succeeded. Units were created in Russia, France and Italy. The Czech Legions, as they became called, were led by their own officers and fought in Russia and on the Western Front. They gained a lot of respect for their discipline and spirit in the field.[2] Beneš recalled a visit he paid his troops on the Italian front in 1918. He had been taken through a narrow mountain defile and into a broad cavity, above which, as though in an amphitheatre, 'were assembled about 2,000 of our troops in a deluge of flags and waving hats. There was a long outburst of cheering, and I was then deeply moved as they intoned the strains of our national hymn, accompanied by the regimental band.'[3]

Throughout the war years, the two components of political activity and military action helped secure recognition for Czecho-slovakia as a belligerent government on the side of the Allies, as the wording of the United States document of 2 July 1918, recognising the legitimacy of the Czechoslovak National Council makes plain.

The Czechoslovak peoples having taken up arms against the German and Austro-Hungarian Empires, and having placed in the field organised armies, which are waging war against these Empires under officers of their own nationality and in accordance with the rule and practices of civilised nations, Czechoslovaks having in the prosecution of their independence in the present war confided the supreme political authority to the Czechoslovak National Council, the

Government of the United States recognises that a state of belligerency exists between the Czechoslovaks thus organised and the German and Austrian-Hungarian Empires.[4]

Masaryk, in Washington on 18 October 1918, made the historic declaration of Czechoslovak independence, spelling out the nature of its governance.

The Czechoslovak State will be a republic. In a continuous effort for progress it will guarantee full freedom of conscience, religion, science, literature and art, speech, press, assembly and of petition. The church will be separated from the state. Our democracy will be based on an equal right to vote; women will be politically, socially and culturally made equal with men. The rights of minorities will be secured by proportionate representation, national minorities will enjoy the same rights ... privileges of the nobility will be abolished.[5]

France, Britain and the United States granted formal recognition; and on 28 October 1918, the new state of Czechoslovakia was legally established. It was to be the easternmost democracy in Europe – and its constitution was influenced by those of France and the United States.

Although much of the planning for statehood took place in council chambers abroad, the aims were not just the expression of an elite group of academics on remote Elysian Fields; they had resonance for the social and democratic feelings of peasant, worker and intellectual in the Czech lands. For most it was a time to walk tall.

Childhood and youth were a happy time for Bozděch. The family were working people from Soběkury in Přeštice, western Bohemia. There was mining in the area, and that was where his father worked. But the surrounding countryside was rich in flora and fauna. Bozděch was the only son; he had two older sisters, Maria and Pavla. There had been a third sister, Anna, but she had died about the age of seven in a childhood mishap: playing a game of make-believe, she had accidentally drunk some poisonous substance she found in an outhouse. Bozděch spent five years at the local primary school at Soběkury, then three years at the Merklin vocational school.

Folk tradition and wood lore were the dominant educators in his early years though. From his elders Bozděch heard the tales of Bohemia, and he was initiated into the mysteries of identifying woodland plants with culinary or medicinal properties. He learned how to recognise edible fungus (a skill he never lost, as will be seen later), and he became proficient in tracking animal spoors. Superimposed on this domain of knowledge and skills were school and vocational training. Much of Czechoslovakia's industry in the 1920s was located in Bohemia and Moravia; a tradition had developed – much as it had in Germany – that vocational training was the route to advancement, so it was quite natural that, at the age of fourteen Bozděch should begin a three-year course at technical college in Pilsen.[6] Those three strands: story telling, affinity with nature, and technology training came together in his adult life, through his relationship with his dog, his flair as an author and the technical nature of his career.

Thanks to the influence of the Sokol movement that began in the later part of the nineteenth century, a culture promoting physical fitness had grown and spread throughout the country. At base it encouraged individual prowess, and inculcated a sense of self-respect. Its disciplined methods and large group displays gave it a semi-military air; and although the movement was not overtly political, from an early stage it had become associated with Czech nationalism, and its displays became part of popular culture. No able-bodied boy could remain indifferent to its influence; so Bozděch became interested in athletics, and he played handball for the Soběkury club.[7] He also had a musical bent: his favourite instrument was the accordion.

As a teenager then, Bozděch had a well-balanced range of interests. He was also lucky, at the time he trained; for students at technical college in the late twenties were comparatively sheltered from the impact of the world-wide economic crisis. His luck continued after that: when he finished his course, which was the same year as the Wall Street crash, he began work as a locksmith. But although life moved along smoothly for many of his generation in this new democracy, the geo-political plates of Europe were beginning to tremble again.

Centuries of subordination to an imperial power had made the Czech and Slovak collective psyche super-sensitive to the dangers of foreign domination. There was less possibility of the Habsburg Empire reappearing in mutated form, but there was a danger of a resurgent Germany; hence defence treaties had to be formed. Since the end of the nineteenth century, Czechs had looked to France and Russia as sources of support, but after the Bolshevik revolution, the Soviet Union's stance on Czechoslovakia turned out to be less than cordial. The Soviet Union had not accepted the Versailles Treaty; and as late as 1929 the Communist Party in the Soviet Union and the Third International adopted a hostile line on an autonomous state for Czechs and Slovaks, describing it as a bourgeois creation.[8] So Czechoslovakia, Europe's most easterly democracy, negotiated an alliance with France. This would provide a bulwark from a democracy in the west, which also shared a border with Germany.

The country also required its own formidable defensive capability; and two strong military arms for ground and air warfare were built up. These were supported by an advanced industrial base and high quality technology. The country already had a cadre of experienced officers and men who had served in the Czech Legions, onto which was grafted a career military; in addition, a two-year period of conscription for men was introduced.

A sense of urgency came into political and military thinking after January 1933, when Adolf Hitler became Chancellor of Germany, and two months later had supreme power in his hands. He rejected the Versailles agreement, and adopted a pan-German policy. Dr Edvard Beneš, Czechoslovakia's Foreign Minister, in an interview that same year, predicted that Hitler wanted to seize Austria and Czechoslovakia, occupy Danzig and crush Poland. Beneš's approach was to work within the collective framework of the League of Nations, to which, he argued, the Soviet Union should be admitted.[9] The rise of Nazism also brought about a change in the Soviet Union's attitude towards Czechoslovakia. In 1935, Beneš met Joseph Stalin, and a defence treaty was signed. In the event of Czechoslovakia being attacked, the Soviet Union would support it militarily. However, the terms of the treaty with the Soviet Union were contingent on France first honouring its treaty obligation by coming to the aid of Czechoslovakia.

At head of state level there were changes within the country. President Masaryk was re-elected overwhelmingly at each presidential election; and at the age of eighty-five, he resigned from office, to be succeeded by Dr Beneš. In political stature and intellectual gravitas, Masaryk could be said to represent Plato's philosopher-king. He had come from a modest background; when he left school, he trained as a locksmith; and in time his abilities were recognised. He duly became a reader in philosophy and then a professor; and he was famous for a courageous stand he took against anti-Semitism. When the time came during the Great War, he was the natural choice as a leader. He had been instrumental in re-establishing statehood, and he led it until 1935. Then he went into modest retirement in the countryside; and he died two years later.

Generally, young men did not look on two years of compulsory military service as an imposition: there was not exactly a pioneering spirit abroad, but their state had re-emerged and they were making their contribution to its security. Bozděch's turn came in October 1934[10], when he was called up. At this stage, he had no intention of making a career in the military; he was doing his stint, and then he would have to serve for a period in the reserve forces. After basic training, he became an aircraft mechanic in the air force. When his two years were up, he was demobilised, placed in the reserves, and he went to work for the Škoda company.

However, the following months were a time for self-assessment: he had served in the branch of the armed forces which was advanced in technology; he had ability, and in the service he had found common interests with a wide range of contemporaries; now he worked in an enterprise that certainly had training opportunities and the structures for career advancement; but he questioned whether industry had the scope for his ambitions. Gradually, he came to the decision that he would make a career in the air force. On 25 October 1937[11] he rejoined the service, and began a process that would continue for more than two decades of training and retraining. He changed trades and trained as an air gunner. The air force had six regional Air Regiments,[12] and when he completed his training, Bozděch flew as an air gunner in the twin-engine heavy bombers, the Bloch MB-200, of the T. G. Masaryk 1st Air Regiment, which was based outside Prague. He was promoted to sergeant and he became a gunnery instructor.

The aspirations and motives of individual servicemen are not often set on the same plane as the great affairs of state, but in the case of Czechoslovakia, in the late thirties and into the forties, they became entwined to such an extent that it is necessary to look briefly at the political developments.

France was the country's primary ally and its constitution was partly modelled on it. In December 1937, the French Foreign Minister, Yvon Delbos, received a warm welcome in Prague at the start of an official visit. He made a trip especially into the country to lay a wreath on the grave of Tomaš Masaryk; and in a speech in

Prague, Delbos expatiated on the nature of the special affinity between France and Czechoslovakia.

> Fraternity is a word which is often used in after-dinner toasts; and it sometimes means little. But in the case of France and Czechoslovakia it defines perfectly their relations. While casting aside every idea of domination, I may say that Czechoslovakia is like an extension of France. We are united by so many ties, we feel things in such a similar way, and our regimes are so similar that a Frenchman in Czechoslovakia feels as though he were in France, and a Czechoslovak in France feels as though he were in Czechoslovakia.[13]

High sentiments! But within less than a year of their expression Czechoslovakia was dismembered, while its fraternal ally stayed supine.

Betrayal and desertion came about in a series of moves. Hitler, in 1937, instructed his generals to draw up plans to smash Czechoslovakia. His first move was Anschluss with Austria; and in March 1938 his troops marched in while France and Britain made no response. Now Czechoslovakia was suddenly vulnerable. But a German invasion of Czechoslovakia had to be paced to take into account the changed situation, as one of Hitler's generals, General Jodl wrote in his diary.

> After the annexation of Austria the Fuehrer mentions that there is no hurry to solve the Czech question, because Austria has to be digested first. Nevertheless, preparations . . . will have to be newly prepared on the basis of the changed strategic position because of the annexation of Austria.[14]

However, he did not have to smash Czechoslovakia: he was handed it on a plate.

Britain had no treaty with Czechoslovakia whereas France had; France had also taken the lead role in European affairs throughout the thirties, while Britain concerned itself with the affairs of its empire; but from the early summer of 1938, Britain took the initiative in dealing with the 'Czech question'.

What became the Czech question resulted from an internal issue. The German-speaking communities of Bohemia and Moravia were much aggrieved by the settlement establishing Czechoslovakia.

Their minority rights were safeguarded within the constitution, but it was a situation waiting to be exploited by a demagogue. Under the leadership of Conrad Henlein, a German party became restyled the German Sudeten Party and emerged as the voice of the ethnic minority. Their claims, orchestrated from Berlin, demanded autonomy within Czechoslovakia – a fascist enclave within a democracy – and were more than matched by Hitler's insistence that he would protect the German-speaking population of that country. The logic of Hitler's position was scarcely analysed in the west – although early on a French Deputy said that it was, 'as if France suddenly claimed a right to exercise control over the French Canadians'.[15]

Beneš and his government could and did yield to an extent; but there was a limit for any sovereign state, beyond which they could not go. Conrad Henlein met Hitler after the annexation of Austria, and he then raised the demands even higher. On 20 May, following rumours that Germany was massing troops on its border with Czechoslovakia, President Beneš ordered a partial mobilisation of his forces.

Within hours partial mobilisation had been achieved. It was a clear warning: Czechoslovakia was prepared to defend its freedom. Its air force had been built up by 1938, and the country's forces were 'at least as efficient and as well-equipped, man for man, as the Germans'.[16] Considerations of scale were another matter altogether. Alone it could not withstand for long the might of the Third Reich – but it did not expect to have to do so: it had its primary pact with France; and if France first came to its aid, the Soviet Union was obliged to fulfil its treaty obligations. Moreover, if France went to war with Germany, how would Britain react?

Britain's Ambassador to Germany, Sir Nevile Henderson, recalling his meeting on 21 May with the German Foreign Minister, Von Ribbentrop, emphasised that his Government was putting pressure on President Beneš to come to an accommodation with Henlein. Then, encapsulating into appropriate diplomatic register the firm line that his Government might (or might not) take:

I warned His Excellency that France had definite obligations to Czechoslovakia, and that, if these had to be fulfilled, His Majesty's Government could not guarantee that they would not be forced by events to become themselves involved.[17]

The last thing the British Prime Minister, Neville Chamberlain wanted, however, was to go to war in support of France defending Czechoslovakia, and he exerted pressure on President Beneš to accept an external mediator. But his idea of mediation was to put further pressure on Czechoslovakia to get a settlement with Germany. Chamberlain had lost sight of principle, and slipped all too easily into the assumption that might is right: he put a time-honoured expedient in place, where an individual, who was not part of the governmental apparatus – and therefore not accountable to the public through ministers – was appointed to investigate and report directly to the Prime Minister, having first been made privy to the preferred outcomes. In this case Lord Runciman, an industrialist was chosen. This approach, in Chamberlain's view, was the first step to getting Hitler off the hook of his own rhetoric; but it was Chamberlain who was to be impaled, by his own policy.

September's events followed one another speedily, and with dire consequences for Europe. Hitler was due to address the Nazi Party's Nuremberg rally on 12 September. Two days before that, President Beneš spoke on Czechoslovak radio; he spoke first in Czech and then in German. The American journalist William Shirer, who had served in Berlin since 1934 and who, in that time, had developed a clear understanding into the regime in Germany, was in the broadcasting station in Prague that evening. Shirer heard Beneš pronounce on basic democratic values: "I firmly believe that nothing other than moral force, goodwill and mutual trust will be needed."[18] After the broadcast, as Beneš came out into the hall of the broadcasting studio, Shirer had the urge to rush up to him and warn him that he was dealing with gangsters;

> But I did not have the nerve and merely nodded good-evening and he walked on, a brave little Czech peasant's son who has made many mistakes in the last two decades, but who, when all is said and done, stands for the democratic decencies that Hitler is out to destroy.[19]

Five days later Neville Chamberlain flew to meet Hitler at Berchtesgaden. It was here that Hitler raised the stakes, demanding not autonomy for the German-speaking areas, but their secession to Germany.

Without demurring, Chamberlain returned immediately to London to discuss the demand with the cabinet. The following day

Lord Runciman was summoned from Czechoslovakia to report verbally to the Prime Minister. Runciman's recommendation was to hand over the area to Germany without bothering with a plebiscite. Meanwhile, Conrad Henlein had been briefed by Berlin and issued a proclamation demanding anschluss with Germany, then fled to Germany. The Czechoslovak government issued a warrant for his arrest for treason. Czech police stormed the hotel, which was his headquarters, and in the gunfight six people were killed.[20]

On 20 September, the Czechoslovak Government refused to concede the secession of the area to Germany, saying that to agree would put the country, 'sooner or later under the complete domination of Germany'.[21] Then President Beneš asked French ministers the question, would France honour its treaty if Germany attacked Czechoslovakia? The answer was that if the Czechoslovak Government did not withdraw its note rejecting the idea of secession, the country would have to fight Nazi Germany alone. With now no choice but accept or perish, the Czechoslovak Government agreed to the plan. And the next day, Prime Minister Chamberlain went to Germany to Godesberg to meet Hitler and deliver to him what he wanted. Hitler spurned the offer, and demanded more concessions. Returning to London, Chamberlain told the House of Commons that he did not think that Hitler had deliberately deceived him. But now he began to face some opposition from within his own Government.

International tension then increased when President Beneš ordered a general mobilisation. This amounted to about one million men, with a field army of about eight hundred thousand.[22] On the German side, a number of influential officers in the army High Command were not at all optimistic of winning a war against Czechoslovakia, if – and only if – France, Britain, and (in the light of the wording of its treaty with Czechoslovakia) the Soviet Union came to its aid. From the outset Germany would have to fight on two fronts; and the extent of their pessimism in such a scenario came to light after the war at the Nuremberg trials.[23] However, what Hitler correctly judged was that the west had not the will to come to the support of Czechoslovakia.

As though to prove it, Prime Minister Chamberlain tightened the screw on Czechoslovakia: if war came about, regardless of the outcome, the German speaking area of the country would be lost to them; and in the House of Commons he announced that a tripartite mission of Italy, Britain and France would go to Munich to attempt to negotiate a settlement with Hitler. In the visitors' gallery of the House sat the Czechoslovak minister, Dr Jan Masaryk. Incredulous, he heard the statement: there was to be no Czechoslovak representation. After the debate he asked for a meeting with the Prime Minister and the Foreign Secretary, and told them,

> If you have sacrificed my nation to preserve the peace of the world, I will be the first to applaud you. But if not, gentlemen, God help your souls.[24]

Munich was the venue for the meeting with Hitler on 29-30 September 1938; and then it was all over: Czechoslovakia was abandoned. On 1 October, German forces marched in to the Sudeten area; the country's defences, the Bohemian 'Maginot Line' were now in their hands. All fortifications, installations and matériel had to be left in place, as the Czechoslovak army withdrew. About 800,000 Czechs in the areas lost their homes overnight.[25] President Beneš resigned as President of the country, under pressure from Germany and shortly after, left the country.

Chamberlain had staked his political credibility on his policy, and now he deployed the repertoire of a politician: on the steps of the plane taking him back from Munich, he played the showman, flourishing a sheet of paper as proof of 'peace in our time'; and then on radio, he cast himself as Pontius Pilate, washing his hands of, 'a quarrel in a far away country between people of whom we know nothing.'[26]

But in the debate in the House of Commons, Winston Churchill spoke out eloquently, amid interruptions, prophesying against the euphoria of the moment:

> We have sustained a total and unmitigated defeat. . . You will find that in a period of time which may be measured by years, but may even be measured by months, Czechoslovakia will be engulfed in the Nazi regime. . . We are in the presence of a disaster of the first magnitude which has befallen Great Britain and France. Do not let us blind ourselves to that.[27]

How prescient Churchill was became clear in less than six months, when on 13 March 1939, Hitler summoned Beneš's successor, President Hacha, to Berlin and threatened to bomb Prague unless his government formally invited the Third Reich to take over the remainder of Bohemia and Moravia as a Protectorate. Slovakia was to be given quasi-independence as a puppet state of the Reich. On 15 March, in early morning snow showers, German armoured columns moved into what was left of Bohemia and Moravia. By evening Hitler was in Prague.

Dr Edvard Beneš was in Chicago the day that Germany marched into what was left of his homeland. He denounced the Munich agreement, and left for Europe with the intention of mustering support to set up a democratic government in exile. The democracy that he had helped bring into being had fallen into the darkness of totalitarianism after only twenty years. It had fallen, not through internal strife and dissension – for the ethnic issue was resolvable – but as a result of external force. But not after armed conflict, for the Czechoslovak military had obeyed their orders from their government; there was no resistance to the Nazi take-over. Over 1,625 aircraft of the Czechoslovak Air Force fell into the hands of the Third Reich.[28]

This, then, was the situation that many soldiers and airmen in Czechoslovakia reacted to. An extraordinary exodus took place, in ones and twos. At the level of the individual, decisions were made to leave the country and try to find a means of taking up arms against the Third Reich. These men were not the political cognoscenti of the forces: they came from all ranks and back-grounds. Hundreds of ground and air crews chose to leave the country, when there was a suitable opportunity. There were no large-scale defections, because of the presence of the occupying power; nor were they slipping over to the other side – for as yet there was no war. These men made their decisions, based on the judgement that, sooner or later, Hitler would have to be stopped; and it would be the western democracies that would go to war with Germany. The route that most of them took was to Poland.

Bozděch made his decision, then bided his time until winter weather had passed, for he was going to go on foot. Carefully, he prepared his ground: he needed to give himself some leeway, for if he were posted missing within hours of his departure, his chance of being caught would be increased; so he adopted the tactic of applying for leave. The German administration now controlled the Czechoslovak military, and requests for leave – once signed by a senior officer – were passed to the local Gestapo office for approval. Bozděch's leave request was granted by a junior officer in his unit,

Lt Decastello, and on 20 June 1939, with his pass signed by the Gestapo, he travelled openly to his home in Soběkury.[29] He wasted no time; he told his parents, and then he bade them farewell. He also told his uncle, Karel Hrubý, who was an innkeeper in Soběkury; and he met the senior police officer in Merklín, Václav Kust, who warned him to be careful. Their discussion, however, was not held in private, for it was in part overheard by a local person, who did nothing with the information – for the moment. Apart from that, Bozděch seems to have been discreet about his intentions, and gave no appearance of preparing for an extended hike.

The area he had chosen to cross over into Poland was Ostrava, in northern Moravia, so he had to travel from the west of Bohemia, a distance of some three hundred miles. If he used public transport, he might be asked to produce his identity, and questioned about why he was so far from his home during a furlough. He had to avoid large troop concentrations; he may have hitched lifts; but largely he covered the distance on foot, and with what money he had he paid for food, and sometimes shelter on the journey. The final stage was the most difficult for him. Whatever the problem – whether it was because of German foot patrols in the area, or activity on the part of some local people – he had to lie low for three days and nights before he was able to cross the border.[30]

Those Czechoslovak airmen who arrived in Poland were directed by the authorities to a reception camp in Male Bronowice; and there, at the end of June, some ten days after he went on leave, Bozděch reported. He had exhausted his supply of money, and the state of his clothing told of the ravages of days and nights spent furtively in the outdoors. Among the comrades he met there was Lt Decastello, the officer who had sanctioned his leave request, and who had himself defected the day after he had done so. Now he and another officer gave Bozděch some money.

At this stage, politically and militarily, the Poles were not interested in absorbing Czechoslovak airmen into their service. However, there were the western democracies. Britain was an unknown quantity for most of them, and so they chose France. And France was receptive. On 5 July 1939, Bozděch's visa, No. 1038, was issued by the French Consulate in Krakov; and on 31 July it was stamped in France by the commissariat in Calais.[31]

In all, between May and August 1939, some 470 Czechoslovak airmen reached France aboard six ships.[32] The efforts of these men were tremendously supportive to their political leaders in the time ahead. As Dr Edvard Beneš put it when he addressed them a year later:

> Our homeland was occupied and enslaved, you went abroad without any clear aim in order to begin fighting again; I myself with my friends began to organise the second resistance both politically and militarily . . . [33]

There was now a long, hard road ahead of them.

CHAPTER THREE

Another Flag

A country is not the sum total of regions, customs and
building materials that my intellect can still grasp. It is an
Essence.

Antoine de Saint-Exupéry, *Flight to Arras*

The French Foreign Legion base at Sidi-bel-Abbès was a far
cry from Bohemia. Nonetheless, it was a journey Czechoslovak military personnel had to make in the hope of
eventually being able to take up arms against the Third Reich.
Traditionally, men joined the Foreign Legion for their own individual reasons, but in the summer of 1939 the surge in enlistments
from Czechoslovaks came about as the result of a policy decision
by the French.

If France created and armed a Czechoslovak army, it would be
construed, at the diplomatic level, as a provocative act signifying
hostile intent; so a delicate alternative strategy was proposed:
Czechoslovak military personnel would sign the standard five-year
contract of the Foreign Legion, and, if France subsequently went to
war with Germany, they would be transferred to Czechoslovak units
under the overall command of the French military. This applied to
both soldiers and airmen – the only way they could attain their long
term goal was to serve France, for the present, in the Foreign Legion.

Situated on a plain about sixty miles south of Oran, the Legion's
base at Sidi-bel-Abbès had been established as a depot almost a

hundred years earlier. A number of depots were built in Algeria at the time to supply Legion excursions into the interior, and these became known as 'biscuitvilles', an allusion to the hard tack that was the staple food for Legionnaires.[1] It had been the lonely site of the grave of a religious hermit until the middle of the nineteenth century when the Legion built a depot there, and over time developed it into its headquarters. By the 1930s, it was a settlement of some size. New recruits were marched along a wide street towards the white painted walls of the Legion's headquarters, and as they passed through its arch they could read the words *caserne de la Légion* on its lintel.[2] Whatever their former rank they were now brought to the same level, *soldat*; and they soon learned that if they were to survive they had to subsume individual or collective motives for being there and accept the Legion's motto 'The Legion is my Country'. They were not allowed to form up in their national groups: this was against Legion policy.

Recruit training followed the same harsh pattern that had been the tradition for generations. Reveille was at five am; breakfast was coffee and hard tack; and then the marching began. Carrying rifle, ammunition and full equipment, recruits were remorselessly put through a regime of forced marches, building up from ten miles to twenty and thirty miles a day in the sweltering heat with minimum amounts of water. It was unremitting; the slogan 'march or die' was drilled into all Legionnaires. A German, Erwin Carlé, who served in the Legion earlier in the century, left a very clear impression of the consequences of this training.

> It is drummed into the Legionnaire that he is intended for nothing else in this world except marching. If the pangs of hunger are gnawing at his stomach or thirst parches his tongue, that is so much the worse for him, but is no sort of reason for not marching on! He may be tired, dead tired, completely exhausted – but he must not stop marching. If his feet are bleeding and the soles burn like fire, that is very sad – but marching pace must not be slackened. The sun may burn until his senses are all awhirl, he must go on. His task in life is to march.[3]

The Czechoslovak airmen had had generic military training, but the purpose of air force training was to enable specialist personnel to man equipment, not serve as foot soldiers. Yet, they acquitted themselves well, and recognised the high calibre of the unit in which they now served. Another airman, Mira Liškutín, who was at Sidi-bel-Abbès at the same time as Bozděch, found the French officers to be very professional and worthy of respect.[4] That these airmen stood up so well to the tough testing regime was noted by a senior officer at the Czechoslovak military administration based in Paris. He wrote of them:

> Czechoslovak airmen were also processed in Foreign Legion boot camps . . . Those men who were willing to trade their young years for an oral promise that, some day, they would be able to fight in their own army were the elite of the Czechoslovak Armed Forces in exile.[5]

War came in September, when Germany invaded Poland, with whom Britain and France were bound by treaty. The French honoured the undertaking they had given the Czechoslovak servicemen: a Czechoslovak depot was set up in the south at Agde; and in due course its country's military personnel were transferred from the Foreign Legion and shipped to France. Airmen were then posted to the French Air Force.

They were now back in the branch of the services for which they had been trained; but first, they had to have refresher training in the areas in which they were qualified; and so on 16 November 1939, Bozděch was posted as a mechanician to the Centre d'instruction de Chasse at Chartres. He successfully completed the course, and on 16 January 1940, he moved on and transferred to a wireless operator/ air gunnery course at Base Arienne at Pau.[6]

There are two different early versions of how Bozděch acquired the Alsatian dog that was to be his inseparable companion for thirteen years. The earlier of the two is in English: a brief allusion in a newspaper article of October 1942,[7] stating that he found the puppy in a ruined house after his aircraft had crashed in France. The second is in Czech and appeared in the journal *Rozlet* in 1945, which has it that Bozděch bought the puppy from a French farmer in Maron near Chateauroux for 80 francs – his friends clubbing in to raise the sum.[8] When Bozděch came to write his story of his life with the dog, the version that he developed was the earlier of the two.[9]

By whatever means he came by the dog, the bonding between them became very strong – on the dog's part exceptionally so, to the extent that it became the stuff of legend: it was written about decades afterwards, and a Hollywood studio planned to make a film about them. That bonding arose out of war; and it is expressed most vividly in an image of the dog sharing with an aircrew lonely combat sorties over enemy territory in a Wellington bomber, rather than be separated from his master. All but three years of the dog's life were to be spent on air force bases. But in those early months of 1940, though, it was a playful puppy, thriving on scraps from the service canteen.

Giving the dog a name turned out to be a collective effort, for Bozděch makes it clear that there was discussion among his Czech friends in the squadron over the choice of name. They thought, for example, that the dog had the markings of an aristocrat of his breed and some suggested noble titles. None of the suggestions seemed appropriate though until one of the group, Joska, suggested the Czech name for a Russian plane, a PE2, a bomber aircraft which the Czechoslovak Air Force purchased from the Russians and which they then designated ANT. So very appropriately the dog was given the name of an aircraft, he became called Ant.

In the spring, still undergoing training, Bozděch was transferred to Cazaux in Gironde.[10] To help them get to know some French people in the civilian population, the Czechoslovak Consulate in Paris gave its countrymen the names of pen friends.[11] This was good for the servicemen's morale, and a spur to improve their knowledge of French. Bozděch, fifteen years later, recalled that he was corresponding with a girl called Yvette who lived in Paris.[12] And indeed there exists an envelope, postmarked 16 April 1940, bearing the initials FM – Franchise Militaire – the free post inscription to the services, addressed to Bozděch as Pilote Tcheque, Bataillon de l'air 724 at Cazaux from Mlle. Yvette Silmudre who lived in the Rue Pierre Dupont in the tenth arrondisement of Paris.[13]

There was not time for the correspondence to develop into anything more significant because the period that was known in France as the *drôle de guerre*, and in English as the phoney war came to an end three weeks later on 10 May, when the German armour unexpectedly thrust through wooded territory in the Ardennes. The audacity of the thrust caught the Allies completely unprepared. In London, the following day, 11 May, Winston Churchill, a long-standing critic of the British Government's pre-war stance on Germany, became Prime Minister.

Bozděch's training came to an end, and on 22 May he was transferred to Chateauroux to a ground attack unit BC (Bombardier Chasseur) 11/8 of 112 Bataillon de l'Armée de l'air. [14] The unit was soon in action, attacking German columns as they crossed the River Somme. The speed of the Panzer drive into France meant that the front was ever changing; strategists were thrown into confusion: orders given and then countermanded. It was about this time that Bozděch began taking his dog with him on sorties, in case he was diverted to another base.[15] The dog 'proved a perfect passenger. Untroubled by flak or violent swaying of the aircraft, he lay quite unperturbed between his master's feet, often dozing.'[16]

Within weeks of the opening of the Wehrmacht's campaign, the British Expeditionary Force was facing the options of having to be evacuated from the country or be annihilated. On 27 May the French port of Calais fell, and the evacuation of British forces began at Dunkirk. General Von Rundstedt, German Commander in Chief of the French campaign, temporarily halted the Panzer columns, fearing their vulnerability; and this gave much needed time for an armada of ships to ferry men to the UK. By the 4th of June the evacuation was complete.

By the end of the first week of June the battle for the capital of France was under way. The ground attack unit in which Bozděch served flew sorties to Vernon where the Germans were trying to establish a bridgehead across the River Seine, and on their return they were taken into the Briefing Room and told that Italy had declared war against France and Britain. It was the 10th of June – one month from the launch of the blitzkrieg; and demoralisation had set in upon the military. Many units had fought well, and the French and the British air forces had inflicted considerable losses on the Luftwaffe, but the completeness of the rout facing the army was bewildering. Large numbers of French troops, whose units had been overrun, too numerous for the swift-moving invaders to control or round up, had been disarmed and turned loose, mingling with civilian refugees and blocking the roads. Panic had already spread. Bozděch gives an airman's perspective of the chaos the speed of the war generated among the civilian population.

The roads from the north were jammed with Paris refugees, easily distinguishable from similar unhappy groups from elsewhere. Large and small cars carried the well-dressed Parisians in the endless stream, while Belgians and country people from the northern parts of France were dragged in their ancient, battered cars by horses and even cows. Rich and poor, however, all had one thing in common – fear. Strained unhappy faces stared out from the vehicles, anxiously scanning the sky for aerial attack.[17]

Then on 14 June, Paris was occupied. By now Bozděch's unit was fragmented, the rump of it, he recalled, made its last move on 16 June to Le Breuil. That same day the French Prime Minister Reynaud resigned and the 84-year-old Marshall Pétain became head of the government.

Pétain's address to the nation on 17 June undermined the morale of the French military: officers and men were confused and shattered by its import. They heard the national hero of the First World War telling them that France would sue for peace terms with Germany. That same day, in the village of Chapelle Vend north of Blois, the Adjutant called Bozděch's depleted squadron together. Overhead planes of the Luftwaffe swooped low. Screened by some trees in the farmyard, the Adjutant called each man forward; to the French airmen he gave each man his papers; to the Czechoslovaks he gave all that he had of theirs – their Foreign Legion pay books; and he told them that the nearest railway station for trains to the south was at Tours.[18]

Similar scenes were being enacted with Czechoslovak soldiers close to the front; and their response was the same as that of their air force comrades: find a way to their base and await orders to be evacuated from the country. Not all French officers understood the situation of the Czechoslovak military personnel in their service. Zdenek Kordina records being brought before the French Garrison Commander at Toulouse, 'who shouted, "La guerre est finie". He was visibly moved when I replied, "Pour vous, mon Colonel. Pour nous autres la guerre commence"'.[19] But there was urgency: until an armistice had been signed, the Panzers advanced further, and the Luftwaffe strafed movement on the roads and railways.

In London, Dr Edvard Beneš petitioned the British Government for assistance in evacuating Czechoslovak troops from France. He proposed that air force personnel should concentrate at Bordeaux on the Atlantic coast and Agde on the Mediterrean.[20] The Air Force Department of the Czechoslovak Military Administration, based in Paris, was headed by General Vicherek. Communication between it and the Czechoslovak personnel attached to about sixteen French Air Force squadrons was difficult, but when the Military

Administration left Paris for a new centre in Béziers in the south, it became impossible. What exactly the remnants of BC 11/8 were told to do with their Czechoslovak comrades is uncertain.

But the group of whom Bozděch was a part decided they would head south east to the Czechoslovak depot at Agde. Reasoning that they stood a better chance if they were less conspicuous from the air, they split into smaller groupings; Bozděch went with six Czechs and two Frenchmen. They decided not to follow the Adjutant's advice to go to Tours; instead they intended to try for Blois. They were in uniform and they had their kit and belongings, so progress would be slow. A foray into a nearby village ended with their commandeering a pony-trap into which they piled their gear. Night was falling as nine men and a dog set out for Blois.

According to Bozděch's account, they came upon a train in a siding before they reached Blois. It was packed with refugees fleeing the advancing forces, but they managed to find space for themselves in a goods wagon. It was safer from air attack by night; and the train set off some time after midnight. They passed through Blois, and took the only undamaged line to the south by way of Nevers. For the next sixty miles or so to Moulins, progress was very slow.[21] The rations the airmen had with them amounted to sardines, chocolate and wine. Whenever the train stopped, they tried to supplement this diet with fresh food. After a time the dog refused to eat. A Belgian woman on the train gave Bozděch a baby's feeding bottle complete with teat; and when the train pulled up at a halt near farm buildings, he produced it and a kindly French woman poured some milk from a can into the bottle, assuming it was for a hungry infant. From that time on, Bozděch recalled, his dog would never again eat chocolate. Their journey continued at a snail's pace via Brioude to Nîmes and Montpellier.

Time was of the essence though. On 22 June the French Government accepted and signed the conditions of the armistice document. Article 12 of the document stipulated: 'The French Government is required to hand over upon demand all Germans whom the German Government may specify by name, whether they be in France proper in French possessions, colonies, protectorates, or territories under mandate.'[22] This had implication for the Czechoslovaks who were considered by the German Government to be citizens of the Protectorate and therefore subjects of the Third Reich. The attitude of some of the French authorities changed after the signing of the armistice: at first, the ship *Appapa* which had been designated to take on board Czechoslovak Air Force personnel did not obtain permission to enter Port-Vendres; but later on, under the protection of the guns of a British warship, *Appapa* entered the port and took on board 237 Czechoslovak airmen.[23]

Communications between the British War Office and the Czechoslovak military administration were frequent and specific. Every effort would be made to evacuate military personnel; if there were no British ships, those of neutral countries should be used.

Because of the urgency of the situation and the need for on-the-spot decisions in the light of whatever ships were available, it is not altogether surprising that there are discrepancies in the official records. For example, according to Bozděch's service record in the Military Archive, he left from the port of Sète on 23 June under the command of Captain Emil Busina;[24] although, in the same Archive, Capt Busina's list of personnel gives their date of departure as 19 June from Port-Vendres on the *Meonia*.[25] Whichever it was, the aim was to get to British territory or to a British ship as soon as possible; but since they had boarded a vessel of a neutral country, they were forced to adapt their plans according to its trading route and so they followed an erratic course.

First they found themselves in Oran in Algeria, the French colony where they had served less than a year earlier as members of the Foreign Legion; then though, France was anticipating going to war with Germany; now its government had signed an Armistice with its enemy, so the position of Czechoslovak military on French territory would be precarious as soon as the colony's administration fell into line with emerging Vichy policy. Capt Busina did not delay: on 27 June they left Oran by train for Casablanca, which was in the French protectorate of Morocco, but whose port was on the major shipping lanes; and on 29 June they sailed from Casablanca the last hundred and ninety nautical miles on the *Gib-el-Dersa* to Gibraltar.

They arrived on British territory with the expectation of being transported to the UK to be rearmed for the fight. Inconsistencies among the sources in the Archive continue: Bozděch's name remains on Capt Busina's list of his on-board group but it also appears on the list of Capt Hlobil on the *Cidonia*.[26] However, Bozděch wrote his own account of this last leg of the journey, which is quite detailed; and the date he gives for his arrival in the UK is confirmed by his military file,[27] so it will be followed here.

Each stage of the escape had held its own difficulties for an airman, determined to keep his young dog with him, and the final part brought him unforeseen problems, which he overcame thanks to his determination and the intensity of his dog's obedience to him. The bonding of the pair had developed and was strengthened by their frequent relocations in the last frenzied weeks of the battle for France then their journeying on the Mediterranean and through North Africa.

Bozděch's group arrived in Gibraltar on 30 June, and he records that they were told that they would be transferred to a ship that same day.[28] The *Northmoor*, a former collier, was to take them, it seemed, on the last leg of their journey to the UK. It rode at anchor for two days while other ships gathered to form a convoy. Then Bozděch's group was transferred to the *Neuralia*, a transport.[29] After the conditions on the old collier this seemed like luxury, but when the third class accommodation became overcrowded with the number of passengers, some of the Czechoslovak troops took to sleeping on deck. Bozděch and his dog joined them in a space beside a gun mounted near the stern. It was congenial for these servicemen from a land-locked country, travelling deck class on a cruise, their attention taken up by the movements of the accompanying warships, as the convoy sailed towards the country now leading the fight against fascism.

Britain's quarantine laws were enforced in wartime with exactly the same rigour as in peacetime. The enemy may have been only twenty miles from Dover – and feverish preparations were being made to repel them – nonetheless, dogs arriving in the UK from overseas would continue to be put into quarantine for six months. Most of the Czechoslovak contingent on board had no knowledge of English, and so through an interpreter, the ship's captain made their officer aware of the situation facing any of his men with a dog: the animal would be taken into custody; if the owner could pay the quarantine costs, well and good; if not the animal would be humanely destroyed. Considering the situation at the time, and relative to the bigger issues that bore in on them, some of the contingent may have thought that they were simply dealing with petty officialdom; and as the ship sailed up the Mersey on 12 July, there seems to have been collusion with their officer: Bozděch and another airman were delegated to be the baggage party, to accompany it by lorry, and unload it at the railway station.[30]

The ship's officers had their own duties to perform as the vessel entered harbour, and were too busy to take a close interest in the foreign servicemen, who were commanded by their own officers. They tied up, and the formalities were efficiently dealt with: thousands of foreign servicemen were arriving at ports in different parts of the UK; and arrangements had been made for them to be taken to designated sites. The men were lined up on deck and filed down the gangway. Kit bags were collected and loaded onto lorries. Bozděch handled one of them very carefully, softly crooning to himself.

Everything went without a hitch until they arrived at the railway station. Welcome as these overseas contingents of military men undoubtedly were, there were security considerations that the UK authorities had to keep in mind: fifth columnists may have infiltrated their ranks; they must be shepherded together until they reached their allocated camp; and so there was a police presence on the station platforms. After the baggage had been unloaded and neatly stacked, the testing time for the dog really began, as the men waited for their train to pull in. Whimpering was heard coming from a kit bag. According to Bozděch it was the quick thinking of a fellow airman, Václav Štětka, that prevented the dog from being discovered by the police.[31] Štětka was a big man, and he had a fine sense of humour; he was a popular figure wherever he went; he had the knack of creating an audience and making himself an attractive presence. Here he leapt into action on the railway platform as the police sauntered along: displaying signs of impatience at the delay, he began fooling around, uttering the convincing sound of a dog whining to be allowed out. It worked. The train steamed in to the station, and the contingent of Czechoslovaks boarded it, along with a smuggled dog.

PART II

CHAPTER FOUR

Rebirth of an Air Force

It is a great honour for you today to be made part of the
British Air Force as an independent Czechoslovak unit.
However, it places great duties upon you.
  President Beneš, Address to his airmen, RAF Duxford 1940

A fter the fall of France, thousands of men from overseas contingents had to be absorbed and rearmed; and until
government policy was sorted out, an administrative
system allocated the different national groups to designated camps.
On 12 July, Bozděch and his small group arrived at Cholmondeley
near Liverpool, a large, attractive park with gracious sweeping
trees where the Czechoslovak Army and Air Force personnel were
bivouacked in tents, waiting to be organised into fighting units
again.

The Polish forces could readily be processed in a legal way into
the British armed forces because Poland had been an ally; and its
invasion was the reason that Britain and France had gone to war.
Czechoslovakia, however, was a different matter altogether: the
recognised government of what was left of that country was based
in Prague, while Dr Edvard Beneš in London headed the Czechoslovak National Committee. Bruce Lockhart, a senior figure in the
Foreign Office, and a man with a lot of experience of Czechoslovakia between the wars, was given the task of drawing up policy
options; and he summarised the position, arguing that the British

should recognise a Provisional Government of Czechoslovakia, and ignore the international consequences.[1] Accordingly, in early July this proposal appeared on the agenda of the War Cabinet.

Events then began to move quickly. On 19 July, Dr Beneš visited the encampment at Cholmondeley and addressed the men.[2] Two days later, the BBC and the press announced that the British Government had recognised the Provisional Government of Czechoslovakia in Exile, under the leadership of President Beneš.[3] Bruce Lockhart was appointed to be the British Government's liaison officer to Dr Beneš and senior members of his Provisional Government in the UK.[4] On 22 July, the Czechoslovak airmen at Cholmondeley Park were assembled, to be marched out on their way to become part of the Czechoslovak Squadrons of the RAF.

It was an emotional scene, symbolising their taking up arms again for their country. The army personnel, who were to remain there until a brigade had been formed, cheered them, then lined up and marched alongside the airmen.

> Half-way down the column a grey haired veteran of the famous Czech Legion in Russia during the First World War marched beside his two sons. With head erect and in perfect step, he kept pace despite his sixty years. At the gate he stepped out of the file and, struggling to hide his emotions, smartly saluted his departing boys.[5]

They were on their way to RAF Cosford, where, as another Czechoslovak aviator, Mira Liškutín saw it, 'this organisational miracle', the rebirth of their national air force was taking place.[6] For the Czechoslovak airmen, who had been through the demoralisation of what happened to their own country in 1939 and then witnessed the defeat of France, first impressions of the RAF had a soaring effect on morale: this was an efficient and well-organised service that had all the signs of self-confidence and determination for the fight. Cosford was a large modern RAF station, dominated by the Fulton Block, which could house about two thousand airmen, but which had to be augmented by rows of wooden huts; and, in addition, a hospital with specialist facilities was sited at the camp's north west corner.

From a legal point of view, the Czechoslovak Air Force had to be incorporated into the RAF: the Reich considered that residents of the Protectorate were German subjects, so if Czechoslovak airmen took up arms with the Allies and were captured, they might not be entitled to the rights of prisoners of war. It also suited the Air Ministry that they came entirely under British control. Accordingly all Czechoslovak airmen were enrolled as members of the Royal Air Force Volunteer Reserve, and integrated into the RAF for the duration of hostilities. This meant that while they retained their Czechoslovak rank, they were given an RAF rank. The Czechoslovak Air Force came under the control of the Czechoslovak Inspectorate within the Air Ministry, and was headed by General Karel Janoušek, whose RAF rank was Air Vice Marshal. Janoušek was an experienced and able administrator, and he was also a veteran of the Czech Legions of the First World War.

No concession of rank was made to the airmen for their previous experience: Bozděch, for example, was a sergeant (četař) in the Czechoslovak Air Force, but until he completed his RAF training he was an aircraftsman. The first element of that training, for those like him who had little or no knowledge of the language, was to be taught elementary English. Teaching was the responsibility of the British Council; lessons were given daily, and the classroom routine followed a strict timetable. Bozděch's Alsatian awaited his return at midday and at 5pm, and for the rest of the time he followed his own inclinations, sniffing out the canteen area, and making friends among the WAAFS and nurses.

Gangly, with disproportionately large ears at this stage, and a beautiful dark streak down his back, the dog was a passport for Bozděch, who became someone of interest; and it was not all that long, he relates, before he began seeing one of the nurses. But he also began appraising his dog, which by now was about eight months old. He knew that Ant was very intelligent; and he also knew that in the domain of his primal social emotions, the dog was exceptionally attached to him – even for a breed which is characterised for its loyalty to only one person – and he suspected that the dog had already shown signs of separation distress when they were parted for long. However, apart from elementary puppy training, Ant was not yet trained. Now Bozděch's background gave him quite a lot of knowledge about animal behaviour and management, and he knew that ordinarily it was too soon to begin formal training; but on the other hand, he felt that the dog's life experiences already had prepared him to be trained in obedience. So Bozděch went about this systematically, patiently and with insight. He was pleased with the results; the dog learned very quickly, and,

Bozděch noted, he was becoming skilled in reading his master's moods.

It was as well that Bozděch used his free time to train his dog at Cosford because this period of stability came to an end in September, when the airmen were posted to the various Czecho- slovak squadrons. Bozděch was part of a group of eight friends, who had gravitated together, some from their days in France, and some from the time they were evacuated; and now they were going to be split up. Joska, Karel, Gustav and Ludva were posted to No. 311 (Czechoslovak) Squadron in Bomber Command, Vlasta remained at Cosford and Bozděch, Josef and Štětka were to go to No. 312 (Czechoslovak) Squadron in Fighter Command. Like so many groups of friends who had to part in such circumstances, they pledged that they would all meet on a certain day at a certain place, and that no other engagement would take priority. The venue they chose was the Czechoslovak National House at Bedford Place in London, and the time was to be Christmas 1940. But as Bozděch put it, 'So many hundreds of similar solemn promises were made when friends were parted through postings, yet so often the Grim Reaper spoiled those plans.'[7] And so it was for them: on 16 October 1940, Joska was killed in action; and two months later so was Karel.

On 5 September, Bozděch,[8] his dog (in the tradition of appur- tenant of an army), and his two friends were posted to No. 312 Squadron at Duxford, near Wolverhampton. As an air-gunner, Bozděch was allocated to fly in Defiant aircraft, but the complement of Defiants had not yet arrived. The best the air-gunners could do in the meantime was to become familiar with the Boulton Paul turrets and the four Browning machine guns with which the Defiants were armed.

Morale was high at Duxford. The previous month President Beneš had addressed the airmen there. Some years later, Bozděch was given permission to quote the transcript of that speech in a book he wrote. It was a clever political speech. The President thanked the airmen for the role they had played in France; he implied a greater degree of recognition by Britain for his office and government than was in fact the case at this time; and then he turned to their present position.

The fall of France has brought you to England and made you close comrades-in-arms of your British comrades-in-arms who, today, with pride and glory, bear the colours of this powerful empire before the entire world, as they fight for a new, free and better Europe, for the freedom of their own British homeland and also for our freedom and the freedom of Czechoslovakia. I can assure you that the British nation shall not lose this war.

You have been welcomed here with sympathy and friendship. You saw already in France how superlative the British Air Force is, what great successes it achieves everywhere it intervenes, and you can see it here yourselves even better with your own eyes. I do not exaggerate if I stress that the British Air Force has proved its worth in this war as the best air force in the world; it will hardly be superseded by another in this war.

It is a great honour for you today to be made part of the British Air Force as an independent Czechoslovak unit. However, it places great duties upon you. I knew our airmen very well at home and I know what they could do; I also know that you fulfilled your duties well in France, and I also know that you will fulfil them well here.[9]

The Czechoslovak squadrons did indeed acquit themselves well in the air war that raged above Britain that summer and early autumn.

Thanks to the prescience of some staff at the BBC, a means was established whereby a highly credible source within the Provisional Government could communicate with his countrymen in Czechoslovakia about the war. In September, Jan Masaryk was invited to broadcast on (what was then called) the foreign services channel of the BBC. He made a series of these broadcasts over the war years; and in Bruce Lockhart's view, he was 'with the exception of Mr Churchill, the most effective allied broadcaster of the war.'[10]

Having failed in its strategy of trying to destroy the RAF, the enemy switched its emphasis to the bombing of cities and industrial targets. No. 312 Squadron was moved to RAF Speke near Liverpool to strengthen the defences of the area. Due to the hasty nature of the move, there was at first insufficient accommodation at the base, and the non-commissioned aircrews were billeted in what had been the passenger waiting rooms of Liverpool airport. This was not too uncomfortable, and a week later they were assigned to huts that had been hurriedly erected. Bozděch and Štětka shared a room with the squadron interpreter, Mírek Čap, the

son of a large textile manufacturer in Czechoslovakia, whom
Bozděch described as 'a true dog lover.'[11] If Čap enjoyed having the
dog's company in the hut, Bozděch's quid pro quo was receiving
one-to-one English language sessions from the squadron's interpreter. The textbook that Čap recommended for him was called
Fundamental English; and Bozděch spent hours studying it. Mírek
Čap also pointed out to him that the name Ant – the way Bozděch
pronounced it – to an English speaker sounded like the homophone
aunt. Clearly there were situations where it could be risible, and so
he had better change it. However, Bozděch did not want to alter it
significantly; and he hit on the idea of adding one syllable /is/, and
from then on, Antis was how the dog was known.

There was still no sign of the Defiant aircraft, and Bozděch was
grounded. To make matters worse, he was involved in a slight car
accident and fractured a bone in his left hand; and the best he could
do was study *Fundamental English* as his contribution to the war
effort. Meanwhile, by night, the blitz on heavy industrial centres
continued; and since August, Liverpool had frequently been a
target. Not far from Speke was the Lockheed Aircraft Company
factory where aircraft were assembled, after having been imported
in sections from the USA. The war was about to come to the
grounded airmen.

Early one evening in September Bozděch took Antis and went
into Liverpool. The nurse he had been seeing at Cosford had a few
days' leave, and was spending them with a relative in Liverpool.
(Their method of communication was by post; he wrote in Czech,
she in English, and each took a letter from the other to the Czech
interpreter at their respective camps.) It was not very late when
Bozděch left his girl friend; he and Antis were coming home when a
rather mellow Stětka appeared from one of the local pubs and
joined them on their way to the camp. Sirens sounded the air raid
alert, and soon the sky was lit up by explosions along Merseyside
and the docks. It was all some distance away, until, from near at
hand came the steady drone of aircraft. Bozděch described what
happened then. 'From a few thousand feet up, three flares spread
a pale scarlet blush over the district.' Then came the high-pitched
scream of falling bombs; and the men who were trained to deal out
destruction from the air were now at the receiving end of it, lying
flat on the pavement, Bozděch clutching his dog to him. The ear-
splitting roar of the exploding bombs was followed by the crash of
falling masonry. Almost as quickly, it was over; 'the light of the

flares faded into the darkness ... and the sudden silence was terrifying by contrast.'[12]

They were unscathed, though blinded and choked by dust; but blocks of homes nearby had been hit. In no time at all, it seemed, people with torches gathered at the scene; and the airmen too made their way over to help. They moved beyond the outer perimeter of rubble to where several people had located a man who was trapped. As they worked to free the man, Bozděch noticed that the dog had got the idea and was scratching with his paws at the rubble. While they were doing this, Bozděch recounted, a uniformed Civil Defence worker arrived and began to form a team. *Fundamental English* had not adequately prepared Bozděch for the exchange that the Civil Defence worker initiated, but when the man saw the Czechoslovak shoulder flash, he used sign language to indicate that he wanted him and his dog to follow him into the centre of the site. Bozděch guessed that the man may have thought that Antis had been trained for this kind of work. But this was not the time to argue.

Whining eagerly, Antis went forward behind the uniformed man into the smoke and dust-filled area, and Bozděch followed. Muffled cries could be heard. The Civil Defence Warden called for silence. They could not tell from where the sound came, but their torch beams located and stayed on Antis; he stopped in front of a heap of rubble, barked and began digging. Immediately the rescuers began removing rubble, and eventually they brought out alive a woman who had been trapped. The process was repeated, and the dog found another person buried. In this way, with the dog stopping and barking at a particular spot, 'they started to work without question – and so four people were rescued from certain death beneath the debris.'[13]

Without warning, an interior wall collapsed, and for a few minutes Bozděch was separated from his dog by a mound of debris and a cloud of dust. Anxiously he called the dog; a moment later eager barking sounded once more; and when the team climbed the rubble their torches found Antis in what remained of a bedroom. There, lay a baby – Bozděch thought about one year old – and a woman, probably the mother. But both were beyond aid.

In the early hours, when it seemed to the Civil Defence Warden that all that could be done until daylight had been accomplished, the two airmen and the dog made their way to camp. With torn uniforms, footwear beyond further use to the RAF and the dog with his bleeding pads, they arrived at the guardroom and thence to first aid. When they finally turned in, the men could not sleep, and talked over their experience, while the dog dropped into a deep sleep. 'The hero of the evening slept, and for once, his snores went unrebuked.'[14]

Heavy bombing of Liverpool and Merseyside docks by night continued; and by the end of September there had been over a hundred and fifty raids. The airfield's defences were manned as soon as the air raid alert sounded, but so long as the explosions were distant sounds, they became part of an evening's background to the airmen in their huts at Speke. By now Bozděch's rank in the RAF was sergeant,[15] and several days after the rescue of survivors from the bombing, he and his two companions were in their hut where they had been joined by pilot sergeant Václav Jicha, who came from a village near where Bozděch had been brought up. Before the war Jicha had been an acrobatic pilot in Czechoslovakia; and he put his skills to good use in Fighter Command.

It was between eight and nine o'clock in the evening; Bozděch and Jicha were talking of rumours that were filtering through about the way families of those who were suspected of serving on the Allied side were being treated by the Gestapo. They had every reason to be concerned. Because it was not simply the case that Germany had marched into Bohemia and Moravia and subdued a mute and hostile populace: there were collaborators. And although Bozděch could not have known it then, that same month – October 1940 – his parents had been denounced to the Gestapo in Pilsen and arrested[16] for having a son serving in the air force of one of the Allies.

The hearing of experienced aircrew, regardless of whatever mental processes they were engaged in at the time, became finely attuned at detecting the particular manoeuvre a plane was making from the note of its engine. Out of nowhere, it seemed, came the roar of an engine opened to full throttle, as an aircraft levelled out of a dive it had gone into with engines throttled back, and shot over the hangars and huts at low level. Jicha read the signs instantly and shouted that a stick of bombs had been released. Bozděch grabbed his pack with its gas mask and steel helmet and the others did the same but before they got as far as the door of the hut, a tornado hit the wooden structure and they felt it heave off its foundations. It did not collapse on top of them, but the timber had given so much that the door's configuration within the door-frame had altered, and it would not budge. Štětka was the most powerfully built of the four, and he threw himself at it until it burst open.

By the time they got out, the searchlight batteries were ablaze and the anti-aircraft guns were firing as the raider, a Dornier 217, made a second pass over the airfield. The nearest air raid shelter was by the NAAFI building about one hundred yards away; and by the reflected lateral light of the searchlights, the ground ahead of them seemed nakedly clear beneath the roar of the Dornier's engine at full throttle and the sustained rattle of its machine guns. The men threw themselves to the ground; Bozděch was vaguely aware that his dog was ahead of them, when all hell broke loose. A succession of delayed explosions tore up the earth. It seemed to him that needles were being driven into his eardrums; and then he felt himself 'lifted up by some giant hand and flung to the earth again.'[17]

None of them was wounded, only temporarily deafened. But there was no sign of Antis. The anti-aircraft guns round the perimeter stopped firing for the lone raider had gone; and eventually the all clear sounded. Bozděch went about for some time calling his dog, but there was no sound. Their hut was matchwood; mounds of earth and timber littered the site, but there were no casualties on the domestic site, and miraculously the NAAFI building was intact. In the hours that followed, they were allocated new accommodation near the Lockheed Aircraft Company premises, and told that they could salvage their kit later. That night Bozděch was without the familiar presence of his dog in the room.

At dawn the operational site was functioning more or less normally, but an unexploded bomb had been found near the billets, and the area was cordoned off. Given the scale of the bombing of Merseyside, the cordoned area of the domestic site was not a priority for a bomb disposal team. Bozděch, still without duties until his fractured bone healed, combed the area beyond the camp's perimeter in case the dog had been badly hurt and crawled away to die. He found not a trace of him. The following day the bomb was defused, and the airmen were able to retrieve what they could from the ruins of their hut. Mounds of earth and detritus from the huts littered the area near the NAAFI. There now was no reasonable hope that his dog could have survived; and Bozděch, rationalising his loss, may have felt – if he had to be parted from him so soon – that the end was perhaps fitting; for the dog had come to him in conditions of war, and it had been taken from him by enemy action.

But that afternoon, a light drizzle that had been falling turned to heavy rain, which continued throughout most of the night. As the routine of the camp got underway next morning, three aircraftsmen mechanics were making their way to the aircraft hangar after breakfast, when they saw a frail, sodden creature trying to haul itself from a pile of wreckage near the NAAFI. Everyone on the camp, of course, knew the squadron mascot, but this could not be Antis. They approached it hesitantly, and when they saw the state it was in, they carried it to the sergeants' mess. Bozděch was having his breakfast when he was called by a sergeant to come to the entrance hall; but he was not told why. He almost broke down, he wrote, when he saw Antis, alive but, it seemed, in dire plight. 'As word of Antis' return spread around the Mess the crowd in the entrance hall grew.'[18] Congratulations were showered on him by the British and Czechoslovak airmen, but, he recalled, hardened as they were, the emotion of the scene touched them, and they silently drifted away.

There was skilled help at the sick bay. No bones seemed to be broken, but there were deep lacerations and much hair had been lost. Later, when the dog slept, Bozděch went and searched the area where the dog had been found; and from the evidence he found, this is what he deduced. It looked as though one of the first stick of bombs had blown a deep crater in the earth about thirty yards from the NAAFI; when the four men and the dog were running in the direction of the shelter, the tell-tale roar of the Dornier, pulling out of its second dive, alerted the men to throw themselves to the ground, but the dog had been caught by the blasts and evidently lifted bodily and thrown through the air, landing in the crater, which was then covered over with falling timbers and soil torn up by the high explosives. Probably unconscious for some time, but getting enough air to keep him alive, the dog was unable to move much, and slowly, over the next day and a half, began to die. What saved him was the rain. The late afternoon rain of the second day seeped through sufficiently to form puddles at the bottom of the crater, which alleviated the dog's dehydration somewhat; and as the rain became heavy and sustained, it slowly loosened the overhead soil, whose particles were not bound together or compacted, but lay on a latticework of wood spars, to the extent that the dog, with whatever strength he had left, painfully clawed his way out of his tomb.

An important part of Bozděch's life had been restored to him, but he was dissatisfied too: he had been thinking – and his friends

Štětka and Josef felt much the same – that Bomber Command was where an air-gunner could best contribute to the fight. Consequently, the three requested a transfer to No. 311 (Czecho-slovak) Squadron of Bomber Command. Confirmation of the transfer came through quickly and on 19 October,[19] he and his two friends were posted to the Operational Training Unit for the squadron at RAF Honington in Suffolk.

CHAPTER FIVE

Night Bombing

In the station, where bombers constantly did not return and
the faces in the Mess were so often changing because of
death, death itself was not discussed.

H. E. Bates, *Fair Stood the Wind for France*

Bozděch got off to a bad start at Honington. The Station
Warrant Officer had shown at their first meeting that he was
ill-disposed towards the dog, so Bozděch knew that there
would be difficulties ahead: 'as many an airman has learned to
his cost, Station Warrant Officers rank next to God and the
Station Commander – with only a short head between them for
second place.'[1] Although he had permission from the Station
Commander to have his dog on the camp, there was a rule that no
dogs were allowed in the crews' rooms. However, as he and Štětka
were sharing a room on the ground floor near a side entrance to the
sergeants' mess, Bozděch thought that he could discreetly take
Antis in and out. When the Station Warrant Officer got wind of it,
he had a letter handed to Bozděch giving him two hours to get his
dog out of his room.

Not prepared to be separated from his dog if he could help it,
Bozděch searched for alternative accommodation, and found some
disused old huts by the camp's boundary fence. The stove in one of
them seemed to be in working order and he was prepared to rough
it there. The uncomfortable arrangement worked for a while until

one evening the hut door was thrown open, and there stood the Station Warrant Officer and the Orderly Sergeant. Bozděch was told to report in the morning. Immediately he went to the officers' mess and asked for an interview with the Czechoslovak interpreter, who assured him that he would speak to the Adjutant and the Station Commander first thing in the morning.

By the time he paraded before the Station Warrant Officer, the clouds had already lifted. All was well; he was told that the CO approved, and he could even have his dog in his room in the mess. But at this point, Bozděch shrewdly declined, saying that he preferred to stay with his dog in the abandoned hut. And in so saying, he established respect from the senior non-commissioned officer, for while the Station Warrant Officer had been overruled by the CO, he still saved face in the sergeants' mess. Bozděch's sensitivity paid off: returning from a training exercise, he found – and learned later it was on the Station Warrant Officer's orders – that the stove had been lit and a goodly quantity of fuel supplied.

When President Beneš addressed the Czechoslovak personnel at Duxford and extolled the prowess and the quality of the RAF, he was implicitly underlining comparative shortfalls, not in the calibre of his own airmen, but in the equipment and practices of his country's air force. The pre-war Czechoslovak Air Force had a role that was designed to support ground troops in a defensive war; its one bomber regiment navigated by map reading, with some use of Dead Reckoning; but there was no knowledge of astro-navigation,[2] a field in whose practice the RAF was advanced. As the new role for the men of No. 311 Squadron was long range bombing, there was much to be learned. Even some senior officers in the early days of the squadron were unaware of this basic deficiency in their airmanship. Herbert Němec was a pilot with the squadron, and he recounts that on one occasion in the early months at Honington, some navigators were practising altitude measurement of the sun with a bubble sextant near one of the hangars, as the senior Czechoslovak officer of the squadron was being driven past. He had the driver stop the car, and he stormed over to the group and upbraided them for taking photographs near a hangar. In the brief silence that followed, each man quickly thought how judicious it would be to disabuse a senior officer and point up his ignorance; and one of them did. Taking refuge in the dignity of his rank, the superior huffed to them to carry on, and smartly returned to his transport.[3]

The squadron were flying Wellington Bombers Mk IC. By this time the Wellington was the old war-horse of the service, but it was still an impressive bomber. Assembled in seven stages, with two and a quarter miles of electrical cable, it had a bomb load of four thousand five hundred pounds, a range of one thousand five hundred miles, and carried a crew of six. For the next two months and two weeks operational training continued for the newcomers. But over Christmas day all training came to a halt, and the sergeants had a big party in their mess. While the evening was still quite young, Bozděch went back to his hut with a special dinner for his dog from the mess. He was content there, but eventually Štětka and Josef thought he had been away too long and decided to join him, bringing with them a goodly supply of booze. Drinking in one's quarters was against the regulations; and they risked demotion if caught. Luckily no one in authority was in the least interested, and the night proceeded as one of serious drinking. Whether bidden or unbidden, the dog went round the glasses, and before very long they were aware that Antis was blundering into them: he was well and truly under the weather. Bozděch had great difficulty waking him next morning; and when he was let out, Antis headed straight for a fire bucket and drank copiously, after which, while his master still suffered from a hangover, he was apparently as right as rain.

In January 1941, his final cross country training completed, Bozděch and his two friends went to East Wretham, the satellite of Honington, where No. 311 Squadron was based. Conditions at East Wretham were very different from the Honington mess: it was a hastily set up satellite on part of Breckland heath in Norfolk, six miles north east of Thetford, comprising huts and tents – even though it was winter. A farmhouse was requisitioned; and it was here that Bozděch and Ludva shared a room on the top floor, with Gustav and Josef in the room next door. Although the farmhouse had been requisitioned, the Manor farm continued to be worked; and the busy life of the farmyard was a welcome respite for the airmen. Antis lived equably with the farm poultry – only the turkeys seemed to pose a potential challenge, but Bozděch firmly warned him off. The camp was about a mile from the farm, and so they acquired whatever form of transport they could; Bozděch bought a bike, and Antis had plenty of exercise trotting around with him. The squadron had been made welcome by the people in the village. Prayers for its work were offered in the small church on Sunday, and its losses were remembered.

Bomber Command at this time – well before the advent of the one thousand bomber raids – played an important role in the public mind. Germany was at the height of its power; Britain was in no position to contemplate a land war on the Continent; only Bomber Command could strike at the heartland of the Reich. According to the thinking and the strategy of the first six months of the war, Bomber Command was forbidden to bomb Germany in case this caused civilian casualties.[4] All that had changed. Whenever the weather permitted, night bombing against industrial and military targets in Germany and military targets in the occupied countries was carried out. The mood of support in the country and the unbowed spirit of the time was reflected – albeit on a grander scale than most could aspire to – in the response of a woman of means who knew something of the grief of war: Lady MacRobert of Cromar in Aberdeenshire lost two sons serving in the RAF; she contributed £25,000 to the production cost of a Stirling bomber; and when the designated aircraft completed its final assembly stage, before it was handed to the Air Transport Auxiliary to be delivered to a squadron, it was named 'MacRobert's Reply'.[5]

Weather conditions prevented operations for much of January. The RAF liaison officer to No. 311 Squadron was Squadron Leader 'Pick' Pickard. Pickard was a very skilled pilot, and, in Bozděch's estimation, an excellent leader, who did a lot to improve the professionalism of the squadron.[6] He also served as instructor and operations officer, developing a strong bond with the Czechoslovaks, and he took his role very seriously. The director of a film that Pickard later took part in reported that when the Germans threatened to shoot captured Czechoslovak aircrew, Pickard wore Czechoslovak shoulder flashes on his tunic.[7] When there was no flying because of the weather, aircrews would often get together in the Ark Royal and Bell hotels in Thetford. Pickard often joined them, without in any way restricting their freedom off duty. Bozděch recalled him standing by the bar, 'a dense cloud of smoke from his well known pipe,' laughing and joking with them, so that 'no man present could for long have held aloof from the fun.'[8]

New aircrews on their first combat mission were known as Freshmen, and they were usually allocated to bomb a military target in France or another occupied country, so that they became familiar with anti-aircraft fire and searchlights; but it was a comparatively gentle baptism of fire before they confronted the intensity of the integrated German air defence system. Pickard, according to Bozděch, often flew with the Freshmen crews to give them support. All in all, he seems to have been an inspiring leader.[9] It is certainly clear from the squadron operations record book that Pickard took on a lot of operational sorties. Another who inspired men and gave himself a heavy operational commitment was Squadron Leader Josef Ocelka.

In February operations began to get under way again. On the night of the 5th six aircraft were detailed to bomb Channel ports; five of them returned. From 7842 T no message was received; its front gunner was Bozděch's friend Gustav Copal.[10] Later it was learned that the plane had been shot down; the crew were able to bale out and Gustav had been taken prisoner. Meanwhile, extensive training was being carried out; and on 9 February, Air Vice Marshal Janoušek visited the squadron.[11] But the enemy was also active: East Wretham was attacked twice that month; the first time it was bombed on the north side; and the second time bombed and machine-gunned, which resulted in the damage of one aircraft.

Another new crew was formed. The Wellington had a crew of six, and in the RAF, unlike the pre-war Czechoslovak Air Force where the observer was in command of the aircraft, the pilot was the captain, regardless of the rank of other members of the crew. In No. 311 Squadron at this time, and for some time to come, the majority of sorties were piloted by sergeants. Bozděch's crew consisted of three officers and three sergeants: Sgt Čapka, the pilot – he had flown as second pilot up until now – FO Šejbl, second pilot, PO Lančik, navigator, PO Kacíř, wireless operator, and Sgts Gruden and Bozděch, gunners. Their aircraft was 1598 C, or C for Cecelia as they tended to call it. Dunkirk, Calais and Bremen were their targets in late March.[12] At Bremen they experienced the effectiveness of the German air defence system. They also learned that it was unwise to relax on their return to base, not even when they were in the circuit to be signalled in to land, for in the early hours of 4 March an enemy plane followed one of the Wellingtons in and bombed the airfield.

The squadron's target for two nights in early April called for precision bombing that, at this point in the development of Bomber Command's technology, was a lot to ask for. Tied up at the French port of Brest was the German battle cruiser *Prinz Eugen*. On 4 April, Bozděch's crew was among the eight that were detailed to carry out the raid. They reached their target and attacked; and they reported that six bursts were seen to the west, indicating that the bomb load had overshot. Two nights later they were off to try again; but this time the cloud was so dense that they could not see the target, and so they bombed in the target area. All seven aircrews had something similar to report. One or two crews, like Sqn Ldr Ocelka's, saw bomb bursts reflected in the cloud base.

Václav Štětka met his death in the night sky over Germany on 17 April. He was front gunner in 1599 J, one of seven aircraft that took off to bomb Berlin.[13] Štětka was a good friend, a most convivial character, and was well liked in the mess. His favourite drinking haunts, though, were the pubs around East Wretham, where he was a popular customer. However, it was borne in on his friends just how cheap life had become when the camp administration swiftly arranged for the clearing out of his room for his replacement. The squadron's losses were not dwelt on, and raids continued in April's favourable weather; Sqn Ldr Ocelka went on eight of them; and Bozděch on five. On the 25th of the month, Bozděch was awarded the Czechoslovak Medal for Valour.[14]

There was less sign of Sqn Ldr Pickard around the squadron in April. This was because the Air Ministry had agreed to the proposal that a documentary film about one of Bomber Command's raids could be a boost to public morale. Some of the very fine films that had been made in 1940 dealt with the response to the blitz and the determination and resilience of those on the home front. But the idea of making a film depicting one aircrew's mission was taken up. Harry Watt was an experienced film director who had worked with the great documentary film-maker Robert Flaherty; and he was commissioned to write and direct a film based on his reading of crew reports. The project became *Target for Tonight*; there would be no actors, but men and women of Bomber Command, with Sqn Ldr Pickard in the role of the pilot of Wellington bomber F for Freddie. The interior shots were filmed in the studio; the external scenes at RAF Millerton. However, from what Bozděch wrote, it seems that Pickard felt that he would like to have included in the footage some acknowledgement of the Czechoslovak squadron with which he worked. He had his own dog, but he was very fond of Antis; and according to Bozděch, Pickard wanted a shot of Antis leading the crew of F for Freddie from the crew room. Such a sequence would not have been strictly correct because the crews were taken by lorry to their dispersals; but a film crew came and took a few shots.[15] In the final edit though no such scene appears: the crew are taken from the crew room by lorry.[16]

To help increase productivity during the war, an extra hour was added to British Summer time. Night bombing required that darkness should have gathered before aircraft crossed the enemy coast, and so, as summer advanced, take-off time became later. On 5 May 1941, starting at 22.15 hours, five aircraft took off; the target was Mannheim; Bozděch's usual crew were flying 1516 U for Ursula. As they headed for the coast of Europe they experienced W/T trouble, and after a brief consultation, Sgt Čapka decided not to proceed to the primary target but to attack installations at Dunkirk. On their approach they were engaged by an enemy fighter, but the Wellington's gunners put in three short bursts, and the hostile was seen going into a shallow dive disappearing into cloud.[17] They then carried on and attacked their target, dropping their bombs in one stick.

That month Bozděch was awarded the Czechoslovak War Cross.[18] Among those who received the award was PO Jan Gellner, who was navigator for Václav Korda, and whose tour of duty with No. 311 Squadron began and ended at much the same time as Bozděch's. Gellner's route to the squadron was different from that taken by most of his comrades. He had been a lawyer in Czechoslovakia in the late 1930s, but fled in 1939. As he was fluent in English he made his way to the USA, but when war broke out, he crossed the border into Canada, which was the nearest country at war with Germany, so that he could enlist. At that time, however, the Czechoslovak authorities in exile had not been able to organise the recruitment of its nationals in Canada – they were then not even recognised as a Provisional Government – and so Gellner joined the Royal Canadian Air Force. After training he was sent to the UK, and in December 1940, was transferred to No. 311 Squadron, as a member of the RCAF.[19]

On 7 June, the port of Brest and the German heavy battle cruiser *Prinz Eugen* were included again on the squadron's repertoire. At two or three minute intervals, from 21.47 hours, nine aircraft, seven of them captained by sergeant pilots, took off for the raid. Bozděch and his crew were in 1598 C as usual, and they were airborne three minutes after the leader. The flight was uneventful. They reached Brest and turned into their approach angle and then released their bomb load; they observed four bursts on a pier, about one hundred yards south of the target.[20] Eight of the nine aircraft successfully reached the target and bombed; but no claims were made for a direct hit on the capital ship. Meanwhile, weather conditions back at base were gradually deteriorating, and several planes had to be diverted.

Fog persisted a day or so, and it was followed by rain. Some Freshmen crews were trained and some cross-country flying at night took place, but there were no operations for four days, and then the pattern continued again with Dusseldorf, Hamm and Cologne as the targets.

Antis' 'Freshman' sortie with Bomber Command, as one might expect, does not appear in the squadron's operations record book among the summarised points of interest which they wanted to flag up for the attention of No. 3 Group. It assuredly did not have the sanction of higher authority; and it seems clear that it did not come about as a result of the crew's decision: the dog took the initiative; and after what turned out to be a rough raid, the crew looked on him as a good omen, and agreed that he would join the combat team. The dog, of course, had flown with Bozděch on active service in France, but that was during low-level reconnaissance with the ground attack unit, and so there was no need for an oxygen supply.[21]

The dog's first combat sortie with Bomber Command came about because he had suffered acute separation stress. When Bozděch left on a sortie, Antis would wait at the dispersal until the aircraft returned. He had the company of the ground crew, and he was particularly fond of Adamek, who led the team responsible for 1598 C. With the acute hearing of a pointed-ear dog, particularly in the higher frequencies, Antis had come to distinguish the exact pitch of 1598 C for Cecelia's engines, even when it was in the circuit with other Wellingtons. Both the ground crew and Bozděch observed this phenomenon – engine parts working at high speed produced sounds whose pitch the human ear could not discriminate between one aircraft and another, but the dog was able to distinguish Cecelia's engines from the rest. However, when 1598 C was grounded, and Bozděch flew in another aircraft, the dog was unable to identify it; his skill in recognising Cecelia's engines seems to have come about through repetition and familiarity. In addition, he was on his home territory, he lived on air force bases; and Bozděch had trained him well: the dog was to become familiar with the presence of aircraft, but the cardinal rule that Bozděch instilled in him was that he must never approach an aircraft until its engines were cut. Then he would bound forward in the early hours of the morning to greet his master, returning from a raid.

When Bozděch wrote up his account of the life of Antis, he did

not have his flying log book with him: it had been left behind in
Czechoslovakia; the squadron's operations record was not yet in
the public domain, and so he had to rely on memory and cross-
references with others who had served in the squadron. He recalled
that it was in June, during the raid on Hamm that he was struck a
glancing blow on the forehead by a piece of shrapnel; the aircraft,
1598 C, was labouring home with its port engine malfunctioning;
and they landed at Coltishall. Bozděch was taken into hospital at
Norwich.[22] Antis, meanwhile, was waiting at East Wretham for the
arrival of his master's plane. He waited two days in the open air;
he refused to eat, and he bared his teeth at anyone who tried to drag
him indoors. It was the squadron's chaplain who suggested to the
Station Commander that since Bozděch was only lightly wounded,
the hospital should be asked if he could be brought to collect his
dog. And this was what happened. Bozděch and Antis shared a
small room for the remaining few days until Bozděch was
pronounced fit to be given a week's leave before resuming
operations.

Sure enough, according to the squadron's operations record
book, after the raid on Hamm (he recalled that it was just after the
German invasion of Russia, but it in fact took place ten days earlier
on 12 June) it was thirteen days before Bozděch was back on
operations again – one of the longest periods that he was not on
operations for the entire period of his tour of duty with the
squadron. When he came back on operational flying again, it was
25 June, and the target was Bremen.

In the early evening, the dog sensed that Bozděch was preparing
for another operation and made his way to Cecelia's dispersal. The
aircraft had already been bombed up; the ground crew were either
having a tea break or were otherwise occupied, and he climbed the
ladder – a skill he had been taught long before – into the belly of
the Wellington, and lay under the canvas sling on the port side that
was used if one of the crew was injured.

This sequence of events, Bozděch reasoned, must have been
what happened. Since no one saw the dog at the time, of course,
this must be conjecture. But there is not another credible explanation for his behaviour. If he had been on board while the ground
crew were working on the plane and gone to sleep, he would have
exuberantly welcomed his master when the crew boarded. Instead
he kept a low profile; he did not reveal himself when the crew came
aboard; it was only when they were committed to their target and

were climbing, as they crossed the Dutch coast that shortage of oxygen forced him to reveal his presence.

Take off was at 23.17 hours. Everything seemed to be going normally on the flight, and Bozděch was intent on his instruments before him.

> Feeling a touch on his elbow, he turned, expecting to see the Navigator asking him for a radio fix, but the Navigator was deep in his charts and took no notice of him. Puzzled he stared into the darkness around him. In the dim glow of the orange light above his panel, he saw the vague shape of the dog motionless on the floor behind him. It was impossible. It couldn't be . . . and yet it was. Antis lay with heaving sides, struggling for breath.[23]

Bozděch undid the straps of his oxygen mask and placed it firmly against the Alsatian's face. After a little the dog stood up, and offered him his paw, but Bozděch ignored it and pointed to the floor at his feet. With the dog between his feet, head raised high, Bozděch found it easier to hold the oxygen mask close to his muzzle.

> In the orange light, brightened occasionally as searchlights swept over the bomber, Antis looked like some creature from another planet. But he appeared quite calm now, and made no attempt to remove the mask. He seemed to sense that the strange refreshing smell of wild thyme, which moistened his nose, was necessary to his breathing.[24]

They were now over Germany; Bozděch needed both hands for his duties and he made the mask on the dog more secure by looping a piece of string through the straps. The oxygen mask, however, also contained the microphone, and as a result of the sequence of exchanging it with the dog the pilot heard what sounded like snoring coming from one of the crew. There was a spare headset and a loose microphone which Bozděch used to keep in contact with the rest of the crew. He told the pilot they had a four-legged passenger. The information registered, but it was instantly relegated in the priorities of the moment. They were flying at fifteen thousand feet to avoid the danger from light flak; and Bozděch managed to work without oxygen without much hardship; but once or twice his heart began to race and sweat dampened his forehead. When that happened he had to remove the mask from the dog, take a few quick gasps through the mask, and then replace it on the dog.

Then the unexpected happened: they began to experience severe icing conditions; and this was followed by a series of violent electrical storms; the aircraft was struck by lightning, and there was instrument failure. There was little choice now but to turn for home and jettison their bomb load over the sea. Three of the four aircraft allocated to the target were affected by the atmospheric conditions, and failed to reach it.[25]

Cecelia had survived Jove's thunderbolts, as well as the ordnance of the enemy that night; and ordinarily that might be thought to be the end of it – a good story about a stowaway dog to tell in the mess and the pubs around East Wretham. But this was war, and they were in Bomber Command and each night greatly at risk. So it was not the end of it: the final component that clinched the decision that Antis should now join their number was the strong superstition that aircrews in wartime were prone to adopt. Bozděch, for example, gave the illustration that a man would wear his girl friend's silk stocking wound round his neck; another might take a photograph of someone dear to him; and even as they left the lorry bringing them to their dispersals, as one crew was dropped off there would be cries of the Czech equivalent of 'break your neck boys' – an absolute guarantee, it was held, that nothing serious would go wrong that night.[26] It was therefore a collective decision, on the part of three sergeants and three officers – the regular crew of 1598 C – that the dog's presence had brought good luck; and they agreed that Antis should be part of the combat team. However, a very important precondition was that the dog had behaved well in circumstances that were difficult enough for a rational human being, but could have terrified an animal: his sense of attachment to his master was greater than his primal instinct of fear. As a result, in the workshops an oxygen mask was adapted for Antis; and the conspiracy was complete. From now on, when Bozděch went on a sortie, six airmen and an Alsatian appeared at the dispersal and boarded a Wellington bomber.

However, all operations were cancelled on 20 June 1941 for a prestigious event in the life of the squadron. Dr Beneš, President of the Provisional Government in Exile visited RAF East Wretham. He was accompanied by Jan Masaryk, Foreign Minister, Air Vice Marshal Janoušek from the Czechoslovak Inspectorate, and one or two senior Czechoslovak Army officers.

When President Beneš addressed his forces that evening, he would have praised their work; and he would have held out hope for the future course of the war – as he had done when he spoke to the Czechoslovak airmen at Duxford a year earlier. However, in that intervening year the number of Allies aligned against the Axis remained much as it had been in 1940. To be sure, the threat of invasion had receded; but Germany's might was still in the ascendancy. Yet less than forty-eight hours after Beneš addressed his servicemen at East Wretham, Adolf Hitler initiated an operation which would greatly accelerate the downfall of his thousand year Reich, and ultimately, would also have profound implications for Central and Eastern Europe, when he launched 187 divisions of the Wehrmacht against Russia.

Bozděch described the mood in the crew room of No. 311 Squadron soon after the Soviet Union had been attacked as one of eagerness; there was expectation that they would be sent to aid their new ally.[27] They were not disappointed: a Bomber Command directive put some emphasis on transportation and communication as priority targets; and this, the aircrews anticipated, would hinder the flow of men and equipment to the eastern front.

There was a flurry of interest at the station in midsummer: on 24 June Sqn Ldr Ocelka was awarded the DFC; the following day the Duke of Kent visited the squadron; and at the end of the month command of the squadron changed hands when Sqn Ldr Ocelka took over from Wg Cdr Schejbal.[28] Ocelka's promotion to the role was popular with the aircrews: he was considered to be an excellent pilot and a fine leader who led by example.

A little over three weeks after their attack on the *Prinz Eugen*, the squadron was detailed to attack it again in Brest harbour. On 1 July eight aircraft took off into the night sky. In Bozděch's crew there was a change of personnel: only he, Sgt Gruden and PO Lančik of the usual crew were together, and since 1598 C was not serviceable, they flew 3221 O. They reached Brest and attacked from 330 degrees, dropping their bombs in one stick, observing them causing a fire north of the dock. Jan Gellner was navigator in Václav Korda's crew in 1015 L, and he wrote more detail in his personal diary than is to be found in the operations record book.

We must have been the first over the target: Brest lay perfectly quiet as we approached. Only when we were already overhead, did the searchlights go on and the anti-aircraft batteries start firing. Our target, the heavy cruiser *Prinz Eugen*, was moored on the east side of the jetty of Dock 8. One of the defences of Brest is a smoke-screen, but the wind was unfavourable to the defenders; it blew the smoke inland, leaving the harbour free. We were very methodical this time, and after cruising over the target area to make sure of the location of Dock 8, made our approach from west to east, along the waterfront. The blacked-out cruiser was invisible against the dark waters, but we got a direct hit on the jetty with our 1,000 pound bomb, while the end of our stick of four 500-pounders should, by my calculations, considering our course and the spacing of the bombs in the attack, have fallen smack on the ship. This was the more probable as all the bombs had obviously fallen on solid ground – I could see this quite clearly from my bombardier's position. Upon our return to base, we did not claim to have hit the *Prinz Eugen*, but reported all the circumstances that made us believe that we may have gotten her, especially the clearly observed hit on the jetty.[29]

Intelligence reports from the French Resistance gave reason to suppose that the ship had indeed been damaged. While all eight aircraft in the attack returned to base, four Freshmen had been sent out that night to bomb Cherbourg. On the way back from the raid, one bomber was shot down by a friendly fighter, with the loss of all six of the crew, having failed to respond to a challenge from the fighter.[30]

Two nights later they were detailed for another raid on Essen. Bozděch's crew were again without their usual aircraft; they were allotted 1718 N, and successfully carried out the attack, reporting that they had caused one small fire. July was a demanding month for the squadron: twelve raids were mounted, involving over one hundred missions. In the course of that month Bozděch was on operations about every second night. Between May and August, he flew on thirty missions. This frequent appearance on the operations roster was typical of just about any member of the squadron.

Night bombing on this scale of regularity took its toll on both men and machines. When Bozděch first went to East Wretham, he noticed that his friends who had been on operations for about two months, looked older and very tired. Now he knew why: the constant strain of facing danger was very demanding, and aircrew had to find ways of coping with it. And when he wrote a book about the bomber crews of No. 311 Squadron, Bozděch depicted them as men whose exposure, night after night, to the stress of the unpredictable made them fatalistic, laconic and able to share their experiences only with their comrades.

> What does it mean to go through a single operation that takes about six hours? The crews who return do not speak much: only when they meet in the Mess to relate the details of the sortie, and expect the return of their friends with anxious looks in their eyes. And others, whose return has been thwarted by the implacable hand of Fate, will keep the secret of their last sortie to themselves.[31]

Taciturnity is implicit in the crews' reports of raids: intention, how it was executed, and any results observed are all that are recorded. Anything else was considered extraneous. Near misses, lucky escapes, shrapnel damage to the plane that did not maim or kill a member of crew or render the aircraft completely unserviceable are not rated worthy of a mention in the aircrews' reports.

The peculiar nature of the stress faced by bomber crews was the subject of study by psychiatrists during the war. They found that there were two dangers the aircrews faced: enemy fighters and anti-aircraft fire (flak). The Allied crews had a high respect for the enemy fighters; but the fighters could be confronted; they could be shot down; or they could be outmanoeuvred. Against anti-aircraft fire, however, they were helpless. Anti-aircraft fire 'is impersonal, inexorable, and as used by the Germans, deadly accurate. It is nothing that can be dealt with'.[32] Faced with this kind of danger night after night, group morale helped them to cope with the threat; and it is that core of comrades that Bozděch wrote about in his aptly titled book, *Gentlemen of the Dusk* (*Gentlemeni Soumraku*). In Bozděch's case, during those summer months of 1941, the presence of his dog would also have been a strength to him; and not only to him: the courage of the dog – his instinctive fears diminished by his greater loyalty – was an example to others.

Equipment became stressed as well. Mechanical failures could lead to an engine overheating. One of the most common problems was simply recorded in the log as engine trouble. What often comes through in the reports though is that when this happened, a discussion took place among the crew, and if the primary target was still some hours ahead, a decision was taken to attack another nearer target – perhaps one they had attacked in the past. After sustaining some damage during one raid, an idiosyncrasy developed in 1598 C so that its heating system stopped working whenever it reached an altitude of about ten thousand feet. During June and July the aircraft was flown by its regular crew on almost all their missions, but after it was damaged by flak in August, it was airworthy on only four occasions that month, and each time there was engine trouble.

Reliance on equipment to such an extent brought out a tremendous commitment on the part of the ground crews. Bozděch paid tribute to their dedication in *Gentlemen of the Dusk*. He described them coming to their work, secured with every serviceman's first priority: the means of victualling himself, with a mug tied to his waist, cutlery rattling in his pocket. As the fitters and mechanics worked through the long hours, servicing and repairing, mates would bring them mugs of tea. They earned the lion's share of the squadron's successes; they gave the aircrews confidence because of their own commitment; and they took great pride 'whenever "their" aircraft, often badly damaged, made it home.'[33]

Highly motivated, the men of the Czechoslovak squadrons knew what they were fighting for; but the politicians of the country under whose leadership they served had still not confronted the shame of Munich, the international agreement that had ceded part of Czechoslovakia to Germany. The compromise that had worked since July 1940 was the recognition of the Provisional Czechoslovak Government in Exile. But provisional upon what? To add to the need to find a long-term political solution, the Soviet Union – now an ally – had never accepted or recognised the Munich agreement. The British Foreign Secretary Anthony Eden, who in 1938 had been one of those against the Munich deal, was sympathetic, and promised his Czechoslovak counterpart, Jan Masaryk that the matter would be pursued. The matter dragged on for months, and stalled in early 1941 when Eden was sent to the Middle East. Whenever Dr Beneš or his Foreign Minister Jan Masaryk put pressure on government officials, they were met with the mantra 'provisional recognition'. Bruce Lockhart, the British Government's Liaison Officer to Dr Beneš and his Government in Britain wrote that an exasperated Jan Masaryk 'asked me if the Czechoslovak airmen who had been killed in the war were provisionally dead, and wrote me a letter signed "Yours provisionally, Jan"'.[34] Finally, however, on 19 July 1941, in the House of Commons,

Foreign Secretary Eden informed the House that the Government had renounced the Munich agreement. The original borders of Czechoslovakia would be restored to it, and so would its democracy.

That future, though, had still to be won; and in July 1941, it looked a long way off. For their part, No. 311 Squadron attacked the invader of their homeland about every second night that month. Bozděch's crew bombed: Essen, Munster, Cologne, Bremen, Hanover, Hamburg, Mannheim and Brest, where the capital ship *Prinz Eugen* lay at berth. On 25 July, he was awarded a bar to the Czechoslovak War Cross.[35]

Antis also served – as the wording on the Dickin Medal reminds us – by accompanying his master on those raids. And he received his first wound during one of them. Bozděch did not remember the date when Antis was first wounded; he recalled that it was over Kiel, but it seems that he misremembered: the squadron did not bomb Kiel that month, but the Czech style of writing Cologne is Köln, and that is how it is recorded in the operations log book. So it was probably on 7 or 10 July when the crew of 1598 C was allocated that target. Bozděch simply wrote that 'a fragment of shell pierced his [Antis'] oxygen mask, scratching his nose and left ear',[36] before lodging in one of Bozděch's flying boots. The dog made no sound, and seemed not to notice the wound; Bozděch was unaware of it until they got back to base and the dog did his usual run around of joy. The shell fragment had cut the dog's paw, nose and ear. The wound seemed nothing at the time, but in later years, as the dog aged, his left ear permanently drooped.

Eventually, it had to come about that the caption 'Dog of War' would appear in the newspapers at a time when editors were looking for good news, or an interesting angle on present strategy. The number of those who knew about the dog that accompanied his master on bombing missions over the Reich led to its being talked about in the pubs in the area; and inevitably it came to the ears of a press reporter. Hence the squadron Adjutant received a request to allow some press photographers to take shots of one particular crew before take off. Publicity for the Czechoslovak comrades-in-arms was to be welcomed, but it was one thing for the squadron's senior officers to turn a blind eye to a crew taking a dog on operations; it was quite another to have proof of it in the newspapers. So although the press turned up, there was no dog in sight as the crew of 1598 C posed in the gathering dusk before boarding.

The photograph was published in a number of papers; and in Prague in 1947, it appeared as the jacket image for Bozděch's book *Gentlemeni Soumraku* (*Gentlemen of the Dusk*).

In August, Antis was more seriously wounded by shrapnel from anti-aircraft fire. Recounting it fourteen years later, without his log book to hand, Bozděch recalled that it was about the middle of the month. But from his description of the damage that 1598 C sustained, and an analysis of the squadron's operations record book, which indicates how long the aircraft was out of service, it is likely that it happened on 5 August, during the raid on Mannheim. There was a particular intensity to the co-ordinated air defences that night, Jan Gellner recorded in his diary. It was his crew's last raid in their tour of duties. 'The target was Mannheim and we had a hard time. The anti-aircraft fire was very heavy.'[37] There is no reference, of course, in the crew's report to the particularly hard time they had. Bozděch described what happened when they were over the target.

> It happened soon after 'Cecelia' had loosed her load of bombs on the target and was turning for home. Whilst still in the turn, a shell exploded under her belly almost causing the aircraft to turn turtle in the air. Showers of metal splinters raked the Wellington, punching holes in the fuselage and floor. 'Cecelia' reeled and staggered under the impact; for tense moments the pilot struggled with his damaged controls, until at last he mastered them. Gently but firmly he eased the bomber back onto a level course and held her there. He knew, as did all the crew, that, come what might, no evasive action would now be possible. 'Cecelia' was lame and must be treated with care. However, though her controls were stiff and slow to respond, the roar of her engines was reassuring.
> 'Everybody OK?' unemotionally asked the captain.
> One by one the crew responded.[38]

Bozděch continued with what then happened, finely illustrating the wartime research findings – that of the two fears aircrew harboured, enemy fighters were the danger against which they were not powerless – because with the aircraft airworthy but slow to respond to the controls, everything now rested on the gunners if they were attacked. And as Bozděch relived those hours in the gun turret, oblivious of his dog's wound, focused entirely on the sky, sensing with such intensity that he imagines he is aware of the presence of the night fighters out there, even anticipating the angle from which the attack would come, tensed to swing round the guns, his use of the third person narrative allowed him to express feelings that he would have been reticent to reveal in the first person. He succeeded too in conveying that strange emotional tie that aviators and mariners can have with the craft on which they depend.

In the rear turret Antis, lying between his master's legs, gazed up into his face. But the man intently scanning the night sky for fighters, could not pay much attention to the shivering dog. He sensed the Alsatian's stare and, without shifting his gaze from the hostile skies, bent down and patted the dog's head. Seconds later 'Cecelia' was pounced upon by the blue glare of a radar controlled searchlight which shot up without wavering or warning. . . It could only be a matter of time now before the fighters arrived. In tense silence the air gunners strove to pierce the blinding curtain of light which dazzled them. They could sense the fighters – but could not see them. The heavy flak ceased suddenly and, almost immediately, was replaced by the weird staccato of cannon from the fighters which had now pounced on the sitting duck. Smoke and sickly cordite fumes filled the cabin, while hot oil splashed the windscreen and the two pilots. Through the large hole in the floor between their seats, cold air rushed in with a whistling sound, clearing the fumes as it came. While one struggled with the controls and nursed the wounded 'Cecelia', the other succeeded in checking the escaping oil. The Wellington shuddered violently under the concentrated cannon blasts; then, for no known reason, the attack broke off. With minds and eyes alert for a resumed onslaught, the crew tensely waited. Meanwhile stubborn 'Cecelia' struggled ever nearer home. Like a wounded bird heading desperately for cover, she throbbed her way towards a mass of cloud. The expected attack did not come, but nerves were strained almost to their limit as the men gazed into the night. At last, blessed relief, 'Cecelia' entered the protective cloud which thickened as she droned westward.[39]

It was only as the eastern sky brightened with the first rays of dawn, and they were making the approach over the town of Thetford a little after 4.30 am[40] and no sign of their being followed by an enemy aircraft into the final circuit that Bozděch felt able to relax and look at his dog. He noticed that the dog held his head very stiffly, and, as he bent down to undo the dog's oxygen mask, he stroked his head. There was no response. In some alarm, Bozděch turned his shielded lamp on Antis and saw the pool of blood that the dog had lain in, his chest badly gashed by a shell splinter. Antis had been wounded hours earlier over the target; and 'never once had he tried to hinder or distract the man from his duty. Silently he had lain there, staring mutely at his master and bearing his pain with a fortitude not often found even amongst the bravest of men.'[41]

He was taken to sick quarters. He could not be given an anaesthetic; a male nurse held his paws, Bozděch cradled his head, and a doctor worked on the wound. The dog seemed to sense the kindness of the men working over him. As Bozděch put it, 'Antis, the only casualty of that raid, was treated with just as much care as if he had been human.'[42] He would pull through all right, but it was made clear to Bozděch that the dog's combat flying days were over for a long time to come.

The crew's report gives the bare information that the aircraft attacked the primary target, came in at 340 degrees and dropped the bombs in one stick. All bursts were observed south of the target.[43] However, 1598 C for Cecelia was out of commission for nine days; and when it came into service again, on three consecutive sorties on 14, 16 and 26 of August, it developed engine trouble; and it happened so early and abruptly on 26 August, that they jettisoned their bomb load in the sea, thirty miles from Clacton.[44]

At admin level it was an eventful month. The squadron commander Sqn Ldr Josef Ocelka was promoted to wing commander. The BBC sent a team to the camp on 21 August, and they made some sound recordings of men; and two days later it was the film world when a crew from British Movietone News shot a few reels of the squadron at work. It must have been suggested that the NAAFI would be a suitable venue for a camp cinema; and on 27 August, the idea was tried out. A number of short films preceded the main feature. And the main feature for this inaugural showing in the NAAFI was not a Hollywood confection, but a gritty British film that had just had its premiere in July, *Target for Tonight*.[45] This film, of course, had layers of special interest for the personnel in the squadron: the captain of F for Freddie, Sqn Ldr Dixon, was played by Sqn Ldr Pickard, who had been the squadron's RAF liaison officer; and the film's story – centred on the crew of Wellington bomber F for Freddie – portrayed the work they themselves were doing – night bombing. On general release this film was already hugely popular in 1941, at a time when the course of the war was still being dictated by the enemy, as it depicted Bomber Command striking at the heart of Germany. The screening was a successful experiment at the camp; and from then on, the NAAFI was to be used regularly as the camp cinema.

By night, the air war continued. Bozděch – if luck held – would complete his tour of duty with the squadron in September. But each man schooled himself not to think ahead. On 1 September, he was awarded a bar to the Czechoslovak Medal for Valour;[46] and his promotion to flight sergeant came through.[47] That night, he was on operations; the aircraft was 8784 U, and the target for his crew was Cologne. Two nights later, it was Brest again to attack the *Gneisenau* and the *Scharnhorst*. Fog descended on East Wretham in their absence and they were diverted to Wittering. His final sortie came four nights later, and the target was Berlin; but their aircraft developed engine trouble and instead they chose a nearer secondary target and bombed the docks at Kiel.[48]

Prolonged exposure to stress created a reliance on group morale among the aircrews; and not surprisingly, when a man completed a tour of duty he was often faced with conflicting emotions – relief and regret: relief that he had made it through; regret that he was leaving others to continue the work; and mingled with regret was a sense of loss. Jan Gellner, who left the squadron the month before Bozděch, expressed it well. 'Losses were also enormous in the one Czechoslovak bomber squadron of the Royal Air Force, and they were hard to bear because they fell on a small group of men who all knew one another personally. Virtually every casualty meant the loss of a friend.'[49] When Bozděch was leaving the squadron to go to the Czechoslovak depot, he went by bus to the railway station. His friend Ludva went with him as far as the station. On the station platform both men put on a show of being cheerful, and Ludva patted the dog affectionately. Then the men shook hands solemnly, and said farewell; and that was the last time that Bozděch saw him.

CHAPTER SIX

Training School

This castle hath a pleasant seat; the air
Nimbly and sweetly recommends itself
Unto our gentle senses.

William Shakespeare, *Macbeth*

The overnight journey from the south in a blacked-out railway carriage gave Bozděch no inkling of the surrounding countryside, but the early morning train from Inverness curved its way through attractive scenery. He had been posted to RAF Evanton. Its setting made an immediate impact on him: he found this part of the Highlands, 'strangely reminiscent'[1] of his homeland in Bohemia. The camp was shielded to the north by Cnoc Fyrish, the start of 'a majestic ridge of hills stretching westward towards Ben Wyvis'.[2] Unlike Bohemia, though, an inlet of the sea set off the contour of the hills, for the southern border of the airfield was bounded by the Cromarty Firth; indeed the airfield had first been established in the 1920s as Royal Naval Air Station, HMS Fieldfare. Woods came right down to the camp's perimeter and to the huts where the airmen were billeted. To say his dog loved the place was a euphemism: 'Antis was in heaven', as Bozděch put it.[3] And this, No. 8 Air Gunnery School, RAF Evanton, to which he had had been posted as an instructor, was to be Bozděch's base for a year and a half.

After his tour of duty with No. 311 Squadron, Bozděch had returned to the Czechoslovak Depot at St Athan, and then to the depot at Wilmslow to await deployment. The result was that his RAF career took a new direction when he was given a training role. His experience with Bomber Command was capitalised on. First, on 14 January 1942,[4] he was sent to the Central Gunnery Training School at RAF Chelveston to train as an air gunnery instructor. He felt – or had been told – that, unlike Bomber Command, which encouraged squadrons to develop their own unique ethos, Training Command might not have a relaxed attitude to trainees bringing their dogs along with them; so Bozděch went through channels and applied for a permit. Meantime, he left Antis in the care of his friend Vladimir Cupak at St Athan, and joined his course.

At Chelveston, he was no longer in a milieu where Czech was the common language in the billets and the mess. If the British are still characterised as being disinclined to learn even a smattering of a foreign tongue, that tendency was much more evident sixty-five years ago, before the burgeoning of foreign travel, and a reconception of the school curriculum. Bozděch had a fair command of English by now; but how were his British friends to address him? The pronunciation of the Czech name Václav defies standard English practice which sounds the letter /c/ as a hard consonant in such a group; his nickname Vašeck was even more problematic. It can be irritating to have one's given name constantly mispronounced; so Bozděch adopted the name Robert (he kept it after returning to Czechoslovakia, and as an author in that country he was described as Václav R. Bozděch). Among his British friends though, he was Robert, which, of course, was abbreviated to Bob.

Permission to have his dog with him on the training course was forthcoming, but before Bozděch had free time to go for Antis, Vladimir phoned RAF Chelveston with serious news for him. Antis had broken away from his control, and had chased some sheep. Before Vladimir arrived on the scene, the farmer who owned the sheep fired his shotgun, wounding Antis. The wounds were not life-threatening (to a dog that bore three shrapnel wounds from the enemy what signified a farmer's buckshot?) but the outcome looked bleak: the farmer had taken Vladimir's name, and he had reported the matter to the police. It was certain that the dog's owner would be brought to court. Bozděch had every right to be worried because the law permits a farmer to shoot a dog found worrying sheep. Failing that the courts usually decide that such a dog must be put down.

In desperation Bozděch wrote to his Czechoslovak Wing Commander of No. 311 Squadron and to the RAF former liaison and operations officer, Sqn Ldr Pickard, asking for their support when the case came up. He received a telegram from Pickard, 'Will see what I can do. Good luck. Pickard.'[5]

The case was heard in Cowbridge Police court on 3 March 1942.[6] Bozděch, however, was not granted leave from his course to attend. The evidence that was adduced galvanised the press reporter in attendance: the dog had made 32 operational flights over Germany; and there followed a garbled version of his progress to the UK, 'from Czechoslovakia through Poland and Russia'.[7] Vladimir had been summoned and told the magistrates that the 'owner wanted the animal back as soon as possible in order to take it on operational flights again.' Not content with relying on the influence of senior officers behind the scenes, Bozděch pulled out all the stops, pleading, as it were, the dog's contribution to the Allied war effort. Although the police had asked for the destruction of the dog, the court ordered that the dog should be kept under control and returned to his owner; and Vladimir was fined eleven shillings.

The evening newspaper, the *South Wales Echo* reported the case that same day on its front page: 'Dog That Flies over Germany'; the subheading continued, 'His Life Spared for More Trips'.[8] This was the point at which media interest in the 'dog of war' really took off. Up until now, it had been rumour and assertion that press reporters and photographers had followed up only to be frustrated by the RAF stonewalling; but here was proof positive: statements in court, pleading that the dog be allowed to continue with Bomber Command. One piece of information was still lacking though – their names.

Bozděch, however, was still left with a problem: he would have to retrain Antis. There were still two weeks of his training course to run, and he had little free time. When it was completed he returned to St Athan to be deployed once more; and in the short time before his next posting, with the co-operation of a local farmer, he set about training his dog not to chase sheep. He did it rigorously and systematically: he kept the dog to heel, and they entered a field of sheep. Alarmed, the sheep scurried to a far corner of the field;

Bozděch took the dog into the centre of the field, and made him sit. Then he spoke to him sternly, treating the dog, as he always had done when he trained him, as though he were a human. They were in full view of the sheep, and Bozděch kept him there for an hour. He took him away, and then he returned in the afternoon, and the process was repeated, but this time Bozděch moved away some distance and left the dog on the spot. This regime of making the dog stay in the presence of the sheep, but still under his master's command went on for three days.[9] Soon after, on 17 March, Bozděch was sent to No. 7 Air Gunnery School on liaison duties for two months.

Then on 14 May 1942, he was posted to No. 8 Air Gunnery School at RAF Evanton.[10] The job entailed training future air gunners. Tom Oddie was Officer in Charge of ground and training.

> I was officer I/C of course training, ground and air, for some sixty cadets, teaching, on the ground:- Browning Mk 2 machine guns, the theory of sighting and use of tracer, pyrotechnics, ditching drills, parachute operation, correct fitting of harness and Mae West. The cadets did PT and drill, and swimming. They got a day off every Monday to go on a free train ride to Inverness to go to the swimming pool there; the rest of the day was theirs. I was involved obviously with cadet welfare. We also had problems with air sickness: some people had to be suspended and taken off [the course] altogether; it was a small percentage, but nevertheless it was rather sad when it happened. Then I set weekly written tests and an end of course exam.[11]

About ten to twenty cadets in each cohort were Czechoslovaks and Poles, and Bozděch's role was to take them through the course, both on the ground and in the air. The aircraft at their disposal for training were not the most modern, as Tom Oddie recalls.

> On the flying side, we had a pretty motley collection of aircraft, and, because of the war, everything was in short supply. The main aircraft was the old Armstrong Whitworth Whitley, which should have been in a museum, and the Blackburn Botha – which I made a note was a bloody death trap, because it had only one escape hatch, and people were

always queuing when it ditched; and since we were flying over the sea, that did happen. Later these aircraft were replaced by the Avro Anson; it was an excellent training aircraft and very stable. In the air we gave instruction in air-to-air firing at a towed drogue at various angles and speeds. We also gave CCG, which is a cine camera gun, which was fitted in place of one of the machine guns, and they filmed attacking aircraft. This enabled us to gauge the accuracy of their sighting, and whether they allowed the correct degree of deflection. To hold the attacking aircraft in your gun sight called for stringent control in the operation of the gun turret, and this was a skill not easily acquired. They also did air-to-ground firing at dummy tanks or anything else that was available, firing off an average of about two hundred rounds. The average flying time for exercise – that was with three cadets on board, each having a go – was roughly one hour and ten minutes.[12]

Arnošt Polak, who is Secretary of the Free Czechoslovak Air Force Association, was then one of Bozděch's cadets. Did he and his colleagues get to know their instructor quite closely?

Not really, except that he was a very friendly chap; but he was so senior to all of us, and he had finished a tour of ops. He was older too, about eleven years older than I, which at that time was an age. He was respected, and because of his Bomber Command experience he was looked up to.[13]

Although the Czechoslovak cadets tended to keep a respectful distance from an instructor with Bozděch's experience, that was not the case with his dog. All the cadets knew Antis; Arnošt said, 'he was everybody's pet. He was a very good dog. I don't think he ever chased sheep.'[14] So the training seems to have paid off.

The war was a world away, and there was time for a good social life. An airman, who was part of the permanent staff of the camp, especially one who had an Alsatian, soon became a familiar figure; and both man and dog were recognised and greeted by the towns-people of Evanton. Soon their fame spread further afield, and they were identified by name.

On 3 October 1942, Antis won a prize for a dog handled by a member of the Allied Forces at a dog show in Dingwall. The following day the *Sunday Mail* ran a half-column story entitled, 'Dog Went With RAF On Raids'; and the article went on, 'Antis, an Alsatian dog that has taken part in thirty-two operational flights over Germany, got a special prize ... and he was shown by Flt Sgt Robert Václav Bozděch a Czechoslovakian airman.'[15] It contained too what is probably the earliest reference to the circumstances in which Bozděch got the dog: his plane crashed in No Man's Land between the French and German lines in March 1940, and he found the puppy in a ruined house. The local newspapers, the *Ross-Shire Journal* and the *North Star*, dealt with the event in Dingwall as a whole,[16] pointing out that the proceeds of this Exemption Dog Show were to go to the Red Cross Prisoners of War Fund, and they were rather low-key in describing Antis. The *Ross-Shire Journal* simply put it, 'This animal has done many operational flights and has been wounded twice.'

However, it was the national press that focused on the exceptional interest in the pair, and the following month the *Sunday Mail* published a photograph of Bozděch and Antis.[17] From now on, whenever there was some opportunity to feature them, pictures of Bozděch and Antis would appear in the press and magazines. Interest in Antis reached the level of the Air Ministry; but none of the attendant publicity redounded to the discredit of the RAF, for the article writers either played down or did not know that taking a dog on operational flights was against regulations; so there were no repercussions for Bozděch. Indeed, as we shall see, knowledge of No. 311 Squadron's exceptional mascot would remain in the Ministry for some years to come.

On 8 November Bozděch was commissioned with the rank of pilot officer; and exactly six months later, he was promoted to flying officer.[18] Tom Oddie and he were good friends; and they kept in touch for a number of years after they parted company. Tom Oddie remembers Bozděch with warmth.

> Dear old Bob, he was a splendid chap, and officer. He was good-natured, totally reliable, and dedicated to his job. Sadly I don't think he ever talked about his home life; I'm surprised about that, but I don't remember him talking about it. He was a first class officer.[19]

Antis, of course, is always remembered by anyone who knew him; and anecdotes are usually remembered.

Antis was a lovely dog. Antis had a loving relationship with Bob; he was gentle and good-tempered. And Bob even taught him how to put out a lit cigarette on the ground using his front paw. Quite an achievement! Another amusing thing in a way was that Bob used to go into the Novar grounds and collect edible fungus. He assured me it was, and I used to eat it for breakfast, with no ill effect. But some people were startled, and asked me what I was eating. Yes he knew his onions there![20]

With all the attention he was getting, Antis was in danger of being spoiled; he began to show signs of becoming indisciplined. Arnošt Polak said that all the cadets knew the dog, and he was everyone's pet. Since he had been a puppy, he had lived on air force bases; so during the day while Bozděch was instructing in the class room, Antis had the freedom of the camp; and he went about with such confidence and playfulness that he was the subject of much attention. Bozděch related how he left the dog in the care of cadets if he was going out in the evenings; and once the dog eluded them and followed his master to a local dance in Dingwall; and another time followed him to the cinema. Because of the way he had been trained, he had no timidity among crowds of men in uniform, and he was quite happy to board a bus with a group of them. One night he boarded the wrong bus in Inverness and ended up at RAF Dalcross. Luckily a Czech pilot there recognised him, took him to his hut and made enquiries to see if Bozděch was in transit, before having a call put through to Evanton. Bozděch had to arrange for a Botha aircraft on a training flight to collect the dog from Dalcross. It would seem that the dog led a charmed life there, but it probably says something about the spirit of that time, when there were few private cars, a dependence on local bus services and a great preparedness among servicemen to co-operate.

However, at the beginning of 1943, Bozděch recounts, Antis responded to the call of his own kind, to one who lived wild in the hills. Local lore had it that before the war an Alsatian bitch that had been maltreated by her owner fled to the hills, and there had her litter of puppies; and then she remained in the wild. She was eventually shot by a gamekeeper who spied her stalking a lamb. One of her litter, a bitch, who had now reached adulthood but who had never been domesticated, was in season. Antis left the camp and was away for five days. When he finally came back, noticeably thinner, and bearing scars as though he had been in a fight with another dog, his route took him through the town of Evanton. Some cadets were about and they spotted him and tried to attract his attention; 'the Alsatian swerved to one side and tried to leap a high iron spiked fence which bordered a garden beside the road. He mistimed his leap, and the spikes cut savagely into his belly as he hung impaled'.[21] The cadets had gently to lift him off the spikes. The camp's medical officer could do little for the dog who had to be taken to a vet in Inverness. He remained in the vet's clinic for four days before he was strong enough to be taken back to camp; but it took a lot longer – almost two months – before Antis was like his old self again. As a sombre memento of the close call his dog had had, Bozděch took a photograph of the iron railings surrounding the house.

The magnificent Novar estate, in which the camp was set, had developed thanks to the foresight of its eighteenth century owner Sir Hector Munro, whose planting and planning had enhanced the sweep of land from the Firth to the hills. At the top of Cnoc Fyrish he had had a folly built, not because he entertained delusions of his own grandeur but to give work to local people who were going through a period of famine. It was 'a monument to a conception of land ownership that still owed something to the old clan feelings of responsibility for kindred.'[22] Its aesthetic intent was to draw the eye up through the woods to the crest of the hill and the sky beyond.

Because he had been brought up in the country, evening walks with his dog in the Novar estate evoked memories of boyhood; and he rediscovered a lost zeal in identifying flora, sharing the secret of edible fungus with Tom Oddie; and, as Antis, following numerous scents, criss-crossed between one rabbit run and another, Bozděch tried to recognise as many different animal tracks as he could find. To his surprise, one day he came across Antis lying, head on paws, close to a small burn that flowed by the camp perimeter, watching with interest, but making no aggressive move towards, a duck and her ducklings.

In a time of war after a period of combat experience, it was a privilege to have had such a posting. But it also brought with it feelings of guilt. Tom Oddie recalled this as he remembered RAF Evanton.

It was a very comfortable, compact peacetime station. Yes it was good. It was a bit remote from the war; at times I used to feel rather guilty about that: people tended to forget that there was a war on. I had to remind them of this on occasions – it was a bit of a struggle at times. When you were posted to Training Command, it was very difficult to extricate yourself: they hung on to you like grim death. But yes it was an excellent little station; I was very happy there really; lovely Scottish countryside. We had good facilities and quarters; the officers' mess had central heating – the quarters were good. Overall it was a happy and busy camp.[23]

In October 1943, Bozděch left. He took away many memories from his time at Evanton; he included some in a book he wrote which was published in Prague after the war; and some in a manuscript he wrote later, which became the basis for a book in English. He remembered men who had served with him there, and who had not survived the war. One of them was the pilot FO Josef Menšik. Menšik had had narrow escapes in the past. On the 8th July 1941, when he was a sergeant pilot with No. 312 (Czechoslovak) Squadron, he was posted missing from an operational flight over France – he was seen making a forced landing in France. But he escaped to Spain and, via Gibraltar, succeeded in returning to the UK on the 22nd October that same year. He then served for a time at Evanton. However, on 22 April 1943, he lost his life, together with his observer R. Sliva during a training flight in a Beaufort, near the village of Swanton Morley.[24]

Before he left, however, Bozděch had made representations through the Czechoslovak Inspectorate that Tom Oddie should receive recognition for the way he had worked with and helped many of the Czechoslovak cadets who had passed through the camp. At the personal level, he and Tom Oddie promised that they would keep in touch; and shortly after Bozděch left, anticipating a time after the war, he wrote to Tom, giving his home address in Soběkury, and expressing his invitation in a rather formal European way.

I would be very glad and proud if you would come to my country after the war. You will always be very welcome in my home.

I am very grateful for your very sincere friendship, and I am really sorry to go.

Very sincerely yours,
Bob,
Robert Václav Bozděch [25]

Shortly afterwards, from Pembray in Wales, where he was based for three months, he followed it up with a newsy letter to him; and Tom replied on 15 December 1943.

My Dear Old Bob,

Very many thanks for your letter and all the news, and I am so very glad to hear that you are now being properly employed, and I am sure that you are fulfilling your duties in your usual efficient way.

Rex is still growing at a terrific rate and will certainly be as big as Antis and perhaps a little bigger. His training is progressing favourably and I intend at a later date to draw up a complete syllabus of training for him. Please tell Antis (in Czech) that Rex misses him and hopes to meet him again one of these days.

There is very little news from here, everything is much the same as when you left except that Ken Chatterton is now posted and I, for one, miss him very much, but I am glad to say that his posting meant promotion and, therefore, it was all for the best.

Gordon Siddall (now Squadron Leader Siddall) has been down here for the last two days with the usual crowd of cronies, but they could not find much wrong and have now departed. Gordon asked me to send you his best regards.

Well old boy, I think this is all for now. Please write as often as you can and I will be writing again in the near future.

Yours very sincerely,
Tom [26]

Bozděch's representations to the Czechoslovak Inspectorate in London to give recognition for Tom Oddie's work brought results, although – by the time the proposal went through channels and passed from one desk to another – it was twelve months later before it was announced. The letter to Tom Oddie was on Air Ministry headed paper from the Czechoslovak Inspectorate at 15 Grosvenor Place:

Flight Lieutenant Thomas Berry Oddie

It gives me great pleasure to inform you that the Czechoslovak Minister of National Defence has awarded you the –
CZECHOSLOVAK AIR FORCE OBSERVER'S BADGE
as a mark of gratitude and appreciation for all the help and co-operation you have given to the members of the Czechoslovak Air Force.

> [signature]
> for Air Vice-Marshal K. Janoušek,
> Inspector General of the C. A. F.[27]

Tom Oddie reflects on how the award came about.

> Bob was keen to see me awarded the Czech wings, but I think there was an uphill struggle for him. Our commanding officer, Group Captain John Marsom, at that time, added his not inconsiderable support to Bob's efforts, and eventually the thing came through. But I think Bob worked very hard to achieve it, because they didn't dish them out too readily. I had go to London to get the wings.[28]

Meanwhile, on 2 February 1944, Bozděch was sent to No. 1 Radio School, RAF Cranwell on a four-month course to retrain as a wireless operator.[29] He kept abreast with the war news; and at the end of his first month of training, among the deaths reported was that of Gp Capt Pickard, who had played such an important training role with No. 311 (Czechoslovak) Squadron (and whose support he had sought when the future of Antis was being decided by the court). Pickard had been killed in action, leading a flight of Mosquito bombers in a daring low-level attack on the Gestapo prison at Amiens. It may have been at this time that Bozděch first began mulling over the idea of, at some later point, putting on record in his own country some acknowledgement of Pickard's work and character.

As his course was nearing completion, Bozděch was earmarked for more extensive training in radio and radar. His first course finished on 6 June (the day the Western Allies landed in France to begin their drive to Germany), and next day he began the advanced course, at the same Radio School.[30] In all he spent almost a year at Cranwell; and it was an intensive time, and one that occupied him fully. He emerged from it highly trained in a field that was to become his specialist area for the rest of his time in the service – both in war and in peacetime. Before the second course was completed, however, he put in a request to return to operational duties.

CHAPTER SEVEN

Bridge of Sand

'Give us work! Give us work!' cried the banshee.
'Very well, build a bridge of sand,' said the man, 'across the
Dornoch Firth.'

Folk Tale, 'The Gizzen Briggs'

When it became evident that Germany would have to capitulate within months rather than years, the Allies began to look towards the postwar reconstruction of the channels of international trade and commerce. Civil aviation was one of the items on their agenda; and in November 1944, the United States convened an International Civil Aviation Conference in Chicago, and invited fifty-four countries to make arrangements for establishing provisional air routes. Czechoslovakia was represented by Air Vice Marshal Janoušek KCB, bearing his Czechoslovak rank of general. It was envisaged that the Czechoslovak Air Force would have an important role in establishing a national airline; and many among its ranks, including Bozděch, would be involved in that transition.

But at the level of high politics, President Beneš and his government were concerned about the vacuum that would follow the withdrawal of German troops from Czechoslovakia, and the reintroduction of democracy, if the country were liberated by the Soviet Red Army. In any event there would be a strong communist presence on the political scene, because the balance of forces in Europe had changed dramatically since the 1930s. However, Beneš saw his country as the bridge between east and west Europe; and in the winter of 1944, he and his Foreign Minister, Jan Masaryk, were beginning to prepare themselves for a difficult meeting, in the spring, in Moscow with Joseph Stalin to discuss the future relations between their countries.

Months of hard fighting on all fronts lay ahead though; and Bozděch was transferred to operational flying again, to his old unit No. 311 (Czechoslovak) Squadron. He had been promoted to flight lieutenant on 8 November 1944.[1] The squadron was stationed at RAF Tain; and he was issued with a rail warrant for himself and his dog. The long train journey, in winter, in wartime, seemed interminable: mugs of insipid tea were available from platform kiosks; but to blot out the present it was a case of reading or think about the future. Bozděch was looking forward, he later wrote, to the prospect of operational flying again; he was particularly pleased that the posting was to his old squadron; and the fact that it was stationed not far from Evanton in a part of the country he had enjoyed so much, made it an attractive prospect. As for meeting old comrades – well that was less likely.

By the end of April 1942, the squadron's manpower losses in Bomber Command had reached the point where they could not be replenished by Czechoslovak personnel, for no new cohorts of recruits could come from the occupied homeland. During its time in Bomber Command it had taken part in some 145 raids, flying well over a thousand sorties; it had lost 180 airmen and 20 aircraft. As there were about twenty aircraft in the squadron at any one time – each with a crew of six, one entire squadron complement had been wiped out in a year, as one who had served with it wrote.[2] At the end of April 1942, it was moved into Coastal Command; its aircrews converted to four-engine aircraft, and they were now flying Liberators. In August 1944, it moved to the north of Scotland to RAF Tain, on the south shore of the Dornoch Firth. Its prime task was anti-submarine patrols.

The U-boat threat to the UK was still a matter of great concern, and its impact was regularly a subject on the War Cabinet's agenda. After the Allies broke out from the Normandy bridgehead, the German U-boat fleet operating in the Atlantic lost its bases in France; Norway became an alternative, and consequently there was an increase in sea traffic between Germany and Norway.[3] The Luftwaffe was still a very formidable force in Norway: in the western European theatre of operations the Allies had complete command of the skies, and the enemy was desperately short of aviation fuel; but in Norway stores of fuel had been accumulated since 1940.

Bozděch rejoined his old squadron in January 1945. The New Year did not augur well. On 1 January, Liberator Y-949 took off from Tain at 22.02 and crashed near Rora Head in Orkney thirty-eight minutes later, killing all its crew of eight;[4] and nine days later an Oxford with a crew of five went missing on a non-operational flight. The weather was very unfavourable, and for five consecutive days no flying took place due to snow and frost; frequently aircraft were recalled by Group because of a sudden deterioration in conditions; and sometimes they had to be diverted.

On 24 January, during a lull in operations, Air Vice Marshal Janoušek, Inspector General of the Czechoslovak Air Force visited the squadron, took the salute at a special parade, and presented medals. Afterwards he gave an address to the squadron in the station cinema; and then Dr Drtina, Personal Secretary to President Beneš gave a political perspective. Servicemen, in wartime, can often be sceptical about a politician's promises – although they have no choice but to listen in silence. Drtina's theme was the future for their country; and as time would show, when he was appointed Minister of Justice in the restored democracy, he stood firm, as a man of integrity, against pressure and intimidation.

There were many new faces in No. 311 Squadron since Bozděch left it in 1941. Among them was Arnošt Polak, who had been one of Bozděch's cadets at RAF Evanton. He was still in his mid teens when, in 1939, his parents sent him and his older brother to the UK. When they were old enough they joined Czechoslovak units. Arnošt recalls the work of the squadron in the north Atlantic and the Baltic.

> It consisted largely of anti-submarine sweeps, and convoy escorts. This must have been among the most boring kind of operation I've ever experienced. The sea was grey, the sky was grey and I was counting the operational flights towards the end of my tour of operations.[5]

For Bozděch operational flying brought back a difficult dilemma. A sortie could last as long as eleven or twelve hours; and sometimes a Liberator was diverted from its base because of the weather. Antis had not experienced his master's long absence since 1941; and he reverted to his old habit of waiting patiently. Bozděch wrote that on one occasion his plane was diverted from Tain. Meanwhile, Antis waited in inclement conditions, although, after some hours, he finally allowed some airmen to cajole him indoors. But when Bozděch returned he found the dog, his nose dry, listlessly curled up on his blanket; and the next day he was not well: when Bozděch took him out, he noticed that the dog was passing blood. Realising the seriousness of this development, he took him to a vet, who told him that the dog's kidneys had been affected.

> The trouble is that he's obviously a very well trained and clean dog, and that's the biggest danger. With his diseased kidneys his bladder is bound to be weaker and, if he's kept locked up for hours, it might well kill him. Don't be fooled by his robust condition; another long spell of exposure to excessive cold will be his last. However, if you take proper care of him, I think you'll find he'll be OK now.[6]

By any scale of values in wartime, Bozděch had few options: he had duties, and it was clear to him that he had to try, to some extent, to break his dog's degree of attachment to him, by turning his back on him, leaving him with others, and having others feed him. Much as it wrenched him to do it, he tried this; and it failed completely. He had not reckoned the extent to which, 'dogs can show a childish obstinacy when their feelings are hurt. Although he was now very hungry, Antis refused to eat and lay motionless on his blanket . . .'[7] The dog's attachment would not be broken; instead he suffered. After another absence, Bozděch came into the room where the dog lay, curled up on his blanket. 'He knew now', he wrote, 'that his experiment had failed and that all their mutual suffering had been in vain.'[8] Fortunately, it seems that a combination of a long winter turning to more stable spring weather, and fewer operational flights for Bozděch[9] spared the dog further suffering. Remarkably resilient, he soon showed his usual zest for life.

Antis, of course, had not only been reinstated as the squadron's mascot, but was accorded even greater status than he had during Bozděch's first tour of duty; he was a veteran; visitors to the mess were told of his prowess; and he was written about by airmen to their friends in the UK. For example, Jaromír Bajer wrote on the back of a photograph he had taken of Antis, and then sent it to a friend, 'This is the famous Bozděch dog that has completed several missions over Germany. Someone from the BBC phoned recently to ask for information about him.'[10]

Social life for the squadron was very important. A few airmen bought cars, or shared in their purchase. However, petrol was rationed; and joy-riding was not a priority in wartime, but engineers in the squadron found a way round the problem. Local people were sometimes surprised when a car with some of 'the Czech boys' (as they were called) would come in sight and pass by, emitting a peculiar odour. Some said it must be aviation fuel. They were right. Arnošt Polak explains how they did it.

> By that time I was experienced in squadron life and I used to drive to a nearby WRNS station in a little Austin Seven, to their weekly dance evening. We used to siphon the petrol from the Liberator. The car would run beautifully on it, except that it was a different colour. There were check-points where the police would check over the carburettor to see what fuel you had. Our flight engineers used to design all sorts of by-pass systems, so that if you saw a check-point coming up you could switch over.[11]

But no large-scale pilfering was required: it happened during operational flying on the four-engine Liberators; and it was done discreetly, with little detriment to the air force or the war effort.

> The flight engineer could pump from one fuel tank to another, because no engine would consume exactly the same amount of fuel. So you would switch tanks as one engine consumed more fuel than another and the weight would be unbalanced; and so the idea was to pump from one side to the other to equalise the weights. And in the process there was a by-pass valve allowing fuel to be diverted into a jerry can of five gallons or so: that was just big enough to fit into a parachute bag.[12]

The squadron was popular in the town. Local people regarded them as quiet men; they found them to have something in common with their own temperament. Liaisons were formed; and Karel Fialka married a Tain girl.[13] Bozděch, it appears, in late spring, was seeing a girl in the town. RAF transport brought some airmen into the town on their off duty hours. From there Bozděch's route took him near the primary school; and he sometimes had Antis with him. After the start of the war, assumptions had been made: food was rationed for the human population, and a large number of dogs – estimated to be a six-digit figure – were put down. By 1945, compared to nowadays, dog ownership was far from common-place. There were working dogs on the farms of course, but, for young children, the sight of an airman and an Alsatian created interest and excitement in the playground.

At the strategic level of war, signs appeared that the collaboration among the Allies, with their conflicting ideologies, was crumbling. When President Beneš and his Foreign Minster Jan Masaryk were preparing their position for their forthcoming visit to Moscow, the British Ambassador to Czechoslovakia, Sir Philip Nichols, sought to go with them; but the Soviet Government refused him entry.[14] Churchill feared Russian expansionism: on 30 April, he wrote to President Truman urging him to ensure that as much of Czecho-slovakia as possible should be liberated by the US Army.

> There can be little doubt that the liberation of Prague and as much as possible of the territory of Western Czechoslovakia by your forces might make the whole difference to the post-war situation in Czechoslovakia, and might well influence that in near-by countries. On the other hand, if the Western Allies play no significant part in Czechoslovakia liberation of that country will go the way of Yugoslavia.
>
> Of course, such a move by Eisenhower must not interfere with his main operations against the Germans, but I think the highly important consideration mentioned above should be brought to his attention.[15]

Eisenhower responded to Truman that the Soviet Staff contem-plated operations into the Vltava valley; if he thought that a move into Czechoslovakia was desirable they would move on to Pilsen and Karlsbad. But Churchill kept up pressure this time by writing directly to Eisenhower.

> I am hoping that your plan does not inhibit you to advance to Prague if you have the troops and do not meet the Russians

earlier. I thought you did not mean to tie yourself down if you had the troops and the country was empty.[16]

Far from their homeland, the airmen of No. 311 Squadron continued with their anti-submarine patrols; and on 5 May, one of its Liberators made its last strike of the war. The weather was fair, visibility was about twenty miles, when Liberator 311, piloted by Warrant Officer Beneš sighted a U-boat, with its conning tower visible. Immediately they attacked with five depth charges. The crew claimed one direct hit; they observed explosions and oil on the surface, and they continued circling and saw the upturned hull of the U-boat under the surface.[17]

That same day, by the time the Liberator arrived back at base, over the airwaves from Prague came the voice of Czechoslovak radio calling on all Czechs to arms: patriots had barricaded themselves inside the building which housed the radio station; the Prague Rising had begun; and pleas were made in Czech, English and Russian for the Allies to come to their assistance. The Czechoslovak Government, represented by Hubert Ripka, immediately appealed to the British to send the RAF to bomb German troop concentrations. As a result, 'on May 7 the Czechoslovak pilots serving with the British Air Force were given an order to be in readiness for take-off.'[18] The news was electrifying for the Czechoslovak squadrons in the UK. The crews of No. 311 Squadron knew that their Liberators had the range to reach Prague; and Bozděch, years later, wrote that some of the crews slept in their Liberators in case they were called to support their compatriots.[19] Such was the enthusiasm of the men. Little flying took place from the base during the period of the Prague Rising. Suddenly, however, the stand-by order to take off for Prague was cancelled.

The die had already been cast: the liberation of Czechoslovakia had no military significance as far as the Allied Supreme Commander was concerned; and General Patton's army reached Pilsen, and halted their advance. Patton, though, was known as a leader who was not afraid to take a degree of latitude to himself. Just how much he took, and how close Prague came to being liberated by the Americans was elaborated on twenty years later, in May 1965, by Josef Smrkovský. He made a statement in which he told that on 7 May 1945, three American tanks reached Prague; and he negotiated with the Americans in the presence of a dozen members of the Czechoslovak National Council.

They brought us a message from General Patton, saying his
armoured units were ready to enter Prague on May 8 at 4.00
am to crush the German forces, provided our Council made
the request. Certain Council members cried joyously: 'Hurrah!
Let's go and see Patton.' But we [communists] realised that if
we let the American troops enter Prague they would be our
liberators. The result would be an important political shift
in the bourgeoisie's favour. We therefore felt duty-bound to
turn the offer down.[20]

Smrkovský, it seems, was economical with the truth in that statement, for three years later in 1968, the year of the Prague Spring, he
added a piece of information that he omitted earlier. He said that
in 1945 the Czechoslovak National Council was by no means dominated by the communists, nor did it turn down General Patton's
offer – it accepted the offer. Smrkovský personally disregarded his
Council's decision and, as negotiator, did not reveal it; thus, by
default he let the offer drop.[21] Whatever the true version of the decision, the opportunity for the west to liberate Prague was lost; and
it was the Soviet Army that swept into the city; while the western
powers' disinterest, symbolised by an American army, poised
indifferent, it seemed, nineteen miles away, was not lost on those
who had suffered under the occupation.

Then came Germany's unconditional surrender. Anti-submarine
sweeps, however, continued as before. On 10 May four Liberators
were on patrol, when one of them sighted two U-boats on the
surface, flying the Black Flag of surrender; and they circled them
and took photographs. Routine work of this kind continued: an
aircraft escorting a surrendering U-boat to Stavanger; others
escorting them to British ports.

With the war in Europe over, and no word of their returning to
their own country, rumours spread among the airmen of No. 311
Squadron. Most prominent among them was that the Soviet Union
was creating obstacles to their return. Recent research, however,
points to another reason: the British government's view that the
return of the Czechoslovak Air Force required the consent of
the Soviet Union.[22] The Foreign Office view was that Prague lay
within the Soviet operational zone and therefore Russian consent
was necessary before the Czechoslovak Air Force could return.
It was proposed to Janoušek that he should have his government
seek Russian consent for the return of the squadrons.[23] But this

would have been an unacceptable condition upon President Beneš, that an independent sovereign country should obtain the agreement of the Russians for the return of its own air force from the UK. The British pussyfooted throughout May; then on 11 June, a Chiefs-of-Staff paper, along with an Annex from the Air Staff went to Churchill, recommending the return of the squadrons. Two days later, Churchill wrote on the document, 'Let them go back forthwith'.[24]

Forthwith was not interpreted as the key word, however, for it was another two months before they were to leave. Partly this was due to Janoušek's astuteness in realising that while No. 311 Squadron was equipped with the up-to-date impressive Liberators, the fighter squadrons had old Spitfires. He wrote to the Air Ministry.

> I am sure that you will realise that it is to a large extent a question of prestige, both from the British and the Czechs' point of view, that we should come back to our homeland with aircraft we could really be proud of.[25]

New Spitfires were procured; politically, the way was now clear for the return of the Czechoslovak Air Force.

However, the Czechoslovak Air Force required not only up-to-date war planes: the service had to be restructured and built to operate as a defensive force; at the same time, it had to contribute to the establishment of a national airline. While negotiations were taking place about the air force's return, administrators in the Czechoslovak Inspectorate were drawing up their development plans, and tentatively slotting in career officers for positions in peacetime; and in so doing, they took advantage of the high quality of the RAF technological training. So, on 20 June, 'with an eye to the future'[26], as Bozděch put it, he was sent to No. 14 Radio School [27] at St Athan on a Signal Leader's Course, accompanied, of course, by his dog. He was there until early August, and returned to No. 311 Squadron in time for its departure for the homeland.

It was while the squadron was preparing to leave for their homeland that a mystery was finally cleared up. On 9 August two hill walkers, one of them an RAF officer on leave, were hill-walking in the Cairngorm mountains on Beinn a Bhuird, when they came across the wreckage of a plane strewn near its summit. Outside the fuselage were two bodies, another two were inside the cockpit and there was a third in the fuselage. Having noted the aircraft's number, the hill walkers reported the find to the police in Elgin. The wreckage, it turned out, belonged to the Oxford trainer PH 404 of No. 311 Squadron which had taken off from Tain with a crew of five on 10 January, disappearing without trace. It had remained undiscovered on the mountainside for seven months. A team from an Indian Army regiment based in the area recovered the bodies.[28] The wreckage of the fuselage was set on fire; the engines were left, and today still remain on the mountain as a symbol of remembrance.

President Beneš had been in Czechoslovakia since May, following in the wake of the advancing Red Army; and he had made a triumphant entry into Prague. The Czechoslovak Armoured Brigade, which had operated in the west, was already on its home soil. Russian troops were due to leave in a matter of months; and a general election was to be held the following year. Beneš's image of his country serving as the bridge between east and west was based on the premise that the Communist Party would work within democratic structures and institutions, and his belief – for he had Joseph Stalin's promise on it – that the Soviet Union would not interfere in the internal governance of a friendly, neighbouring country. The return of the Czechoslovak Air Force was awaited.

The complexity of the logistics in moving an entire squadron comes across in its drafting on paper. A three-page document with two copious appendices was drawn up, and thirty-eight copies were made. Flt Sgt Rennison who was one of the British personnel attached to the squadron kept his copy after the war; and thirty years later his son sent it to Bozděch. On 25 June, the squadron had been transferred from Coastal Command to Transport Command,[29] whose headquarters authorised the movement by signal on 30 July and 3 August.[30] The move from RAF Tain to RAF Manston was to be by rail, road and plane; No. 311 Squadron would ferry the squadrons back to Prague; and the date for departure was to be Monday 6 August. Those who had permission to travel by car had to leave four days earlier. Dress for the officers of the main rail party was ceremonial caps, walking out uniform and gloves.

Ironically, at the time he was leaving the country, Bozděch was officer in charge of the loading party at the base for kit bags, personal luggage and (a category of transport that was very important for many airmen) private bicycles. He had been put in charge of the loading and unloading of baggage when he first docked at Liverpool in 1940; but then it had been part of a ploy to bring a dog into the country. Now there was nothing covert about the make up of the squadron. Although Antis does not appear in the list of personnel, he was there; and while he may have entered the UK surreptitiously in 1940, five years later he was leaving it in style.

At 8.00 am on Monday 13 August, after a week's postponement, the Liberators took off from RAF Tain for RAF Manston on the first leg of their flight to Prague. At last they were going home. They had followed in the footsteps of their forefathers, the Czech Legions of the First World War; they had fought for their country and the freedom of other countries in a second war; and after six years of it they were now going home.

Part III

PART II

CHAPTER EIGHT

Laurels and Ashes

I hope that our people in the future will always remain as
close in solidarity, as united in thought and effort as the
airmen who are the subject of this book. If they do, then they
will certainly be able to keep and defend their freedom.

General Vicherek, Preface to Bozděch's
Gentlemen of the Dusk

Twelve converted Liberator bombers of No. 311 Squadron
approached the western boundary of Czechoslovakia on 15
August 1945; they rendezvoused with a formation of fifteen
Spitfires bearing the Czechoslovakian markings, and were escorted
in a low sweep of triumph over Prague before circling and landing
at Ruzyn airfield. Setting foot on the homeland for the first time in
six years was an emotional experience. 'Ruzyn airfield,' Bozděch
wrote, 'presented an unforgettable sight. On the vast expanse of
concrete before the main building, which was decorated with flags,
bands played as people swarmed to meet the returning exiles, and
crowds of schoolchildren danced in their national costumes.'[1]

The airmen got a tumultuous reception; but euphoria did not
dim their underlying fears. What had the Gestapo meted out to the
families of those who had fled and fought against Nazism? This
was a concern felt at the highest levels. In May, Air Vice Marshal
Janoušek wrote to the British Government urging the speedy return
of the Czechoslovak squadrons. Although there were also weighty

political reasons for their return, he spelled out one compelling consideration:

> We have learned . . . that, almost without exception, one or more members of the family of our officers and airmen serving in this country have not only suffered under Nazi domination, but have actually been killed in the most ghastly manner.[2]

Anxiously scanning the sea of faces, Bozděch saw no sign of his parents. An officer of the Czechoslovak Inspectorate approached him and took him to his office. There he found relatives who told him what had happened.

In October 1940, a local person in Sobĕkury had denounced his parents for having a son in the air force of the Allies, and they were arrested by the Gestapo in Klatovy. The same individual also informed the Gestapo in Pilsen that Bozděch's parents had had written contact with their son, in 1939, through his uncle, Karel Hrubý, an inn-keeper in Sobĕkury; and he too was arrested by the Gestapo, and all three were interrogated in Klatovy. After several weeks of interrogation, his mother and his uncle were released on the basis of insufficient evidence. On the instruction of the prison doctor, his father was released earlier due to his ill health. However, this was not the end of it: in 1942, his mother was re-arrested and sent to the internment camp in Svatobořice near Kyjov in Moravia. Since May 1945, the alleged informant had been in the Pilsen Regional Court detention pending trial.[3] The health of both parents had been so affected that they could not make the journey to Prague. Reassurances were all that could be given until the legal formalities of demobilisation from the RAF were completed.

First, however, came the victory celebrations; and Antis paraded on the streets of Prague with No. 311 Squadron. After five years of life on air force operational stations, the dog was not distracted by the noise and the crowds. The crowd loved the spectacle; and the magazine *Rozlet (Flight)*, seeing the potential of a story, soon began collecting material – a lot of it from Bozděch – for a series of articles about a faithful dog accompanying his master on bombing missions over Germany.

Then there were formal gestures of thanks from a grateful State to individual members of the Allies: senior British officers of the RAF were honoured, and so too was the brilliant plastic surgeon Archibald McIndoe,[4] who had restructured the faces and restored the lives of airmen who had been badly burned; he received the Order of the White Lion. One Czech pilot who had been treated by McIndoe was Frankie Truhlář; and so successfully had he overcome his injuries and been rehabilitated that he was going to continue flying with the Czechoslovak Air Force.

The legal process of releasing the Czechoslovak airmen from the RAF completed, Bozděch was granted three weeks' leave before taking up his career again where he had left off six years earlier as a member of the Czechoslovak Air Force. He took the dog and together they went to his home at Soběkury. It was a joyful homecoming; the parents, their daughters Pavla and Maria and their son were reunited; but it was painful too. His father was now lame and his mother had heart trouble as a result of the conditions at Svatobořice internment camp. They had aged quickly and painfully.

Life at his old home took on a rhythm that he had forgotten existed; and he and Antis spent hours in the haunts of his boyhood. The dog revelled in the freedom of the country. However, for a young man returning from war to his native heath, it was also a time for introspection. There was the loss of an innocence that could never be recovered: the comrades who had died; and the suffering that his own sense of duty and subsequent actions had brought on his family.

It may have been then that he thought of writing about his comrades. There were good reasons for putting the deeds of the bomber squadron on record: their achievements were not widely known about in the homeland; for unlike the public in the UK, who were informed about the bombing campaigns of the RAF by radio, press and newsreel film, Czechoslovaks – apart from those who, braving detection or exposure by informers, listened to broadcasts in Czech by the BBC – were fed what the occupying power determined. Although Bozděch's training had been technologically biased, and not in the literary field, he had a feeling for story and a sense of structure; his writing style was direct, he was very familiar with his subject – and more importantly, he was passionate that it should be told.

When he returned from leave, Bozděch was posted to Ruzyn airfield where his former squadron had been restructured as an air transport unit, pending the formation of Czechoslovak airlines. He and other aircrew officers stayed in the Palace Hotel; and so did his dog. Not that Antis was merely tolerated: he had status; he was now officially recognised as a military dog, with a permit to prove it, signed by General Janoušek. In the short term, Bozděch's duties required that he often had to fly to the UK and other European countries, which meant absences of two or three nights; but the dog was well looked after and settled contentedly into hotel living.

Arnošt Polak too continued to serve in the Air Force until the country's airline was established, and his duties at the time were similar to Bozděch's.

> I was serving in Transport Command until Czechoslovak airlines would start up. I had hoped to join the airline. At the time we took over what the Germans had left behind, Junkers 52s. You'll have seen the three-engined planes that the Germans used during the war, they were designed in 1927, made of corrugated iron. But they flew, and we flew with them. Our flights would start from Prague airport and include trips to London via Frankfurt, to Paris, to the Hague, Belgrade etc. The aircraft we flew, apart from the JU52s, also included twin-engined Siebels.[5]

It was not until October that Bozděch met his old friend Gustav Copal. Four and a half years earlier Gustav had been shot down on the night of 5 February 1941, when he flew as front gunner of a Wellington of No. 311 Squadron. He was taken prisoner and sent to a POW camp. At some point, he was involved in a break out; but he was subsequently recaptured, and handed over to the Gestapo. He was then taken to Czechoslovakia where he was told that he was to be executed. While he awaited his fate, his prison was liberated by the advancing Red Army. He too seemed set to continue his career in the Air Force.

That first autumn after the war was a golden time. In late 1945 Bozděch was transferred to the Ministry of Defence as a technical adviser to the Czechoslovak Air Force, with the rank of captain. In November, he met Tatiana Zilka at a student ball at The National House. They had already seen each other fleetingly when No. 311 Squadron landed at Ruzyn airfield, and she had stepped forward and kissed him as one of the returning exiles. Two months later, in February 1946, they married. Tatiana was the daughter of an army colonel who had played a prominent part in the Prague Rising in May 1945, and so the wedding was quite a social occasion. Bozděch's mother was able to make the journey to attend; and his best man was Gustav, the recently returned POW. Among the guests were Bozděch's commanding officer Colonel Vlastimil Chrast and his English wife, Pamela. Vlastimil (or Vlasta as he was familiarly called) had met Pamela in London in 1942, when he was a wing commander in the Czechoslovak Inspectorate, and they married in 1945.[6]

After the church ceremony, which he was not allowed into, Antis nearly stole the show from the bride, during the photo shoot, getting himself entangled in the bride's train in his enthusiasm to be part of it. The newly married couple and their dog moved into a flat in Prague, which was in the gift of the Minister of Foreign Affairs, Dr Jan Masaryk. It was situated at the Stromovka Park, a lovely area which swept down under a canopy of elegant trees to the Vltava river.

Masaryk first got to know Bozděch in the UK when he toured the stations where the Czechoslovak squadrons were based.[7] His mother was American, and, as a young man, Masaryk had spent ten years in the United States; he well understood the workings of democratic institutions, and the importance of the means of communication with the public. A collection of his wartime speeches, under the title, *Speaking to my Country* was being published; and it may have been he who encouraged Bozděch to go into print, for, as we shall see, it seems that the office of the Presidency facilitated the inclusion of correspondence in one of Bozděch's books.

Already the magazine *Rozlet* was carrying a series of articles about the mascot of No. 311 Squadron. Bozděch had given the editor a lot of materials, including photographs,[8] but none of the writing appeared under his name. Other former members of the squadron seem to have contributed information as well.

At a number of levels powerful political forces were positioning themselves to shape the country's destiny. General Janoušek was pushed aside as head of the country's air force, and was replaced by General Vicherek; and the head of Defence was General Svoboda, who had served on the eastern front. So positions at the top echelon of the military were being filled by personnel acceptable to the Russians; those who had served in the west were regarded as suspect.

One month after the Czechoslovak squadrons returned from the UK, the writer Edwin Muir arrived in Prague – the city he had last seen twenty-four years earlier – to work for the British Council. There were Russian troops much in evidence; and Muir noticed that most shop windows, it seemed, displayed a grouping of three portraits: one of Tomaš Masaryk, founder and first President of the republic; one of President Beneš; and, always in the centre, and usually slightly higher than the other two, one of Joseph Stalin. However, on 28 October, the anniversary of the founding of the republic, he noticed something strange: the photographs of Stalin were all removed and were not replaced.[9] Russian troops began pulling out a few weeks later, and, according to Muir, they seemed as happy to be leaving the country as the Czechs were to see them go. After one occupying power in their country, they did not hanker for another. The last of the Russian troops left at the end of 1945.

Elections for the re-established republic were to be held in May 1946. However, shortly before the date of the election, the Soviet command in Vienna informed the Czechoslovak government that units of the Red Army would cross the country from Austria and Hungary to the Soviet zone in Germany. It required the intervention of Foreign Minister Jan Masaryk to have this incursion prevented;[10] but it was intimidatory.

Then there was the internal dimension; and in the cafes, in the work places, wherever politics and alliances were discussed, one word resonated: Munich. As the British journalist Sheila Duff Cooper found, on revisiting Czechoslovakia, in the collective psyche there was deep resentment of the western allies who had betrayed the country in 1938. The Soviet Union, however, had not recognised the Munich agreement; and in 1945, it was the Red Army that liberated the country, while an American army had halted its advance at Pilsen – there was a message to be exploited here: the west were not interested in the postwar development of the country. Although President Beneš arrived in Prague in May to an enthusiastic welcome, on the ground the dominant impression was of one victorious ally from the east. And the delay in returning the Czechoslovak Air Force from the UK reinforced it. Britain's insistence that the Czechoslovak government obtain prior approval for its return from the Russians unwittingly played into the hands of the country's Communist Party.

The outcome of the elections gave the communists 38% of the vote; they were the largest party, but they did not have an outright majority. A government called the National Front was formed for a two-year term of office; the communist Klement Gottwald became Prime Minister; and the party took control of key ministries such as the Ministry of the Interior and the Ministry of Information.

Less perceptible was the manoeuvring at local level, as Arnošt Polak found.

> As I told you before, I had a little flat which I shared with some other people. One day we got an order from the mayor of Prague at the town hall, that we had to vacate the flat by order. I went to the town hall wearing my medals, thinking I'll sort it out. But no way! That's the order, and there was no reason given. So on the appointed day an armed policeman came, and he escorted us out. After that I made enquiries and I found out – the flat was a very nice flat in central Prague – that the deputy mayor was a communist, and he had his eye on the flat and compulsorily acquired it. And there was no appeal. The communists had already infiltrated all sorts of key positions to such an extent. It was not obvious, but nevertheless true.[11]

As far as Arnošt was concerned, it was a sign of the way that arbitrary authority might go in the future. His older brother had applied to the University of London to study chemistry; so Arnošt, without any other obligations, resigned from the air force and obtained a visa for the UK.

However, for Bozděch, 'life flowed along pleasantly';[12] he bought a car and he and Tatiana drove out for week-ends to his parents' home. Tom Oddie, who had been a colleague with him at No. 8 Air Gunnery school wrote to him, and received a very warm reply containing one of his wedding photographs.[13] In the autumn Tatiana became pregnant. Life flowing pleasantly did not mean indolence – far from it; he was in the flow. He was now an Air Staff Officer at the Ministry; and he wrote in his spare time. It was an intensely productive period; he wrote four books and a script for radio. His topic was the air war against Germany, and his themes were loyalty and sacrifice. In two years he wrote: *Gentlemen of the Dusk* (*Gentlemeni Soumraku*), *Enemy in Sight* (*Nepřitel v Dohledu*), *Bombers Attack* (*Bombardery Utoei*), *Fighting with Fate* (*Souboj s osudem*),[14] and a drama/documentary script for radio about Gp Capt Pickard's bomber raid on the Gestapo prison at Amiens.

In *Gentlemen of the Dusk* (*Gentlemeni Soumraku*), which was published in 1947, Bozděch wrote about the early night bombing raids of No. 311 Squadron. It was a short book of one hundred and

fifteen pages, which Bozděch dedicated to those brave comrades-
in-arms who did not hesitate to sacrifice their lives for their
homeland.[15] What is striking about the book is the level of official
support that Bozděch attracted: a Preface by Gen Vicherek
Commander of the Czechoslovak Air Force followed by two
addresses – over 2000 words in all – by President Dr Edvard Beneš.
For Bozděch, a junior officer in the Air Force, albeit a staff captain
in the Ministry, this was impressive backing. Gen Vicherek
applauded the book's aim.

> I welcome with great pleasure the occasion of the publication
> of this book as one of the documents testifying to the activity
> of our airmen who served abroad and who, with their British
> comrades-in-arms, from the very beginning until the end of a
> bloody world drama sparked off by megalomaniac Germany,
> fought bravely and died.
> ... Among the airmen who survived this fight is the author
> of this book. He describes real experiences, which he lived
> through with his Czechoslovak and British comrades-in-arms,
> in order to tell his readers of devotion and love of homeland
> that inspired heroic deeds, which should remain shining
> examples for future generations – should it be necessary once
> again to defend the hard won freedom of our people and
> humanity in general.[16]

Bozděch had authorisation to quote from the transcripts of two
speeches by President Dr Edvard Beneš. They were both politically
and strategically important. Beneš delivered the first in England at
RAF Duxford on 6 August 1940, and the second at a victory
celebration in Prague on 21 August 1945. The readership that Gen
Vicherek envisaged for the book was one that had gone through the
occupation and had not had access to the pronouncements of its
government in exile, so the inclusion of Beneš's speech in England
in 1940 is particularly significant.

> Czechoslovak airmen!
>   Last week, for the first time in two harsh years of fate for all
> of us, when I stood in front of our small Czechoslovak army as
> its Commander-in-Chief, I could barely suppress my deepest
> emotions. All that has happened since the May mobilisation of

1938! Our homeland was occupied and enslaved, you went abroad without any clear aim in order to begin fighting again; I myself with my friends began to organise the second resistance both politically and militarily, and when the war really broke out, we prepared our army in France; and you yourselves got to work immediately as part of the French army. May I declare here that my first duty is to thank our airmen for everything they did in France. You were the first from our ranks to take part in war operations. You displayed great courage and you have documents and evidence to testify to that. Official French authorities in both military and government circles issued public testimonials about this. Here in England, we were very happy to hear about it; and please accept my words as words of thanks and recognition to our air force from the Commander-in-Chief of our armed forces, from the President of the Republic, once again recognised and continuing to exist; accept this as thanks on behalf of our entire nation whose interest we are all defending together today, and whose freedom we shall once again restore, with Great Britain as our leader.

The fall of France has brought you to England and made you close comrades-in-arms of your British comrades-in-arms, who today with pride and glory bear the colours of this powerful empire before the entire world and fight for a new, free and better Europe, for the freedom of their own British homeland and also for our freedom and the freedom of Czechoslovakia. I can assure you that the British nation shall not lose this war.

You have been welcomed here with sympathy and friendship. You saw already in France how superlative the British Air Force is, what great successes it reaps everywhere it intervenes, and you can see it here for yourselves with your own eyes even better. I will not exaggerate if I stress that the British Air Force has proved its worth in this war as the best air force in the world and that it will hardly be superseded by another in this war.

It is a great honour for you today to be made part of the British Air Force as an independent Czechoslovak unit. However, it places great duties upon you. I knew our airmen very well at home and I know what they could do; I know too that you fulfilled your duties well in France, and I know that you will also fulfil them well here.[17]

Consummate politician that he was, Beneš was prematurely
claiming official recognition by the British Government; generating
emotion by his passion for the fight for the homeland and for
democracy; and – though his own belief was that his country's
interest lay in good relations with both east and west – acknowledging Britain as the leader in the fight against Nazism, and
praising the superlative quality of the RAF.

The second speech, which is very much longer, was made by
Beneš on 21 August 1945, in Prague. He recapitulated the events of
the early years of the Czechoslovak military units in France and the
UK; and then he turned to the political dimension.

> Then came a difficult road towards recognition of us as a real
> and legitimate government and towards the breaking up of
> stipulations arising from the Munich agreement. The entry
> of the Soviet Union into war – after a year-long unaided fight
> by Great Britain against Germany – which I counted on from
> the first moments of the beginning of the Second World War,
> was a great turning point in our entire political and military
> activity. There were successful trips to the United States and
> Soviet Russia and the signing of the alliance treaty with the
> Soviet Union. In all this, government officials found priceless
> support in the military activities of our army units, of which
> the Czechoslovak Air Force was most prominent in the eyes
> of the world; the air force which has been active up until now
> in the West European theatre of military and political events
> – in Great Britain.[18]

That last paragraph summed up Beneš's ideal, that the country
would continue to exist as a sovereign state with good relations
with east and west. These two-thousand word speeches by Beneš
gave a tremendously authoritative context for Bozděch to set his
narration of some of the operations of No. 311 Squadron.

The structure that he adopted was to write an overview chapter
of the war in the air from the perspective of a Czechoslovak airman
based in the UK in 1940. He rendered into Czech Winston
Churchill's sombre speech to the House of Commons on 12 May
1940 when he became Prime Minister: 'I have nothing to offer but
blood, toil, tears and sweat. . . '[19] Bozděch then went on to
enumerate the representatives of the countries arrayed against
Germany: the Free French, Poles, Czechoslovaks, Norwegians, the

countries of the Commonwealth, all under the leadership of Britain. To the Czechoslovak reader of 1947 one omission stood out starkly – the Soviet Union. And in the simmering politicised climate of the time, in certain quarters, this was noted.

Bozděch's style in describing the bombing raids resembles that of the documentary film screenwriter. He begins his chapter called 'Invulnerable Enemy' with a description of night falling over the small village of East Wretham; children, who have been playing near the airfield earlier in the day, have now gone to bed; but the stillness over the village is deceptive. A car passes the guard house at the crossroads to turn into the command headquarters, for this is the headquarters of No. 311 Czechoslovak Squadron; and it was going 'out' again; its ninth operation in twelve days. The first airmen we meet, though, are the ground crew; and Bozděch salutes their dedication.

> Long runways at the airport are being lit up. Mechanics, weapons experts, electricians and other technical personnel are coming here. Many of them have mugs attached to their belts and cutlery rattling in the pockets of their overalls. . . . These mechanics, weapons experts and electricians have a lion's share in the successes of 311 Czechoslovak Squadron.[20]

After establishing the scene, Bozděch takes the reader into the briefing room, where a large map hangs on the wall.

> It is 25 June 1941. Three days ago, German troops attacked the Soviet Union. No other nation welcomed its ally in the fight against Germany with more joy than Britain, which until that time was alone in its fight. With great eagerness, we were expecting to be sent to aid our new ally. And we were not mistaken.[21]

The Wing Commander approaches the dais and points with his pencil to the target: 'Hamm. I am sure I do not have to tell you why you are going there!' No, it is not really necessary: the crews know from earlier operations that Hamm is the biggest railway junction in western Germany. 'I would like to add,' the commander continues, 'that at the moment large scale movements of the German army going to the east are taking place there.'[22]

What Bozděch narrated was the simple truth: the Czechoslovak

Air Force squadrons, based in Britain, were in action against Nazi Germany in 1940, at a time when Stalin and Hitler were observing their non aggression pact. But that simple truth, in certain powerful quarters, was a truth that had to be abolished: history was in the process of being rewritten. For at the very time that Beneš was addressing his troops in the war zone of the UK, the present Prime Minister of Czechoslovakia, Klement Gottwald was safe on the side-lines in Moscow, making no public utterance whatsoever about the war; and the Communist Party in the Protectorate in Prague was reviling Beneš and warning the Czech nation not to be misled by him.[23] Indeed in December 1940, while the Czechoslovak squadrons in the UK were engaging the enemy, the Executive Committee of the Communist Party in Prague had carried a resolution stating that, 'The Soviet-German friendship represents the cornerstone of the international situation against which the anti-Soviet plans of the Anglo-French bloc have already been dashed to pieces.'[24] All that changed, of course, after the German invasion of the USSR in June 1941, but in *Gentlemen of the Dusk* it was being revisited, and highlighted.

Not by any stretch of the imagination could Bozděch have been described as a political polemicist. His book, however, was directed to a wide readership, and it had an authenticity: a united struggle, from the perspectives of the highest political level to the operational levels. And, as a result, his writing would be held against him, both in the short term and in the long term; for over twenty-five years later, as we shall see, although rehabilitated, he would be denied a visa to return to Czechoslovakia.

In his book, *Fighting with Fate*,[25] Bozděch wrote about the brave Czech airman František Truhlář, who was one of the first members of Archibald McIndoe's Guinea Pig Club.[26] Frankie Truhlář was a rear gunner in No. 311 Squadron in the months before Bozděch was posted to it; his Wellington bomber, returning from a raid, crashed near London. He was the only survivor, but he suffered severe burns to his face. He became one of McIndoe's patients. McIndoe was not only a brilliant plastic surgeon, painstaking in his research and innovative in his methods, he was a good psychologist; and he realised that in giving his patients their lives back, he had to restore their sense of self-worth. His Guinea Pig Club developed their own social community; and he brought them into the wider community of which they would ultimately be a part. So successfully did Frankie Truhlář recover, that he retrained as a fighter pilot.

Lightning struck twice. Over France he was shot down in flames and he again suffered severe burns to his face, and endured more painful treatment. After the war he remained in the Czechoslovak Air Force and was stationed in Prague, and he flew Spitfires. In the winter of 1946, on forty-eight hours' leave, he went by train to visit his parents. He opened the door of a compartment, in which there was a mother with her young child, and he went in. When the child saw Truhlář's face, she became hysterical; the mother angrily rebuked him for appearing in public with such grotesque features. Frankie Truhlář said nothing; he went out and stood in the corridor for the rest of the journey. He was rather silent during his short stay with his parents. When he returned from his leave, he reported for duty next morning; and he took off in his Spitfire for a cross-country exercise. He had given just about all that a young man could give for the motherland; and now he flew over it in the clear winter light, as one of its guardians. Then he turned his Spitfire into a vertical dive to the earth.

Bozděch wrote *Fighting with Fate* as a tribute to a brave man. He was given support from a high level by being allowed to quote private correspondence from the wife of the President, Hana Benešová.

In May 1947, Bozděch worked on the script for a radio drama-tisation of Gp Capt Charles Pickard's final bombing raid. Pickard, who had been the RAF liaison and training officer with No. 311 Squadron in its early days, had made an important contribution to the squadron; but the operation that Bozděch chose to write about was the one in which Pickard met his death. It was the daring daylight bombing raid on the Gestapo prison at Amiens, which was designed to breach the walls of the prison in two places to allow a number of important figures in the French underground to escape. It required contact between British Intelligence and key members of the Resistance who had got caught up in a dragnet search and were awaiting questioning by the Gestapo, who, at this stage, did not know their true identity. The pinpoint accuracy that was required for this raid to succeed could not have been achieved at an earlier stage in the war; it was possible now thanks to the low level Mosquito bomber. Pickard led the raid, and it was very successful: it took place just after mid-day when a large number of guards were having a meal in their canteen. The canteen was targeted to cause maximum casualties to the guards; it was bombed, and the walls were breached in two places, allowing many prisoners to escape. Pickard, having ordered the remainder of the flight to return to base, made a final low-level survey of their results; but the enemy had now had time to call up a fighter unit, and Pickard was shot down.

Bozděch's research for the script entailed close contact and collaboration with the British Air Attaché in Prague, who was able to loan him the RT tape of the raid.[27] He did not know it at the time, but this kind of contact with the military of a foreign power could be used against him in a year's time.

For the present though, life moved serenely for him and his wife. On 20 July 1947, they had a son; and they decided to call him Jan. The baby's godfather was Dr Jan Masaryk, Minister of Foreign Affairs. The christening ceremony was attended by a range of social classes: country people, city dwellers and a sprinkling from some social elites; the congregation in the church in the beautiful city of Prague may have seemed to reflect an idyllic middle European way of life in a reborn democracy.

However, the fragility of this idyll was becoming more and more apparent. President Beneš suffered the first of two strokes in July; his speech was slower, but he was able to carry on his duties. The country's parliament decided that it would accept financial aid under the Marshall Plan, a US financial package designed to help war-torn Europe as a short term boost. When this was announced, Stalin summoned Prime Minister, Klement Gottwald, and Foreign Minister Jan Masaryk to Moscow in July to discuss the implications of accepting western financial aid. Stalin told the delegation that Czechoslovak acceptance of the Marshall Plan would be regarded as a violation of the 1943 treaty between the two countries and a hostile act against the Soviet Union. Czechoslovakia would have to renounce its intention of accepting the Marshall Plan. Masaryk commented to friends on his return to Prague: 'It is a new Munich. I left for Moscow as a Minister of Foreign Affairs of a sovereign state. I am returning as Stalin's stooge.'[28] Then two months later there was a glimpse of the extent to which violent means could be used to bring about political change: Jan Masaryk and two other democratic ministers were sent parcel bombs, disguised as bottles of perfume. Fortunately the weapons were detected in time. The police, under the control of the Ministry of the Interior, which was in Communist Party hands, began an investigation – it led nowhere.

Autumn, however, heralded a brief Indian summer for democracy: a public opinion poll showed that support for the Communist Party was falling away (internal findings by the communists pointed to the same conclusion). The retired British diplomat Bruce Lockhart visited Prague, and because of the status that he had held during the war as their chief means of liaison with the British Government, and the fact that he was a close friend of Masaryk, both President Beneš and Masaryk shared their thinking with him. Politically, 'The failure of Gen Patton to liberate Prague was regarded by both men as a cardinal error on the part of the Western Allies'.[29] The first year after the war had been very difficult for democrats in Czechoslovakia, but the second year was different: they both felt that the communists were losing ground, and would not fare well during the 1948 elections. As if to clinch matters, following investigations by a District Attorney into the source of the parcel bombs that had been sent to the three democratic Ministers, the Department of Justice – without involving the Ministry of the Interior – was able to bring a case to the courts which directly implicated the Communist Party. A trial was fixed for March the following year.

Before it could be held, however, the communist coup took place. In February, as a result of the Ministry of the Interior's refusal to comply with a Ministerial Council decision against its witch hunt of non-communist police commanders, twelve democratic members resigned, confident that their action would result in an earlier election of a new government, in which the communists would be less strong. However, the Communist Party stepped in and took control; Klement Gottwald was able to give a veneer of legality to a coup d'état; and by the end of February 1948, the country had fallen into the Soviet fold. The dilemma for the democrats was whether to remain until they would be ousted.

On 7 March, Bozděch met Jan Masaryk. It may have been at, or after, a reception that followed a ceremony in Prague to mark the ninety-eighth anniversary of the birth of Jan Masaryk's father, Tomaš Masaryk, first President of the republic.[30] Whenever it was that they met that day, they spoke in private; for Bozděch wrote, 'the deeply worried Masaryk'[31] warned him to flee, telling him that, 'he knew the airman was now high on the Red purge list.' It was a hammer blow; but one could not act on the strength of it. Then three days later on 10 March, the thunderbolt fell: radio broadcasts were interrupted with the announcement that the body of Dr Jan Masaryk, Minister for Foreign Affairs, had been found in the courtyard beneath the open window of one of the rooms in his suite of offices. It was put about that he had committed suicide by jumping from a window at the Foreign Office.

Some years later Bozděch wrote:

> Dr Masaryk did not commit suicide. He was murdered on the previous night at a military airfield near Prague, shot beside a plane in which he had planned to leave Czechoslovakia to organise resistance against Communism.[32]

What evidence he had for making this statement is not known. But at the time of Masaryk's death, Bozděch's fellow officers, and their wives, did not believe it was suicide: as Pamela, wife of his commanding officer put it: 'none of us did; we never thought that he committed suicide.'[33] There is confirmation, however, from another source that Masaryk intended to flee the country. On the same day that he spoke to Bozděch, Masaryk met a friend of his, the American novelist, Marcia Davenport. She was leaving Prague later that day for London; and Masaryk gave her a verbal message, which she was to give to Bruce Lockhart:

> The message to me was that he would escape later at some conference. The resignation of the twelve [democrats] had been a grave mistake. He was being spied on by his own people.[34]

Right from the beginning suspicion surrounded the circumstances of Masaryk's death: no public inquiry was held; and a few weeks afterwards, the police doctor who had been called to the scene where Masaryk's body lay outside the Ministry, and who was said to have given a verdict of suicide, was found dead in his office in the Police Department. The communists announced that he too had committed suicide.

However, immediately after Masaryk's death Bozděch procrastinated for some weeks. He did so with good reason. He knew that Masaryk's advice was good,[35] but he was now torn. He vacillated between a best-case scenario, in which he might be left untouched, and the cold realisation that this was the era of Joseph Stalin.

There were still glimmerings that the gathering darkness would not completely eclipse all freedom of expression. On 6 April, President Beneš made, what turned out to be, his last public statement; it was at the celebration of the six-hundredth anniversary of Charles University; and to the end, he remained an outspoken champion of democratic values. Beneš reminded his audience that Czech universities, 'have always stood on the side of truth, freedom and morality.'[36] He went on to speak of man's natural longing for peace, and for freedom of conscience, of science, of thought and religion.

But as far as the forces now in power were concerned, those fine ideas were already being extinguished in the very seat of learning in which Beneš gave them expression: less than two weeks later, when Edwin Muir, Director of the British Council in Prague, returned from the Easter vacation to resume his lectures on English literature at Charles University, he found that two communist observers sat in on his lectures. The atmosphere in the lecture room was changed completely: he was still able to speak to his class, but he no longer had contact with it.[37]

Bozděch experienced this close observation a little earlier. He was first summoned before an internal investigating committee and questioned about his writing. He was told that it was re-actionary and contained anti-state propaganda. He explained that what he had published had already been vetted. Certainly his radio script would have been keenly scrutinised because the Ministry of Information had been in communist hands since 1946. Officially, there was no censorship of other publications, but publishers might find that supplies of paper – which was scarce after the war – were not available for a particular book. But no matter the medium of expression, no criticism of the Soviet Union had been tolerated since the end of the war. Bozděch's *Gentlemen of the Dusk*, with its high level of official backing, its references to the entry of the Soviets into the war would certainly have been closely scrutinised. He reminded the committee of that. But now, in 1948, after the coup, that book with Beneš's addresses was even more potent as a testament to the truth, and Bozděch's writing was, 'evidence . . . of reactionary anti-state propaganda'.[38] Threats were implied, and he was asked to name others who were reactionaries. He told them that he had no information to give. For the moment it went no further than that; and he was allowed to continue with his role at the Ministry; but two observers were installed, ostensibly to shadow his work.

He now had to face the fact that his days were numbered. Even a political innocent would have come to the conclusion that

Masaryk's murder must have been authorised at the highest level – and almost certainly from outside Czechoslovakia. There would be a systemic purging, starting with those in positions of influence; and although he was not a senior officer, he worked closely with that level in the Ministry; already his commanding officer, Vlastimil Chrast had been transferred from the Defence Ministry to Brno.[39]

He could not keep his fears from his wife; and they had anguished discussions. When they discussed alternatives, they realised that the family would be stopped at the normal exit points in the country; if they tried to go on foot, it would be impossible with an eight-month-old child, who was ill and was being treated for a parathyroid gland. The only option was for her husband to leave alone.

If he were to flee the country, he would require assistance. People in all walks of life in Czechoslovakia had gained experience in covert activity during the German occupation, and vestiges of cells from resistance networks were reactivated. Among the officer corps in the Czechoslovakian military were some who had worked in the democratic underground networks during the occupation. The democratic groups existed before the communist underground (which only came into being after the Nazi invasion of the USSR) and they largely distrusted it. Contact was made, and air force officers who had served in the west were sounded out.

On or about 12 April, Col Náprstek of the air force took Gen Janoušek into his confidence, and told him that a group of airmen were organising their escape.[40] Janoušek decided that he would join their number. However, although he had been ousted as head of the country's Air Force, he was still a general, and because of the high level he had held in the service in the UK during the war, he was likely to be closely watched. He knew it too; and so he looked for someone with whom he could make his escape. He went to Pamela Chrast, who was still in Prague although her husband had been transferred to Brno.

> I remember Janoušek came to the flat; and I always remember that he said, 'I would like you please to persuade your husband to leave with me.' And I can always remember my saying to him, 'I cannot persuade my husband to go with you because I don't want him to go with you.' I knew that he possibly had papers on him or that sort of thing. I might have been young, but I wasn't stupid.[41]

Vlastimil Chrast and Pamela had already had the same kind of discussion that Bozděch and Tatiana had had, and their decision was they must go; they too had a young son, Vivian. Pamela though, had married a Czechoslovak, and under the British regulations of the time, and those of Czechoslovakia, she had to give up her British citizenship in order to obtain a Czechoslovak passport. However, there was a way that she could leave the country, through the good offices of the British Embassy. Her sister had come over to Prague, and had been staying with her for a while. Together they went to the British Embassy.

> The British gave us a 'safe conduct' pass, and it lasted forty-eight hours; and you had to get out in the forty-eight hours. And I remember going to the British Embassy, and by that time we had all the Czech communist guards on the gate, watching us go in and out – because my sister was with me. My sister came to stay with me in Prague, and she came home with me. Her passport was all right, but mine wasn't: I had a Czech passport, and I had to get this 'safe conduct' pass.[42]

Once she obtained the pass, her husband prepared for his escape – only to be thwarted at the last minute. He returned to Prague.

> He was going to be taken across the frontier by the German guards, but the moon came up; and he couldn't go: they wouldn't take him. And he came back to Prague; and I remember I had quite a shock when he came back. Then he was there for another week, arranging to go again. But I couldn't wait anyway, because I had this forty-eight hour pass.[43]

He would have to make some other arrangement, but Pamela had to leave before the deadline for her safe conduct pass expired, and therefore at a point where the situation had suddenly become fluid again.

> I don't know if he was going to go with Janoušek, because he was still in Prague when I left. And I didn't know actually who he was going to go with by that time, because there was a point when he was in contact with Bozděch, and there was some

thought that he might have been going with him, or with somebody else.[44]

It was not to be with Bozděch though. Since others were to be involved with him, it is almost certain that Bozděch would not have given details in advance to his wife – perhaps not even on the morning he was going to leave, for she would be questioned. She would understand why; and the assumption they would most likely have worked on was that, in time, after making petition to the authorities, Tatiana and her child would be permitted to leave the country and join him. However, while Bozděch could not take his family with him, he was determined to take his dog.

Now it might be thought that he was unwisely increasing the level of risk to himself by taking his dog: photographs of them had appeared in magazines and newspapers; he would be in uniform on the streets of Prague with the dog; and they could be recognised by anyone who made the connection. But on the other hand, during the first crucial hours of the attempt, if he found a means of having the dog with him at his work, it would not arouse suspicion. When Bozděch eventually wrote about his escape, he gave nothing away that could incriminate anyone who had conspired with him; but the early part of his plan implicated no one; and he gives a credible account of how he was able to take the first steps of his escape on a working day from the Defence Ministry in Prague, accompanied by his dog. His plan was bold and it was simple.

In his office on the morning of Tuesday 27 April, he casually announced to the two work shadowers that his wife had been complaining that the dog's claws had been causing damage to fabrics in the flat, so he would have to take him to the vet to have the claws cut; he would send one of the clerical staff to his flat later in the morning to bring the dog to the office, and then he would take him to the vet before lunch. Antis, of course, was still recognised as a military dog, and his presence for a short time in the Defence Ministry would be unremarkable. Later in the morning, Bozděch called in one of his clerical staff, a capable man and someone who was fond of animals. Explaining that his wife was attending a medical clinic with their baby, he gave the clerk the keys of his flat and his gloves, and told him to collect Antis and bring him to the office, so that he could take him to the vet. The dog, he assured the man, would follow him placidly as he had his master's gloves. The elements of phase one fell into place as planned; and about an hour before lunch, he took Antis and left the Ministry.

Heading in the direction of the vet's – probably by tram – he alighted, and veered off to a pre-arranged rendezvous. The sequence now was to change out of uniform, and be picked up by a working vehicle that a trusted man had driven in from the country: a lot of experience and ingenuity had been learned over the years of the occupation. From an allusion Bozděch made in his own account, it is a fair assumption that he had not simply given himself the best part of two hours leeway before his absence from his office raised questions: it is more likely that he had been timetabled to be out of the Ministry of Defence in the afternoon, for example, to attend a meeting or a training course. With luck, he was giving himself the best part of twenty hours' grace.

It was less than three years since he and his air force comrades had made their triumphal return. Now he was a fugitive. And as he climbed into the vehicle that would take him away from the city towards the south west, he cast eyes for the last time on the enchanting city of Prague.

CHAPTER NINE

Path into Exile

Then came the second war, passed and repassed,
And now you see our town, the fine new prison,
The house-doors shut and barred, the frightened faces
Peeping round corners, secret police, informers,
And all afraid of all.

Edwin Muir, 'The Good Town'

For the second time in a decade democracy in Czechoslovakia was extinguished. Many again took the exile's route; but in 1939, it was German troops who had to be evaded, now compatriot border guards shot their own people; Poland then had been a refuge, now it too was part of the Soviet bloc, while West Germany was a haven.

The escape route that Bozděch took is not known; and there is little scope for cross-referencing. However, in 1953, he wrote an account of it in English, for serialisation in either the press or a journal; then later, he incorporated a slightly amended version in a manuscript, which he intended as the basis for a book.

As with his writing about the air force squadrons, it is characterised by precision of detail, and it is this specificity with regard to distances, topography, proximity of a railway line and place names in Germany that helps the reader plot the crossing point. His stance as writer was that of anonymous narrator; so it is written in the third person. He concealed behind fictional names the identities of those who went with him; nor did he name the village near the border which was the starting point for their trek on foot. The journey was not completed the day he left Prague; it was the end of April; and they did not spend the first night in the open, but there is no clue about where they stayed. All he wrote was that there were three in the group, and that the escape plans were arranged in Prague.

But the identity of someone who escaped with Bozděch is known. Franta Kraliček, who was only about 18 (and therefore had not served in the Czech forces in the west), was allocated the task of driving the pair from Prague part of the way; he was then to return and go about his usual work. Franta, though, on the spur of the moment, it would seem, decided that he would leave the country with them. He eventually settled in England, and Bozděch and he were in contact infrequently in later years. However, Franta does not correspond to the character whom Bozděch called Anton in his account, a local man who was to take them across the border and return to Czechoslovakia. The third member of the trio seems to have been an officer in the Czechoslovakian forces, who may also have served in the UK during the war. Bozděch gave very little away about him, only that he was the older of the two from Prague. So, in his account, he gave no information that the authorities did not already have: two high profile officers from Prague escaped on 27 April 1948.

It is therefore to Bozděch's account that we have to turn. He was probably writing under less pressure of time than when he wrote in Prague, and he was able to build on his instincts as a story teller, for the tale of their escape is well structured, tense and absorbing. Their direction was south west from Prague, through Bohemia towards Bavaria, in the American Zone of Occupation in West Germany; and their targeted crossing place was close to the small Bavarian town of Furth Im Wald. Their final approach on foot may have been from either Česka Kubice or Spaleny. In his earlier paper he made no reference to how they travelled on the first leg of the way from the city, but in his second version Bozděch wrote that it was by a series of pre-arranged lifts in working vehicles.

One of the group, however, required no anonymity – Antis. Bozděch wrote fulsomely about the part that Antis played in their escape. He acknowledged, however, that his fellow escapee from Prague challenged him at the outset about the wisdom of taking the dog with them: it was known that the frontier guards used dogs on some sectors of the border. Whatever Bozděch's deeper reasons were for taking the dog, he simply argued that he trusted the dog 'to smell out danger long before you or I could hear or see it.'[1] Then when the pair reached the point where they were met by someone with local knowledge – to whom he gave the name Anton – who would lead them to the crossing point, there was further heated discussion. According to Bozděch, he insisted that Antis was a remarkable dog; if they felt so strongly they could go without him: he would take his chances, alone with Antis. It was resolved by their staying together.

The final approach to the border area had to be on foot; it was daylight; and they had to traverse a thickly wooded area before it got dark, and position themselves there for the final crossing at night. Bozděch put the dog to work. He used a game that he had played with Antis many times in the past when they were on air force stations and had gone for long walks in the country. He kept the animal close to heel, but as they approached an open glade, or a track intersecting their line of march, he whispered to the dog and signalled it forward. The dog went forward, sniffing the air, listening intently, 'every movement he made was purposeful',[2] while the three men waited; sometimes for only a few minutes; sometimes it seemed an age before Antis returned. When he did, they assumed the area to be clear. Avoiding well-trodden paths, they sometimes had to crawl on all fours; progress was difficult and slow.

They continued in this fashion, for about three hours, until the trees thinned out and gave way to a valley, consisting of a strip of pasture land through which coursed a fast-flowing, shallow and, at this point, turbulent river, strewn here and there with boulders. This was the sort of spot where it could be forded without much difficulty. Bozděch's description of the topography pinpoints the area. The river rose in Germany and flowed into Czechoslovakia; and about ten yards from its bank on the other side was a narrow road that led to Germany; the border lay a few hundred yards further along. The road was frequently patrolled by Czechoslovakian border guards. There were still some hours of daylight left; although it was tempting to make a wild dash for it, they would be exposed in the open pasture, and as they waded through the river; so they withdrew a little way into the wood and lay concealed, waiting for dusk.

As the hours dragged by, like animals, their senses were alert;

but they were more than instinctive creatures, and inevitably – for the two escapees from Prague – the mind flitted into ruminative pattern, going over the situation they had left, and the consequences for their families. Bozděch thought of Tatiana. She would first have begun to suspect something had happened when she discovered the dog had been taken from the flat; her suspicion would be reinforced when her husband failed to return after office hours; and then it would be confirmed by the arrival of the security police. She had no information to give them; but that would not make the abrupt, threatening manner any easier. They would not likely remove her for questioning, for she had such a young child. But it would not take the authorities long to evict them from the flat in the Stromovka; she would probably pre-empt that by going to her parents. There emerged in his ruminating a trace of bitterness that, in time, might change into guilt. Then, particularly for a veteran, there was the underlying political hopelessness of the situation: in 1939 there was conviction among many that the western powers ultimately would act against Hitler; now there was no possibility of outside intervention to restore democracy; they were without hope – all that mattered was survival.

Beside him lay Antis, who had been part of family life in Prague, and who had been his faithful companion, sharing danger with him in the gun turret of a Wellington bomber. However, as they lay in the forest, waiting while the gloaming deepened, the roles of man and dog were reversed: the dog had superior senses; they were now in his domain. Certainly Bozděch was right that the dog could smell and see danger before they could, but there was an unpredictability about being led by a dog; for Antis' ancestors were night hunters, whose visual acuity was superb in twilight or night time. Bozděch was startled by the dog suddenly adopting a crouching position, looking fixedly in the direction of a clump of small trees. Recalling it, he wrote that the dog then rose and remained in this position for some minutes. As he slowly raised his hand to soothe the trembling dog, he felt Antis' hackles rise. From the thicket there emerged a roe-deer, and suddenly, before Bozděch could stop him, Antis bounded after it, all his training overtaken by natural instinct. The men were powerless; Bozděch dare not call out. Then a remarkable thing happened.

Even as they watched, Antis stopped in his tracks and, with head and tail held low, slunk back to his master's side.[3]

In the way humans interpret a dog's behaviour, Bozděch described Antis as showing signs of contrition; then he settled again, and the men waited. Darkness gathered, and when they thought it deep enough they moved forward to the perimeter of the forest, then waited a little longer.

They began to advance through the strip of pasture with its long straggling grass, ungrazed and untended. But they had not gone far when Antis suddenly dropped flat to the ground. The three men lay prone in the scant cover provided by the long grass. What had he picked up, by smell, sound or sight? Antis, with a much larger field of vision than a human, was facing towards the forest, to the direction from which they had come. Bozděch put his hand on the collar; he could feel him, tense and rigid. They listened and waited. Soon they heard a different sound from the constant background note of the river: it was footsteps swishing through the grass; a number of people were silently advancing along a line which seemed to be converging with theirs. Was it a patrol of border guards or some escapees like themselves? It was nerve-wracking, Bozděch recounted; and Antis was poised to spring and challenge, but Bozděch restrained him, and the dog silently obeyed. The silhouettes of the unknown group passed within several yards of the men lying in the straggly grass; and were swallowed by the dark. The trio lay perfectly still for some more minutes, but breathed more easily. During this time, Antis, Bozděch wrote, made no attempt to rise. Then 'he touched his owner's hand with his muzzle',[4] and slowly stretched on to his four paws. The men rose too and began to move forward silently.

Suddenly, from about three hundred yards beyond the river on the other side, the darkness was pierced by the harsh glare of first one searchlight and then another from a portable unit on higher ground. The three men dived to the ground. Bozděch held the dog. The beams of light, they could see through the long grass, were moving restlessly in arcs, and were followed by prolonged bursts of machine-gun fire. To their horror they could see fleeing figures, trapped in the cones of light, cut down by the machine guns. The group had been escapees like themselves – the crossing point had been compromised and lay like bait. Not daring to move, the men lay flat while the searchlights played over the water and on both sides of the river.

After some minutes, they heard the sound of vehicles, and the lights of two speeding cars came sweeping along the narrow road,

1. Young minstrels in Bohemia. Bozděch is the accordionist
(*Maureen Bozděch collection*)

2. Off duty in Prague during compulsory military service 1934–36. Bozděch standing third from right. (*Jiři Malik collection*)

3. Career serviceman in 1938, Bozděch, course instructor in the centre with cadets. (*Jiři Malik collection*)

4. Port-Vendres, France June 1940. Protected by the guns of a British warship Czechoslovak personnel wait to embark for the UK. (*Maureen Bozděch collection*)

5. Cholmondeley park July 1940, the Czechoslovak military encampment. (*Maureen Bozděch collection*)

6. Antis, as a puppy, on board ship with Bozděch en route from Gibraltar to UK, to be smuggled ashore. (*Maureen Bozděch collection*)

7. President Beneš with his airmen, Cholmondeley July 1940. (*Maureen Bozděch collection*)

8. Arrival of Czechoslovak airmen at RAF Cosford. (*Maureen Bozděch collection*)

9. An informal session with President Beneš and airmen. (*Maureen Bozděch collection*)

0. Incorporated in the RAF, Czechoslovak airmen drawn up for review before being posted to their squadrons. (*Maureen Bozděch collection*)

1. No. 311 (Czechoslovak) Squadron of Bomber Command at Honington 1940. (*Maureen Bozděch collection*)

12. RAF East Wretham in the spring 1941. From left PO Eduard Šimon, Sqn Ldr Charles Pickard, who was instructor/liaison officer and then operations officer with No. 311 (Czechoslovak) Squadron, his dog Ming and Sqn Ldr Josef Ocelka, who became squadron CO in July 1941 Šimon was shot by communist security men in 1949; Pickard, who was captain of 'F for Freddie' in the film *Target for Tonight,* was killed in February 1944 leading a daring low-level attack on the Gestapo prison at Amiens; and Ocelka was killed in an air crash in July 1942. (*Zdeněk Hurt collection*)

13. The King and Queen visiting No. 311 (Czeckoslovak) Squadron at East Wretham in 1941. (*Maureen Bozděch collection*)

14. Wellington bombers of No. 311 Squadron (*Arnošt Polak collection*)

15. Aircrew comrades in arms. Bozděch and Antis (*Iveta Irvingová collection*)

16. Relaxing in sunshine in front of C for Cecelia, before the night's operation, are three of its regular crew of the summer of 1941: Čapka, first on the left, Bozděch, third from right (in dark glasses) and Antis, along with three other members of the squadron. (*Ludvik Klimek collection*)

17. (*Right*) '...you have inspired others by
your courage and steadfastness'. Antis
with bandaged head, after having been
wounded on a night bombing raid.
(*Iveta Irvingová collection*)

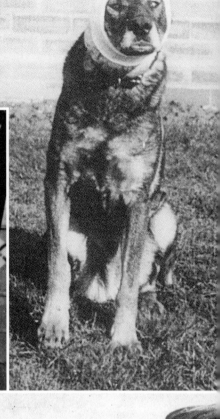

18. (*Above*) C for Cecelia, the
Wellington bomber whose
crew included Bozděch and
Antis, here with its pilot
Josef Čapka DFM. This
picture was taken in
January 1942, after Cecelia
had completed 52 missions.
Along side the numerical
pattern of bomb symbols
representing its raids is the
V-for Victory sign in Morse
code.
(*Zdeněk Hurt collection*)

19. Making an official visit to the squadron. Air Vice Marshal
Janoušek, on the left, talking to Wg Cdr Ocelka, on the rig
(*Maureen Bozděch collection*)

20. No. 8 Air Gunnery School at RAF Evanton, 1942. A group of cadets have completed their training. Bozděch, their instructor, in the centre with Antis.
(*Arnošt Polak collection*)

21. As each intake of cadets passed out as air gunners, there is a formal picture round Antis and Bozděch. Back row, second from the left, Arnošt Polak.
(*Arnošt Polak collection*)

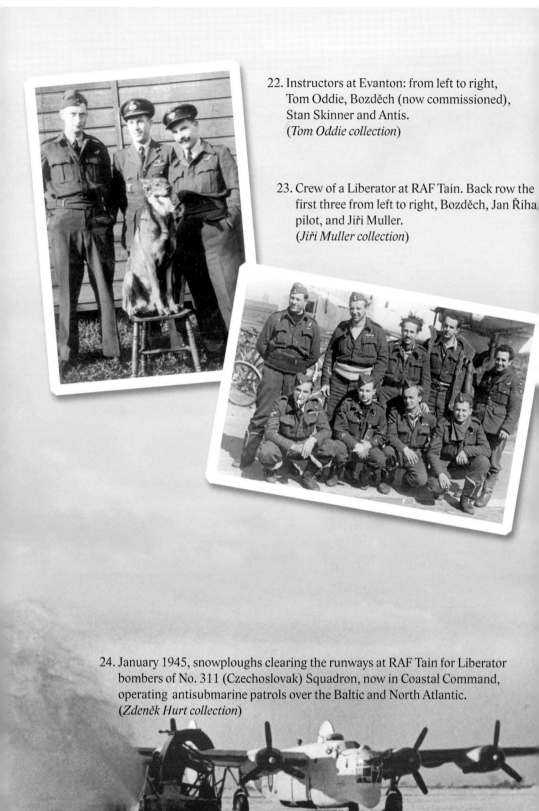

22. Instructors at Evanton: from left to right, Tom Oddie, Bozděch (now commissioned), Stan Skinner and Antis. (*Tom Oddie collection*)

23. Crew of a Liberator at RAF Tain. Back row the first three from left to right, Bozděch, Jan Řiha pilot, and Jiři Muller. (*Jiři Muller collection*)

24. January 1945, snowploughs clearing the runways at RAF Tain for Liberator bombers of No. 311 (Czechoslovak) Squadron, now in Coastal Command, operating antisubmarine patrols over the Baltic and North Atlantic. (*Zdeněk Hurt collection*)

25. Teacher and pupil in the same crew. From the left, Irving, 1st pilot, Hayek, Weiss, Spitz, a
    WAAF driver, Shaw, Polak, Sedlak and Sukany. Dr Geoff Shaw, the only Englishman flying
    with No. 311 Squadron, before the war taught at an English grammar school in Prague
    which shared the same building as the Czech grammar school where Arnošt Polak was a
    pupil. (*Arnošt Polak collection*).

26. The wedding of Wg Cdr Vlastimil (Vlasta) Chrast and Pamela in London 1945. After the war
    Vlasta Chrast became Bozděch's CO at the Defence Ministry in Prague. (*Pamela
    Schutzmann collection*).

27. Return of the Czechoslovak fighter squadrons to Prague August 1945. Spitfires in the background, on the left, Lt Col Jaroslav Hlado formally reports their arrival to Generals Bohumil Boček and Karel Janoušek. On right General Brigadier Heliodor Pika whose son served in the RAF. Under the Stalinist policy after the communist coup, Pika was executed; Janoušek and Chrast (previous photo) were sentenced to 16 years and 12 years in prison respectively for their involvement with the west. (*Zdeněk Hurt collection*)

28. Victory Parade in Prague, August 1945. The airmen, still in RAF uniform, march past, accompanied by Antis. (*Rozlet*)

29. Bozděch, staff captain at the Defence Ministry. (*Maureen Bozděch collection*)

30. On his wedding day, Bozděch escorting his mother into the church. (*Maureen Bozděch collection*)

31. Bozděch and his bride Tatiana. Antis is entangled in the bride's train. (*Maureen Bozděch collection*)

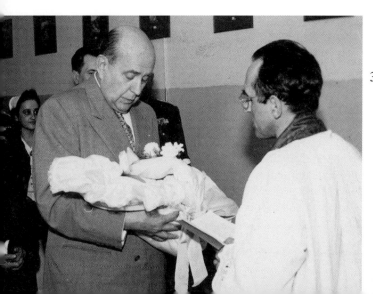

32. Aged about seven months, Jan Bozděch with Antis at home in Prague. (*Jan Bozděch collection*)

33. Christening of Bozděch's son Jan. Dr Jan Masaryk, Foreign Minister, is the godfather and he is holding his godson. Bozděch behind Masaryk and slightly to the left. (*Maureen Bozděch collection*)

34. Jan Masaryk and Bozděch on 7 March 1948, two weeks after the communist coup. On the wall a picture of Joseph Stalin. Three days after this photograph was taken the body of Masaryk was found in the courtyard of the Ministry building. (*Maureen Bozděch collection*)

35. Dieburg refugee camp, West Germany. In the room of this old school building are the bunks of several former RAF officers. Antis on the top bunk to the centre. (*Maureen Bozděch collection*)

36. Earls Court London, March 1949- ceremony of the award of the Dickin Medal to Antis. Field Marshall the Earl Wavell, his granddaughter and the hero. (*Maureen Bozděch collection*)

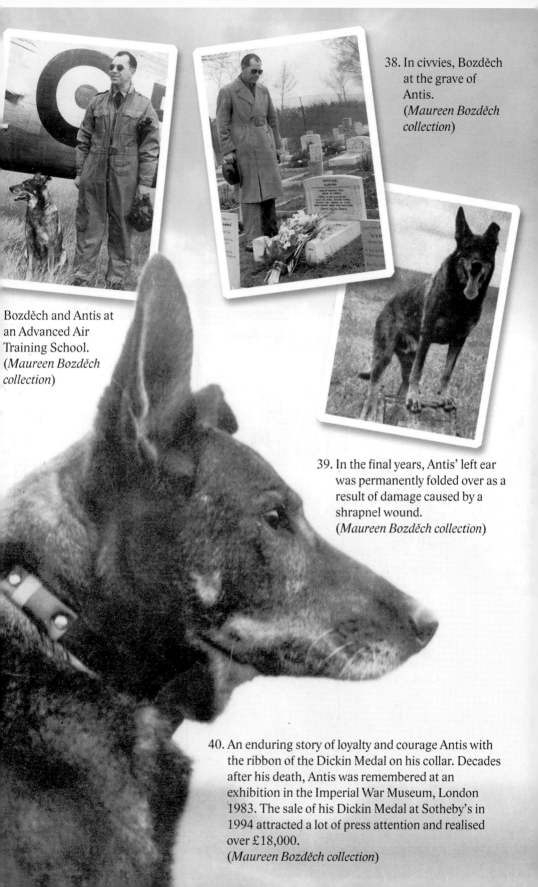

38. In civvies, Bozděch at the grave of Antis. (*Maureen Bozděch collection*)

Bozděch and Antis at an Advanced Air Training School. (*Maureen Bozděch collection*)

39. In the final years, Antis' left ear was permanently folded over as a result of damage caused by a shrapnel wound. (*Maureen Bozděch collection*)

40. An enduring story of loyalty and courage Antis with the ribbon of the Dickin Medal on his collar. Decades after his death, Antis was remembered at an exhibition in the Imperial War Museum, London 1983. The sale of his Dickin Medal at Sotheby's in 1994 attracted a lot of press attention and realised over £18,000. (*Maureen Bozděch collection*)

41. The wedding of Bozděch and Maureen, 1962. As he had just left the RAF, Bozděch was not able to be married in uniform, but for the reception he donned his best blue for the last time. (*Maureen Bozděch collection*)

42. Remembrance in Prague 2005. Flanked by a Czech guard of honour of a new generation, General Frank Elston, on the right, and Lt Col Arnošt Polak of the Free Czechoslovak Air Force Association after laying a wreath at the memorial to the Czechoslovak airmen who died during World War II. (*Pavel Vančata collection*)

and, within fifty yards of the forest, swerved in a wide arc towards the scene where the searchlights were now settled. Several men in uniform got out, and from where they lay the trio could hear the excited whining of a dog. Immediately Antis raised his head and sniffed the air, 'as if estimating the strength of this new enemy.'[5] The men in uniform searched for their victims; then, satisfied with their haul for one night, guards and their dogs returned to their vehicles; the searchlights were switched off and the cars drove away. Darkness reclaimed the valley. Predators had efficiently killed their prey; and the river's discourse with its gravelly bed was indifferent to the slaughter.

The sickening thought sank in: their salvation had been at the cost of the lives of some of their countrymen, like themselves bent on escaping. 'Seconds had decided which group of escapees would be watching the pitiful end of the other's bid for freedom.'[6] Antis' warning had delayed them. Waiting a while longer to make sure no foot patrol had been sent, they turned in the direction they had come and silently made for the trees to confer.

Attempting to cross at that point was suicidal. Hesitating before he spoke, the local man, their guide, said that there was no option but to move further west through the forest, and make their way to the other side of a hill, which was about 1000 metres high, whose western base was almost in Germany. Such a detour in this wooded area in the dark would take them perhaps five or six hours. Making their way first north, then westward, they had to avoid the main road and carry on until they reached a river near the eastern base of the hill. Bozděch assumed that it must be a loop of the same one near whose bank they had lain up hours before. It flows into the forest then loops round the hill on the Czechoslovak side; they had to cross it before they got to the hill.

Progress through the trees was painfully slow, but they were encouraged when they heard the sound of running water. Reaching the river, they explored from its bank: the difficulty in the dark was to gauge a place where it was not too deep and where the current was not overpoweringly strong. Eventually they just had to chance it. Jumping into the water, one by one, each took hold of another's hand. Bozděch came last, holding a companion and Antis' collar with his other hand. The river was waist deep a little way out from the bank, but it was wider at this point than they had estimated, and soon the power of the current buffeted them. Each of them stumbled, lost his companion's grip, and they became separated.

Bozděch managed to keep hold of the dog's collar, and they got to the other side. Exhausted and chilled through, he could see no sign of the others.

They were still on Czechoslovakian soil, so calling out was unwise; but regardless, the noise of the river would drown the human voice. Bozděch knelt beside the dog and told him to seek; and then he waited, shivering in his sodden clothing in the April night air. Minutes later through the darkness loomed a figure holding Antis' collar: it was their local companion, who, when the dog came up to him, understood from his behaviour that he would lead him to Bozděch. Again Antis was told to seek. This time he was away longer before he returned with the third member, who had been carried furthest down stream. Wet through and weary the escapers had now to cover the last stretch to the border – a fairly densely wooded hill, then a further strip of arable land bounded by a river. Their options were a contour walk round the hill, which would take longer, or climb to its summit or one of its shoulders and down the other side, which would be quicker. The decision was to climb; and this turned out to be, as Bozděch put it, an unfortunate error of judgement.

In the dark the climb was difficult; they kept stumbling and were persistently impeded by branches and caught on thorns. Then their misjudgement soon became obvious: a heavy night mist began to form, and with 'appalling suddenness it came upon them', shrouding the top of the hill; they could no longer see the stars and they were unable to get their bearings. However, they could still climb blind, as it were, so long as they knew they were making a steep ascent. And this they did until, around 1am, they reached a shoulder of the hill. They dare not risk descending though, in case they lost their way and wandered away from the border; there was no alternative but to await the dawn, huddled together for warmth, chilled by their sodden clothing. Aware of their indebtedness to Antis, Bozděch 'stroked the dog's head, then bending forward, he whispered the words of praise which Antis had earned so richly. . . Antis pressed against his master's chest. He loved praise from the man.'[7] And the man became aware that he was absorbing warmth from the dog's body, and it gave him an idea. Each of them took turns in hugging the dog's body for warmth for a few minutes. They spent a miserable two hours on the hillside until the first faint light of dawn glimmered on the horizon.

As the mist slowly began to clear they could see to their right the track they must follow. Their plan was to wait a little longer then continue, so Bozděch told Antis to stay: the dog was at a rocky outcrop, effectively guarding the path. The mist dissipated a little more, and they decided it was time to go, when, without any warning growl, there came the sounds of falling stones. The three men ran to the rocky outcrop where they had left the dog.

> On the ground in front of them sprawled a man in dark uniform and on top of him stood Antis, growling savagely. With the Alsatian's front legs planted on his chest, the frontier guard was helplessly pinned to the ground.[8]

Antis had never bitten anyone, but Bozděch wrote that he had never seen such savage fury in the dog: he thought it was the animal's courage and sense of loyalty that had transformed it. They disarmed the guard – he had been on his own not part of a patrol. Bozděch's depiction of him is very disparaging: callow and callous, he was one of the new indoctrinated breed of border guard that had replaced the old style of frontier guardsman, and unhesitatingly would have shot his fellow countrymen. They rendered him helpless by gagging him and tying him to a tree; then swiftly, they set off down the track.

The descent was easy, and within half an hour they were at the edge of the trees. In front of them lay a stretch of grass, bounded by a bend of a river, and on its farther side Germany. So too, in the near ground, in the grass area was what appeared to be a recently constructed wooden hut with two phone lines running to it – the base of the guard who had been climbing the path. But the question was whether he was alone on duty, or shared the watch in rotation with a colleague. The distance to the river bank was about two hundred yards; they could see a line of stones on the nearer bank, marking the country's boundary. The lateral dimension of the grassland was about six hundred yards; there were little wooden houses of a small settlement on each side.

These, before and during the war, had belonged to the German population of this part of the frontier area of Czechoslovakia, who, in terms of the decision of the Big Three Powers, had been expelled in 1945/46 and repatriated to Germany. Their property was given over to the National Land Fund to be apportioned to Czech land workers. This arrangement came under the aegis of the Ministry of Agriculture, which was in the hands of the Communist Party. The

way the Communist Party implemented the policy caused great
bitterness with the democratic parties in the National Assembly:
party members were receiving preferential treatment in the alloca-
tion of land.[9] In the election of 1946 the majority of voters in the
frontier area voted for the Communist Party. Surveying the area
before them, however, the three needed no psephologist to advise
them to bring that factor into the equation: they knew intuitively
that the occupants of those properties, living only yards from the
border, would be highly unlikely to be sympathetic to countrymen
fleeing the regime. It was far too risky to try skirting the perimeter;
it had to be a quick dash down the middle of the grassland to the
river.

But that could mean a bullet in the back. Kneeling beside the dog,
Bozděch whispered to him, and immediately gained his focused
attention; then he pointed to the hut and commanded Antis to go.
The men waited. This was not a game the dog was familiar with,
but he padded out into the cleared area sniffing the early morning
smells in the open, picking up the scent of rabbits, and wandered
over to the hut and sniffed around it. Bozděch felt guilty that the
dog was being made to take the risk, while they watched. Not satisfied with sniffing round the door, Antis then did what he had done
so often to a billet door on an airfield station after he had been out,
he scratched at it. There was no response from within. Once this
seemed certain, the men emerged from their cover and sprinted
through the field, Antis joyfully frisking alongside them. They
plunged into the river, waded across and clambered up the far
bank. 'They were in Germany. The last barrier to freedom had been
crossed.'[10]

Bozděch ended his first paper there. He wrote it in 1953, a few
months after the death of Antis. It was a tribute to the dog. His
introduction to the account refers to the death of Antis, 'famous
Alsatian war-dog',[11] being reported in the newspapers. However,
what had been written about Antis, up to that point – both in the
British press, and in the Czechoslovakian newspapers – dealt with
the dog's service during the war; he wanted to put on the public
record, in journal or newspaper article, 'the leading role'[12] that
Antis had played in the escape from Czechoslovakia. However, he
had to be careful not to identify himself prominently in a story of
escape from behind the Iron Curtain, a story which might well
attract large circulation: although Stalin had recently died his
legacy was very much alive throughout the Soviet bloc; there could

be repercussions for Bozděch's family. The distancing device he adopted was to claim that, as anonymous narrator of the story, he had been told it by Antis' master, to whom he gave the name Jan. So in 1953, Bozděch's limited aim, according to his introduction to the document, was to include this episode in what was already known about the dog.

But later, Bozděch wrote the more extensive manuscript about his life with the dog, and the earlier version of the escape from Czechoslovakia was amended and incorporated into it. He took up the story from the point at which they crossed into Germany. When the three men and the dog ran dripping from the river bank on to German soil, the sparsely wooded slopes were still within sight and range of the Czechoslovak border posts; and since bullets did not respect boundary lines, they ran until they were in cover. Then they headed for the nearby small town of Furth Im Wald, which was about two miles away in the United States Zone of Occupation. On their approach they came across one or two locals. Bozděch asked in German the way to the police station.

In the years they had been together, Bozděch developed insights into his dog's psychology and had become very sensitive to his signals; and he realised that Antis seemed to be suffering from strain, as a result of the watchfulness that had been expected of him: the dog kept looking enquiringly at him and seemed confused about what was now being demanded of him. All their time on air force stations, Antis had been very much a social animal, in constant contact with humans; he had never before come across man's inhumanity to man at close quarters. When the dog had been with Bozděch and the rest of the combat team in the Wellington bomber, anti-aircraft explosions and armour piercing cannon fire from a Messerschmitt ME 109 were not associated with human hand. For the first time, though, the dog had been made aware that man might be an enemy; and as they moved along from its outskirts through the streets of the town encountering an early rising citizen, who nodded with a *Gruß Gott*, he seemed confused. But as they continued, Bozděch noticed, and though the dog still received no sign from his master, he gradually relaxed.

At the police station they gave their identities, claimed asylum, and Bozděch and his colleague from Prague handed over their service revolvers. As the area was in the American Zone of Occupation, incoming refugees were passed through its military administration. With very little delay, the men were taken by jeep to the United States Air Force base at Straubing, which was several miles to the west. There they met three Czech airmen, who had also been officers in the RAF.

During his second day at Straubing Bozděch heard news of his family from other refugees who had arrived. His wife had taken their child and had moved to her father's home. He thought, at the time, that this would give her sanctuary from the authorities for a short while; and he had hopes that later she would be able to join him. In the longer term he had a clear idea what he wanted to do: rejoin the RAF.

The British Air Ministry was quick to recognise the value of the professional experience that former members of the Czechoslovak Air Force who had served in the RAF, and who were now fleeing their county for political reasons, could bring to Britain's peace time air force, which was heavily dependent on National Servicemen. So in 1948, as former ex-RAF personnel began arriving in camps in Germany, volunteering to rejoin the service, the Air Council relaxed enlistment procedures for overseas applicants in the case of those who had served with the RAF during the war,[13] on condition that they became naturalised British citizens. A number of escapees who were presently being processed at the US Air Force base at Straubing volunteered for the RAF, and they were moved in a party to Regensburg to await approval of visas.

Some mechanism had had to be set up to receive the influx of Czechoslovak refugees; the German Lender authorities could not take on responsibility for them: they were fully committed trying to cope with postwar reconstruction, and in resettling thousands of Germans who had been compulsorily removed from their homes in parts of Poland and Czechoslovakia; nor could the Allied military fill the gap – except as a short-term holding measure – as their role was to prevent the Soviet empire moving further westward in the wake of its tanks. Organisations like the International Refugee Organisation (IRO) filled the void, but as the numbers escaping grew, speed of response could not keep pace with the demand. During the time they were at Straubing, due to the comprehensive logistical and support systems of the US military, living conditions were comfortable and food was plentiful. There was also a preliminary security screening carried out at the base, for Bozděch wrote that the group had been warned by a friendly security officer that conditions at Regensburg were dire at this stage: inadequate food and no eating utensils; and so he arranged that some be given them, and for Bozděch to take with him a large bag of dog food for Antis.

If anything the conditions at Regensburg were even worse than they had imagined. Bozděch glossed over it, referring to its being demoralising, and instead described the plight of Antis. The dog refused to eat the dog food, after having lived on the products of the canteen at Straubing; he became thin, his ribs showing through his coat, and it lost its glossy shine. Bozděch had no alternative but to force-feed him the dog food from a spoon. The dog hated the experience; their overcrowded communal setting made things worse; and as some concession to the animal's dignity, Bozděch took him to a partly ruined attic where he fed him. However, he also made a point of exercising him; and the dog loved swimming in the river Danube.

Thanks to the method Bozděch used to create the final manuscript, and due to his own circumstances at the time he worked on it, there are some vivid impressions of postwar Germany which do not find their way into the finished work. Drafting the text in Czech, he translated it into English, and then dictated it on tape for an audio typist, carefully spelling out German place names and proper nouns. However, he was serving in the RAF at the time, and he required permission for his project: he dealt, after all, with recent events in the British military, and the contemporary situation of the cold war. Bozděch's decision to write in the third person as anonymous narrator may have made it easier for approval to be given; but the transcription of the typed material was first read by a senior RAF officer. And as the tapes were completed and the narrative built up, a dialogue between Bozděch and the senior officer took place on the tape. For example, at the beginning of the tape that he designated 'Germany 1', he began by addressing the officer with a biographical detail from the end of the war years.

If it's not too late and if you consider it of any importance, I should like to add that on 5 June 1945, with an eye to the future, I was sent to St Athan, to Number 14 Radio and Radar School for six weeks on a Signal Leader Course – Antis of course went along. The camp had changed quite a bit since we were there last in 1941-2. And now back to Regensburg in Germany.[14]

Thus there are, on tape, some fascinating tableaux of either side of the exile's road, that reflect the shared context of experienced airmen, which do not appear in the final manuscript.

Bozděch included an interesting aside – absent from the later manuscript – which explains why a group of them were moved from Regensburg. Each of these camps had a Committee to provide some organisation and structure; and Bozděch said on tape that 'owing to the puzzling activity'[15] of some of the Committee members who were taking an inordinately keen interest in learning the details of the escape routes, the ex-RAF personnel, with the approval of Allied security staff, were transferred to another Czech refugee camp at Dieburg near Frankfurt. The aural mode of communication brings with it the inflexion of the human voice, and both here and further on Bozděch, with economy of detail, gives stark glimpses of the destruction and aftermath of war for Germany. The group were to go to Dieburg by rail: 'It was half past midnight when an absolutely packed train arrived at Regensburg's roofless railway station.'[16]

The journey to Dieburg took about eleven hours; Bozděch and his eleven companions stood in the corridor all the way; the dog lay under the feet of people who had seats in a compartment. Their new quarters, Dieburg camp, were an old school, set amid fields of corn and turnips, and linked by a small country road to the main route to Darmstadt. The twelve airmen were accommodated in one room containing twelve double tiered bunks; Antis had the lower bunk beneath Bozděch. Conditions were not much better than at Regensburg; and Bozděch has left images of the pathos of the refugees' plight; human dignity amid privation; his care for his dog; and an incident, brought about by their meagre diet, which turns out to be a humorous tale at his own expense.

Dieburg camp was run by a Committee under the chairmanship of a 'highly respected priest, himself a refugee, and assisted by a splendid IRO (International Refugee Organisation).'[17] By the second half of June conditions at the camp became much better: there were rations, milk for the babies and they had their own kitchen. The bag of dog food from Straubing had long run out; Antis began to lose weight, and his coat suffered; Bozděch had to resort to feeding him from the daily mixture they called raison soup. On balmy June evenings someone would start gathering wood, and the refugees would light a camp fire on the ground adjacent to the school; a 'charming girl' began playing the accordion, and they joined in the patriotic songs of their homeland. These were unashamedly sentimental; and the pathos of the refugees' lot was brought home, Bozděch recalled, by the sight of a young face, 'untried yet by hard life', gazing tear-stained into the flames.

As new refugees arrived at various centres throughout West Germany, they brought news of the most recent developments in the circles they had left. In this way Bozděch learned that on 30 April, three days after he made his own escape from Prague, his commanding officer, Col Vlastimil Chrast had been caught, along with Gen Janoušek near Preštice making for the frontier. Now within the circle of officers with whom Bozděch conspired there were held, or memorised, certain addresses in the UK; and one of them was that of Pamela Chrast's mother. Guessing that it would be some time before the communist authorities chose to announce the arrest of her husband, Bozděch wrote to Pamela to break the news.

On 4 June 1948, Pamela replied.

Dear Captain Bozděch

Thank you for your letter. I was glad to know you got through safely. I begged my husband to go with you on the 27th (that was the day I left Prague) but he wanted to know that the furniture was safely out of the country first. I always knew we should not have bothered about the furniture, my husband's life and safety were much more important to me. He was not really waiting to go with Janoušek but only for this reason which I have told you. I knew it would be fatal to go with Janoušek as he was very nervous and I knew he must be watched.

The news was a terrible shock to me as you must know. The first I heard about it was through a letter which was sent here for you but it was addressed to my mother so I opened it, as it had a German postmark and hoped it concerned me. In it someone told you about my husband's arrest, this was the first I knew of it. After that I made intense enquiries and everyone said the same and then I had confirmation which made it quite definite, also Mrs Hanaš's husband is in prison, which you probably know.

I am sorry I opened your letter but as I said it wasn't addressed to you and my anxiety by this time was so great I hoped to learn something from it. I have heard that Janoušek gave away the names of twelve officers among which was my husband's name, but one hears so many rumours it is difficult to know what to believe. I do hope that my husband's valise was not with him as everything helps. I wish I could get some news here but no one knows anything. If I could only know when Vlasta will be tried, on what charge, and what kind of defence he can get etc. I have made up my mind to go back to Prague within the next ten days or so, I can't stand it any longer, I must be near my husband and at least see him once a week. A girlfriend of mine in Prague visits him every week and told me he is well, but I want to see him and find out what is going to happen. The only thing that would stop me going back is if I thought it would make things any worse for Vlasta and I don't think I can do that now. I am glad to hear that he is fairly well treated, but as I know my husband he is very restless and cannot stand to be anywhere when he knows he is not free so I think it will have pretty bad effects on him eventually. It seems so wicked that all these people should be treated like this when they have done nothing.

You have been very kind to us and I don't know how to thank you. I do appreciate what you did for us in Prague and that you offer to help me now. You will need your money when you come here, as the first few months will probably be difficult for you. I don't care that I haven't got any money, I only wish my husband were here and we would manage somehow. My furniture, glass etc arrived last week and it upset me to think that just for these paltry things my husband is where he is now.

If there is anything you want done in England about your visa or anything else let me know. In case we shall not be here I shall tell my mother and sister and they will deal with it. Now there is another thing, where will you stay when you come to England? My mother said you can stay here if you would like to, we have enough room. The only thing though I must warn you about is that it is an old house and rather dilapidated, not like our nice flats in Prague with central heating and hot and cold water, but you really can stay here if you want to until you get fixed up; just write and if I am not here you know my sister. We should be glad to do something even if it's not much.

Can you get in touch with Major Richter and give him my address, I don't believe he knows it, also tell him that I said if he has nowhere to go (which I don't believe he has) he can put up here also.

I am glad to hear you have Antis with you. Was he good?

I shall enclose the letter which was sent for you. Do you need anything while you are in Germany? Let me know if you do, and in case I am not here, as I said before, my sister would be pleased to do anything.

Don't advise me not to go to Prague, everyone does. But I feel I must and want to. It's a thing I can only decide for myself. You know, I think, how much my husband and I mean to each other. I shall leave Vivian in England. Hoping you are well.

Yours very sincerely

Pamela Chrast

PS If you hear any other news do please let me know, and don't forget to write if you need something. I should be glad to be able to do something for you.

I crossed out these things only as an afterthought, but I hope this letter is safe.[18]

After she had written the letter, as a precaution, Pamela obliterated the address and her second name.

In the middle of June, Bozděch went by train with Antis from Dieburg to meet some Czech friends in other refugee camps. What purpose these trips were to serve he did not reveal in the tape; and they are not referred to at all in his later manuscript. It is difficult to believe that he was doing a social whirl around the camps, so it may be inferred that there was some significance behind them: meeting with colleagues like Maj Richter, and, of course, his only source of information about his family was from the refugee community. From what Bozděch wrote there was also the possibility of finding a way for his wife and child to join him. The likelihood of their making a clandestine exit from the country seems remote, but there may have been soundings made in Prague to find out if Bozděch's family would be allowed an exit visa. His wife and son had moved in with her parents; Tatiana's father had been an army colonel and played a part in the Prague uprising in May 1945 – an event the Communist Party liked to claim responsibility for – and therefore someone of standing with the authorities.

It would be reasonable to speculate that he may have had the ear of Gen Svoboda, Defence Minister.

Gen Svoboda was untainted by contact with the west: his military experience as a field commander had been in the east. In the tradition of the military in the Czechoslovak Republic he had not been overtly political, and may not have been a member of the Communist Party; but he was a fellow traveller. During the war he was reluctant to contradict the decisions of the army political advisers.[19] He was careful not to put a foot wrong with the communists: Miroslav Kerner was an official in the Ministry of Food in Czechoslovakia after the war, and he relates how, some three months before the communist coup, he was asked by Václav Holub, a member of the Czechoslovak parliament and chairman of its National Defence Committee to invite Svoboda and three other generals to dinner at his flat to find out what would be their attitude in the event of President Beneš calling a mobilisation of the army to protect the country's democracy. Svoboda, Kerner reports, made an excuse that he was too busy, and only two of the four turned up (in their opinion it was unthinkable for the President to make such an order and antagonise the Soviet Union).[20] No, Gen Svoboda was not the man to stick his neck out for anyone. To entertain the very idea that his family might be allowed to leave may have been disingenuous of Bozděch; but perhaps not many people, at the time, could foresee the extent of the purges and their harshness.

At any rate, by late June Bozděch had not given up hope that they might be reunited. All that he described of those trips, however, was the view from the train windows, and his mood was reflective as he surveyed the devastation, with a sense of his share of responsibility for it.

On their way to those camps they passed through many demolished towns including Bremen, Hanover and Hamburg; the places they used to bomb during the war. A strange, depressing feeling seeing the terrible destruction they once helped to accomplish.[21]

The final scenes of refugee camp life that Bozděch depicted are of a humorous, inept attempt to supplement their meagre diet; but it is an account that shows the resilience of the refugees and their ability to find laughter, despite their conditions. It was a wild pig hunt: it is not altogether in the genre of the three little pigs and the big bad wolf; nonetheless the pigs win. The cerebral drive came from a former violinist in a Prague orchestra. He and his wife had been there three months; they hoped to emigrate to Australia, but were having difficulty because priority admission went to skilled artisans and labourers. He had learned from a local farmer that there were wild pigs in the area (he had also been told that they were vicious, but he made light of that); they often liked to wallow in the mud of a bend in the nearby stream. His hare-brained scheme was to have Bozděch send Antis after one of the younger pigs, separate it from the others; then when the pig was preoccupied with the dog, a circle of men would close in on it and the violinist would fell it with a blow from a stick, and hold it in a full Nelson grip. He seems not to have given too much thought to how its final dispatch would be made. Bozděch said that he had no intention of putting the dog at risk, and was against it, but reluctantly he went along with the violinist and three compatriots.

It was around 5 pm on a hot June afternoon when the hunters set off; and soon they trod the soft grass of the forest. Eventually they spotted their quarry: the wild pigs looked small from a distance. Excitement gripped the men; Antis suddenly lunged forward. 'It was fascinating to watch him,' Bozděch said, 'as he cut across at right angles to the pigs.' In his stalking manner Antis soon caught up with the little shadows; and not until he was certain that they had spotted him did he bark. The barking produced a piercing squealing from a little pig; and the 'musician darted forward like an otter, with the rest of the team right behind him'. They had not gone half way when a deep warning rumble came from a nearby thicket. The men turned and ran; and Bozděch, fearing a life and death struggle between the dog and a wild boar, with the irrational surge of protectiveness that can overtake a dog owner, ran forward calling to Antis. He stumbled and fell. As he regained his feet, he found the dog was standing beside him; and the angry snorting changed into a soothing sort of wail. Bozděch realised that the wild beasts were as frightened of him and the dog as he was of them. With shaking hands he fixed the broken lead on Antis' collar; and left the field of disgrace. He ruefully recorded, 'What fun the people in the camp had that evening when the hunters returned home.'

On 4 July a British Air Ministry representative arrived at Dieburg to meet those who intended to rejoin the RAF; and the following day, twelve volunteers left Dieburg by lorry for RAF headquarters in Wiesbaden where they were enlisted in the RAF. The next step was the British Embassy at Frankfurt, where they were issued with passports; and it was only then, at Frankfurt, that Bozděch realised, when an official told him, that he would have to part with the dog when he arrived in the UK. This was a prospect that had not even occurred to him up to this point. In 1940, amid the confusion of thousands of servicemen from the Continent arriving in the UK, and the imminent threat of invasion, it had been possible to hoodwink authority on the dock side; and the poor grasp of English that Bozděch and his Czech friends had at the time meant that they probably thought they were merely outwitting petty officials. But not now; Antis would have to go into quarantine in the UK for six months. However, a senior RAF officer assured him that the dog would not be left behind. From then on things happened quickly: two days later their orders to leave for England came through; they were to travel to the Hague in Holland by rail; and a railway warrant was issued for twelve airmen and a dog.

As 9 July dawned, Bozděch realised, as he put it, that his last hope of being reunited with his family in Germany was gone, and he and his eleven compatriots boarded a train for the Hague. They travelled more comfortably this time, and they arrived at 5pm. Their ship was scheduled to sail that night for Harwich; but another problem presented itself: the dog would not be allowed to travel on a British ship without a permit from the British Ministry of Agriculture. The Commanding Officer of No. 110 Movement, Royal Air Force BAFO was sympathetic (Bozděch interjected in his tape recording that as he recalled the CO held the rank of flight lieutenant or squadron leader), but he could not circumvent the regulations. Bozděch's response, he said, was to refuse to sail without the dog; he would have no peace of mind; besides he owed him too much, and Antis was his last link with his family. The officer warned him of the consequences: he had signed on, so this would mean trouble for him. However, the CO offered to phone the Air Ministry in London to put the case and ask for instructions. Bozděch was now in a sweat; he was service-minded; he was already branded a deserter from one country's forces, and he had re-enlisted in the RAF on 5 July.[22] As he described how he tried to wrestle with his feelings, he left an image of war-damaged installations when he said on tape that he took the dog, 'and went for a stroll along the demolished harbour to think the thing out.'[23] He was away about an hour, and on his return he was no nearer resolving the matter for himself, when he saw the CO, accompanied by an NCO coming to meet him.

From this point onwards it is clear from decisions that were made at higher levels, as well as from Bozděch's service record over the next five years,[24] that Antis' wartime exploits were a matter of some significance to the RAF. The CO began by telling him that the fame of Antis was indeed known at the Air Ministry, and he had been given instructions on how to handle procedures: the regulations could not be waived, but arrangements would be made for documentation to be completed and for the dog to travel to the UK within a few weeks; meanwhile the unit CO made himself responsible for the dog, and proposed delegating care of him to the NCO, Corporal Hughes. With his understanding of service life and procedures, Bozděch knew that this was the best outcome he could hope for. He found at once in Corp Hughes that quality that is so fundamental to servicemen who have faced difficulties and danger as part of a team – trust; 'the type of fellow that doesn't usually let one down.'[25] Antis, wagging his tail gently took to his new guardian; and, with an anthropomorphic touch, Bozděch felt he could safely leave him: 'knowing how good a judge of the human character he was'. Then he inspected Corp Hughes' quarters, saw the bunk that would be the dog's, and stayed with him until it was time to go aboard. He had on him 135 krona in bank notes, bearing the likeness of Tomaš Masaryk, which today are still in an envelope among his papers.

The overnight crossing from the Hague to Harwich for the twelve airmen was but a continuation of other journeys, made eight or nine years earlier, when they had fled the eclipse of democracy in their country. Then they had rallied in their Czechoslovak units in France, where they gained a sense of purpose and renewed confidence in their national identity; now their hopes, like those of so many of their countrymen and women, leaving Bremerhaven and various ports in Germany, were to disperse in the west, and assimilate; but not forget.

CHAPTER TEN

Antis DM

Why bother to learn to read when you can smell meat a mile away?

Mikhail Bulgakov, *The Heart of a Dog*

To an airman of Bozděch's experience, RAF Cardington, with its tall hangars, built in 1917 to house the airships R-31 and R-32, could have been the starting point of a time line representing aerial warfare. For the best part of fourteen years of that period, from the Zeppelin to the jet engine, Bozděch had served variously in the forces of Czechoslovakia, France and Britain; and he was able to accept with stoicism that he must again don the uniform of one of them, and also find himself, for the fifth time in that career, at the bottom of the heap. He was not alone: former wing commanders and squadron leaders in the wartime Czechoslovak squadrons of the RAF, who had escaped from their country and rejoined, had all, under the conditions of enlistment, to revert to the rank of aircraftsman until posted to units.

His enlistment began on 5 July in Frankfurt am Main;[1] his previous service in the RAF during the war was accrued, but he was given a new number, 788941. He signed on at the recruitment centre at RAF Cardington for a period of five years. He was thirty-six; he would be forty-one at the end of the period of engagement, and he was giving himself options, for he could not foresee what might happen on the political scene. Documentation had to be completed;

and when Bozděch filled in the form naming his next of kin, he must have given some thought to where Tatiana might live in the longer term: she could not stay with her parents indefinitely; and he did not know how she would be treated by the authorities. In RAF personnel files, the names and addresses of next of kin were completed in pencil – to make later amendment simpler; in Bozděch's file a new address for his next of kin: wife Tatiana, was later interpolated.

Within days of arriving at Cardington, he received a letter from Corp Hughes telling him that Antis was well and not pining too much. The undertaking the Air Ministry had given was fulfilled; the RAF made the arrangements, and two weeks later Antis arrived at Hackbridge kennels in Surrey, where he was to remain in quarantine for six months. The day after Bozděch learned this, he was given a pass and went to see his dog. Hackbridge kennels were the largest quarantine kennels in England at the time; and as Bozděch approached them from the railway station, he had the impression of a large modern farm; then as he reached the compounds, he felt it was more like a hospital and the dogs the patients, looking expectantly for a visitor.

Antis recognised him by his step before he saw him, and greeted him exuberantly. Bozděch was delighted by his appearance, and the care Corp Hughes had taken of him: his coat was glossy and he looked well-fed. It had been the longest period Bozděch had been apart from his dog in the eight years he had had him. He groomed him, played with him, and stayed until late. Then came the time to part. He knelt beside the dog and, in the way he had during the war when he was on operations, he explained in a quiet voice that he would have to leave again.

The exceptionally strong bonding between man and dog was obviously manifest in the dog's behaviour, but Bozděch's devotion to the animal was great. It is apparent in the decision he made to take Antis when he fled from Czechoslovakia. Although he had to leave his family behind, whatever the reasoning he gave his fellow escapees, he was not going to leave the dog. And now that Antis was in quarantine, Bozděch came regularly to see him. Indeed while he was stationed at Cardington, he came every Wednesday and Saturday afternoon to see him. Regardless of the weather, twice a week, he went to Hackbridge; and he felt that the dog, in some strange way, knew when 'the great days of the week' arrived: for as he approached, he would see him, 'stiffly sitting, waiting'. On the tape, Bozděch describing the dog's posture, interjected a piece of information for the officer who would read the transcript:

> By the way, Antis' left ear, which was holed by a splinter during the war, was so weak now that it remained continuously flat.[2]

On 24 September, Bozděch was posted to an Air Ambulance Unit at RAF Innsworth as a Signaller IVA.[3] The designation Sig IVA (now obsolete) equated to the non commissioned officer rank of sergeant.[4] Each week, however, he went from Innsworth to Hackbridge, and this continued throughout October.

What seared Bozděch in his life with the dog were those occasions when, because of his enforced absence, Antis' loyalty to him brought the dog near the point of death. It happened during the war when Bozděch's plane had been diverted to another airfield, and, as a result, the dog feeling abandoned, refused food, became ill and fell into a decline. The worst was yet to come.

At the end of October Bozděch's visits suddenly ceased: he had an accident to his leg on the station's sports field; and he was taken to Innsworth hospital[5] where his leg was set in plaster. He was a patient for two weeks there.[6] Life for a serviceman, who was not in married quarters, was not his own when it came to a decision on where he would spend a period of convalescence; and on 11 November, he was admitted to Collaton Cross Military Rehabilitation Unit[7] near Plymouth. It had been impossible to get permission to travel while he was a hospital patient; and now the MO at Collaton would not give approval for a long journey.

Two weeks after he arrived at Collaton, Bozděch received an urgent letter from Hackbridge kennels: Antis was very ill and was likely to die; and he was courteously but strongly advised that he should come without delay.[8] With a heavy heart Bozděch went to the MO, who was also the unit's CO. Showing him the letter, he asked if, in these circumstances, he could have permission to travel to Hackbridge. The MO, whom he described as having a kindly face, was sympathetic and asked him about his dog. Bozděch briefly recounted Antis' experience in their life together. 'Yes I think I remember that Alsatian dog,'[9] said the MO, referring to newspaper articles he had read during the war. However, he was firm in refusing to sanction a journey of such a distance; but he said that he would arrange to have Bozděch transferred immediately to another medical rehabilitation centre in Surrey. And two hours later, according to Bozděch,[10] on 24 November,[11] he was on his way to No.1 Military Rehabilitation Unit at Chessington.

The MO at Collaton seems to have briefed his counterpart at Chessington, for next morning Bozděch was given permission to go to Hackbridge; and he travelled by bus. He found the kennels shrouded in autumn mist, as he hobbled towards them. A member of the staff prepared him for the worst as they made their way towards Antis' compound. The stress of confinement became too much for the dog: at first he tried to escape, then he refused food and he went downhill quickly. The best efforts of very experienced staff were of no avail.

When Bozděch came to write his memoir of the life of Antis, he selected an approach that would serve to tell the dog's story with dignity. His writings in Prague had dealt with men at war, and the tone of his work respected the qualities of self-sacrifice, bravery and the bonds of friendship. Five years later, when he constructed his narrative about Antis, he adopted a similar respect; and he avoided a Disneyesque style: he wrote from the perspective of dog owner; and because he used the third person, giving his persona the name Jan, he introduced a distancing element, which worked well for his topic. But in certain parts of the story, particularly when the dog was under great stress, Bozděch altered his stance and wrote from the dog's point of view, projecting into him some of the most deeply felt human emotions, and attributing to him a rational, cognitive capability. This can be quite a difficult technique to adopt convincingly; some writers, however, have successfully handled it in a sustained way. He used it sparingly, but effectively. For example, he described Antis' response in the Hague as he was about to board ship for Harwich. 'Antis made no effort to follow him, for the situation was perfectly clear to him. . . he appeared sad, but quite calm.'[12]

Again, recounting what had happened at the end of his first visit to Hackbridge, Bozděch took it from the dog's perspective. 'He knew that there was some mysterious reason which prevented his master from taking him away, and his sombre eyes kept on asking one question, when is this going to end?' Then, picturing the dog's response to his prolonged absence, as a result of injury, Bozděch, in the translation of his first draft in Czech (which had still to be polished), brought to the dog's reasoning themes that, by this time, lay deep in his own psyche – loyalty and betrayal.

> Antis paced up and down in his enclosure and stared for hours. He did not suspect that his trust in his master's promise had been betrayed, for in their long life together he got no reason to consider such a betrayal.[13]

When he revised this for his manuscript, Bozděch kept the same themes, but inverted the ideas to give more poignancy to the dog's plight.

> Despite all the efforts of the kennel authorities, nothing could rouse Antis to fight for his life. He felt he had, at last, been deserted by the man he loved, and just did not want to live.[14]

Although the kennel authorities had warned him, Bozděch was not really prepared for what he saw.

Through the wire mesh of his enclosure Antis looked a shadow of his former self, lying motionless with his head on the edge of his straw bed, his eyes closed, showing no sign of life. You cannot plead extenuating circumstances to a dog, and, in his narrative, he shouldered blame and guilt. At one glance he felt 'remorse, love and a sense of disaster.' Even when he went into Antis' compound and stood beside him, and gently called his name, the dog did not raise his head.

> Perhaps he recognised his voice, but in his long abandonment, he heard that voice in his dreams so often that he grew used to such phantoms.[15]

Bozděch struggled to get down on one knee; then, holding the dog's head in his hands, he talked to him, encouraging him and stroking him. Slowly, the dog responded. At first he raised his head; then let it fall, as though in self pity; but when he lifted it again, Bozděch received, what he called, a forgiving glance. Within half an hour, to please his master, the dog lapped a bowl of milk – the first food he had taken for days. Later Bozděch was able to coax him into the run behind his kennel, but after only a few minutes the dog had to go back to his kennel. It was clear that Antis was very ill. Bozděch stayed with him for hours until well into the afternoon. But the pain would be renewed when the time came to leave. And when it came,

> Antis began to tremble, and there was a sudden terror in his
> damp eyes, as he looked up into his master's face.[16]

Bozděch then did the only thing that he could think of, the trick that
had worked in the past: he left his gloves beside Antis' bed.

Having asked for an interview with the vet, he made his way to
the kennel's administrative offices. Wryly Bozděch observed on
tape that the vet's assessment was so guarded that whatever the
outcome he would not be wrong. In the vet's professional opinion,
the dog was very ill and his age was against his recovering; but on
the other hand, he might pull through.

At this point, his tape comes to an end. There is no signal that it
was to be the conclusion of the taped material, so it has to be
assumed that the narrative continued on another tape which,
unfortunately, is missing from the materials that he kept. His
manuscript, of course, continues and is now the main source for the
remainder of Antis' story.

Despondently, as dusk was gathering, he returned to the bus
stop, lost in thought. The year that was coming to an end did not
bear reviewing, yet it kept intruding: he had lost his family and his
country; only months earlier he had had a promising career,
moving among circles of power in Prague; a man whom he had
looked on as a friend, a Minister of State, had been murdered; and
now he was being riven because his dog was dying. A bus pulled
up, but he made no move to board it. It was not just Antis'
wonderful courage and loyalty, accompanying him and his
comrades night after night over enemy skies, that pierced him: his
dog was now his only link with that period and with his family and
country.

There was no one with whom he could share his feelings; he had
just moved to the rehabilitation unit at Chessington, and he knew
no one there. He saw a church close by, and he went into it.
Haltingly, he approached the altar. Unable to kneel in the confined
space, he sat in a pew. He was not a religious man; he had given up
churchgoing as a boy; and now as he tried to remember some set
phrases, none would come to him. So in the empty church he 'spoke
to his God from the fullness of his heart'.[17] Then he made his way
back to the bus stop.

Next morning the CO at Chessington again granted him a pass

to go to Hackbridge. To his joy and astonishment, he found that Antis had taken on a new lease of life: his bark was still very weak, but his eyes were brighter. Each day that followed the CO allowed him to visit his dog; and each day the dog visibly improved.

Malevolent fate then twisted the screw another turn. In the scale of consecutive negativities, which he had experienced that year, the new setback that Bozděch faced was not overwhelming; nonetheless, he had not the means to deal with it. Although the RAF had arranged to have Antis put into quarantine at Hackbridge, Bozděch had to pay for the kennelling. The cost was twenty-five shillings[18] a week – about sixty per cent of the pay of an AC2 [19] – and therefore insupportable over a long period. There was nothing else for it: he had to borrow money from a friend in Thetford. But that could not go on, because Antis would be in kennels until late in January. His advance to Sig IVA would have enabled him to pay back his friend; but doing that and continuing to pay the kennelling costs was very demanding. So, 'in despair', he went to the offices of the People's Dispensary for Sick Animals (PDSA).[20] The PDSA, a charitable organisation, the largest veterinary organisation in the UK, existed to provide free treatment for the animals of those who were unable to pay; and it did this by attracting patronage. Bozděch described it as, 'that grand society, which does such wonderful work for animals'. On 20 January 1949, the PDSA responded confirming that they would meet some outstanding cost.[21]

At the end of January 1949, the period of quarantine came to an end; Bozděch collected Antis from Hackbridge and took him to RAF Innsworth. Although the dog was now nine years old, reunited with his master, the familiar RAF uniforms and the camp life that he had known for five of those years all acted like a tonic for him, Bozděch observed, and he was soon his former playful self.

The Air Ministry's policy of recruiting Czechoslovak airmen who had escaped from their country, but keeping them at the lowest rank of the service was exposed by the *Sunday Express* on 30 January 1949. The paper's headline read, 'Is this the way to treat heroes?' The article claimed that about one hundred and fifty former members of the RAF escaped from communist oppression and rejoined the service. The paper's Air Correspondent was well informed about Gen Janoušek, pointing out that he had been knighted in this country during the war for his services as Inspector-General of the Czechoslovak Inspectorate, and reported that the general had been trapped trying to cross the frontier. However, the paper's thrust was the policy of the RAF, citing that officers had to accept the lowest non-commissioned rank, and went on:

> Thirty-five of them, several wearing the ribbon of the Distinguished Flying Cross, are today at the Cardington (Bedford) recruiting centre sweeping floors, scrubbing tables, dishing up food, and cleaning lavatories for British conscripts.[22]

Bozděch had cut out the front page of the paper; he quibbled over the Air Correspondent's choosing to highlight only those of the former Czechoslovak Air Force who had served in Fighter Command, by putting a question mark against it; but he kept the article.

Around this time he was invited for a short stay at the home of Pamela Chrast's mother. Pamela, the wife of his former commanding officer in Prague, who had been arrested as he attempted to escape, had invited him earlier when she wrote to him at Dieburg refugee camp. Pamela recalls the visit.

> When he returned to the UK he stayed with us; in my mother's flat. That's what I said in the letter, if you remember. And he did, he came there with the dog. And I knew the dog, but when Bozděch went out and left the dog with me, the dog wouldn't let me go into the room anymore. He was a guard dog, he was a good guard, but he wouldn't let me go in the room anymore; and then we took him out for a walk, he didn't want to go too far away from where he was either.[23]

On 2 March Bozděch was posted to No. 4 Radio School at Swanton Morley, and of course, in the RAF, where Bozděch was posted Antis went too. That same month honour was to come to the dog, which redounded on the air force.

The PDSA had taken careful note of what Bozděch had told them of Antis' life and had made their own enquiries about the dog's wartime record. Clearly it was felt that Antis met all the criteria for the award of the Dickin Medal, or as it is more commonly known the 'Animal VC'. The Dickin Medal is only awarded on recommendation; and like the Victoria Cross it has to be earned in conditions of war. It is awarded to animals associated with the armed forces that have shown gallantry and devotion to duty. In Bomber Command during the war, it was no small effort for even highly motivated men to resubmit to the lonely sorties over enemy territory, or face the classification 'lack of moral fibre'; but it was quite another for a dog, who had joined a crew, and sensed their fear, not to follow instinct and avoid that situation in future. Instead during the bombing phase of 1941, among the contributions made by No. 311 (Czechoslovak) Squadron of Bomber Command one team of six airmen and an Alsatian went to the dispersal point night after night.

On 14 March 1949, Bozděch with Antis, groomed and bright eyed, arrived at Earls Court London. The distinguished guest who was to confer the award on Antis was Field Marshal the Earl Wavell. A soldier-scholar, Wavell was a fine choice. His great adversary in the desert battles of the North African campaign of the Second World War, the charismatic commander of the Afrika Korps, Erwin Rommel, thought highly of Wavell and carried a translated version of Wavell's essays on generalship with him on the campaign.[24] Wavell's interests, however, were wider than the military field: he had an anthology of his favourite poetry published in 1944, under the title *Other Men's Flowers*. So when it came to honouring the contribution that a dog, by his example of courage and devotion, had made to men at war, Wavell, reflective and sensitive soldier that he was, could rise to the occasion. And he made it a family affair by bringing his five-year-old granddaughter to meet Antis.

A large audience was assembled; benefactors of the PDSA from among the great and the good were there; and the media were out in force. Television transmissions had restarted after the Second World War, although access to the medium was fairly limited, and TV cameramen were in attendance. The principal media coverage of the event would come through movie newsreels and the press; the term 'dog of war' would feature in a number of the national dailies the next day. After addressing the audience, Field Marshal Wavell avoided any trace of mawkishness, as he found both a means of praising Antis and bringing home the symbolism of the animal and human relationship. He fastened to the dog's collar the blue and brown ribbon of the Dickin Medal; then he addressed the audience.

I am just going to say a few words to the Dog. Dog Antis, it gives me great pleasure to make this presentation for 'outstanding courage, devotion to duty and life-saving on several occasions while serving with the Royal Air Force and French Air Force from 1940-45 in England and Overseas,' and devotion to your master. You have had many adventures by land and by air, and if you have not yet been in a naval battle it is only because you have not had the opportunity. You have been in action a great many times, and have been wounded, and you have inspired others by your courage and steadfastness on many occasions, and have been adopted as Mascot by your Squadron. You are the first foreign Dog to receive this award, which you have worthily earned by the steadfastness, endurance, and intelligence for which your race is well known. You have been your master's guardian and saviour. I am sure everyone will join me in congratulating you on your award, and we wish you many years in which to wear it.[25]

The Dickin Medal, which is cast in bronze, has 'For Gallantry' written in the middle, and underneath the words, 'We Also Serve'. Antis calmly faced the flashbulbs and the cameras. As for Bozděch, he simply sat back, 'basking', as he put it, in the reflected glory of his dog.[26]

The publicity that the occasion generated reached some people who had known the pair during the war. His former comrade Tom Oddie, who had corresponded with him after the war, sent a letter to Bozděch's flat in Prague after the communist coup. He heard nothing more – it would have been intercepted by the security services. Then there came an opportunity for Tom to make contact in the UK, via what would seem impeccable channels; but the outcome was surprising.

Some time later, my mother, who knew all about Antis – she had a great love of Alsatians – saw a cutting in a national newspaper of Bob and Antis, in this country. So I wrote to the Air Ministry, asking where he was and what it was all about, but they stonewalled me, and tried to make out that he wasn't even here. Incredible. I gave up; I thought, well they won't tell me anything. So that was that. I should have tried harder; I should have been more persistent.[27]

A Norfolk couple who knew Bozděch during the war tried another avenue with better results. They wrote to the PDSA who passed the letter on to him; and a link was re-established that would be kept for some years.[28]

Service life soon took over again. He completed a refresher course in signalling at No. 4 Radio School in top position in the order of merit list.[29] On 26 May 1949, he was posted to 240 Operational Conversion Unit at North Luffenham.[30] An intensive period of staff development followed: he undertook a signals course, where he achieved 81%,[31] followed the next month by a masters' course at Upper Heyford; and in September a course at a supply training unit. In this way summer, for both man and dog, passed quite agreeably, and on 15 September Bozděch was posted to Netheravon;[32] and two months later he was promoted to Sig IA.

While they were stationed at Netheravon, Antis made his last flight. A far cry from Wellington bombers on night raids, the short flight was in a Dakota, but it was a nostalgic occasion; and it happened during a parachute dropping exercise over what used to be East Wretham airfield – the base from which Bozděch and Antis left on operational flights with No. 311 Squadron. That had been eight years ago, and the war had been over for four years; swords had been beaten into ploughshares; the control tower had been demolished and the huts dismantled; the former airfield had been returned to heath land and farming.

On 1 March 1950, Bozděch was posted to 27 Squadron[33] as a signaller. Two weeks later, on 16 March the address of his next of kin was changed on his personnel record. He had thought of a way of ensuring that in the event of his death, his wife would be contacted by giving her address as Mrs T. Bozděch, Soběkury – his home village: his sisters would know, or find out, the whereabouts of Tatiana. Eight months later he again was sent to 240 Operational Conversion Unit at North Luffenham as a signaller instructor, with the rank of flight sergeant.[34]

He was now back at the rank he had held in the RAF nine years earlier. Although a person does not need possessions or status to survive (as a man with his record of service knew better than most), a definition of oneself is important for the individual. During the war years that sense of identity had come as a result of being a Czech airman – whether in the Foreign Legion, the French Air Force or the RAF – now the RAF continued to give a sense of identity to Czechs who had rejoined its ranks. But to wider society Bozděch was an emigré. In the quaint phraseology of the briefing note that the PDSA prepared (Field Marshal Wavell picked it up, and so did the newspapers) Antis was the first 'foreign dog' to be awarded the Dickin Medal; and by extension, Bozděch was probably the first foreign owner of a dog to be so honoured. Therefore, 22 June 1951 was a particularly significant date for him; he was no longer technically an alien in the UK; he was given British Nationality.[35] He may not have been able to quote the certificate number by heart, as he could his service number, but he kept it close at hand and was able to refer to it, No. BNA 19472. Although he had now British Nationality, the Home Office document made it clear that he still retained his Czechoslovakian citizenship.[36]

By this time, of course, he used his second name, Robert rather than Václav; but he did not officially change his name: his RAF documents and papers continued with the sequence of first and second names, but when he now signed his name he simply switched the order. And when writing in English he no longer observed the diacritic ě in the family name.

His next posting took place on 7 August 1951.[37] It may have happened by chance, or it may have come about as a result of a degree of sensitivity on the part of higher authority. From a scrutiny of his official record, it looks as though it was the latter, because the posting lasted for over two years: one of the longest periods that Bozděch spent in a station during his entire postwar career; and it was also the final stage of Antis' life, and appropriate that it should end on an air force base. Certainly it would have reflected badly on the RAF had Bozděch been given a posting that necessitated separating him from his dog: the press would have got hold of it, for this dog was newsworthy. He described the new move thus.

> It could not have been a better posting. This was the country-side which both man and dog loved so well, a fitting place for Antis to spend his declining years. He looked fit and still enjoyed the chase of rabbits during the evening walks, but he was ageing and his muzzle was now snow white.[38]

The posting was as an instructor to No. 8 Advanced Flying Training School at RAF Dalcross (which is present day Inverness airport). Dalcross was set on the south shore of the Moray Firth, not far, as the crow flies, from Evanton. The area reminded him of his part of

Bohemia. At the time, and for some years to come, he felt it was the part of the country to which he would like to retire. However, the winter of 1951 was quite severe in the north; it took a toll on Antis' health; and Bozděch became aware that the heart of the dog was weakening.

During leave the following summer, Bozděch and Antis made, what turned out to be for Bozděch, a poignant visit to Evanton. They stayed at a local hotel. In a small town, word gets around quickly: people recognised them; but the order in which they did so was first the dog then the man. On the following morning Bozděch took Antis to the abandoned former airfield. It had ceased to be in use for some years. At the former guard house of its main gate an Air Ministry constable was on duty; the station was not accessible to the public, but the gate was open. The dog padded forward, and Bozděch, making no attempt to call him back, spoke to the constable for a few minutes, doubtless telling him that he used to be stationed there. Then with the constable's permission, he went in to fetch his dog. From that brief visit, Bozděch has left a series of elegiac images of the deserted air station.

In some respects, his description is reminiscent of an early scene in that fine film, *Twelve O'Clock High*, directed by Henry King (1950). The film concerns the early days of an American Army Air Force bomber group in England during the war, their difficulties and different styles of leadership. In an early scene, established as 1947, the former Ground Executive Officer of the group (played by Dean Jagger, who won an Oscar for best supporting actor) has come back to the UK and visits the abandoned airfield. As he walks over the neglected runways towards the derelict huts, he seems to hear again the voices of the aircrews singing in the mess, and by means of a slow dissolve, the story of the film takes place in retrospect in his mind. However, in Bozděch's description of Evanton airfield, the focus is different: the past remains unchanged, but he and the dog have changed.

The last time he had written about Evanton was when he lived in Prague in 1947, in his book *Gentlemen of the Dusk*,[39] where he recalled by name some of the airmen who had been stationed there. One of them was Terry, an instructor colleague: 'Czechoslovak airmen who took part in the RAF Evanton training school in Scotland can surely remember a charming Scot who taught them how to tackle inflating and boarding a dinghy during an emergency landing at sea.'[40] He also referred to the Czechoslovak pilot Josef

Menšík who had served there, and who later tragically died in England. Now he remembered again some of those faces, and the sound of their voices came back to him. As he walked through the deserted station, he saw Antis, sitting by the edge of its boundary stream, watching a mother duck and her ducklings in the water, just as he had watched another bird on that same stream all those years ago.

> The camp, now silent and deserted, brought memories flooding back to Jan. Before him stretched the same majestic line of trees leading to the Officers' Mess, and it seemed to the man that time had stood still in this place while only he and Antis had changed. Antis moved unerringly towards the hut in which they had lived. Though age may have sapped his strength, his memory remained undimmed. To satisfy the dog, Jan pushed open the creaking outer door of the hut. In a moment Antis stood before their old room, on the door of which the scratch marks of his paws showed clearly despite the passage of time.[41]

Reluctantly, as Bozděch put it, he left the past; he led the dog back through the main gate of the camp, and made for the hotel.

Interestingly, the producer of the film *Twelve O'Clock High* for Twentieth Century Fox was Darryl F. Zanuck (who had served in both world wars and whose writings as a young soldier in the First World War had been published in the magazine *Stars and Stripes*), and, as we shall see later, within a decade of this visit to Evanton, Bozděch, on the strength of the manuscript he had written, was invited to meet Zanuck.

That winter the different trajectory arcs of the life of man and dog impacted sharply on Bozděch. Within months, it seemed, Antis had reached the geriatric stage. Seldom, in Bozděch's manuscript, does any hint of self pity come through – until the end of 1952. He stayed on camp during the Christmas period. One night after he had put out the light, he felt the weight of the dog's head on his chest. This was not unusual, and Bozděch spoke to him for a while and then ordered him to bed. Ordinarily the dog would have responded at once, but not this time; it was as though he had not heard the command. Then Antis slowly moved towards his bed, but collapsed on the floor before reaching it. Lifting the dog on to his bed, Bozděch could see that he was ill; his legs seemed to have lost all power. The following day there was some improvement, but the dog was unable to take even a short walk. In the evening Bozděch stayed in his room; he had photographs of his family arranged round a small Christmas tree on a table. 'He had abandoned hope of ever seeing his loved ones again, and now his last remaining link, Antis, was slowly slipping from him.'[42]

A vet in Inverness recommended radiant heat treatment, and this was carried out twice a day at the camp's sick quarters. By the summer the dog's sight and hearing were very impaired: he would sit on top of an air-raid shelter near their hut at mid-day and in the evening, waiting for Bozděch to return. Walking was very painful for him, and he had difficulty in eating. The vet advised that it would be humane to end the pain. Bozděch was not squeamish; he had been in combat and had a warrior's fatalistic outlook; and he knew that the vet's advice was correct – but taking the final decision was difficult. There must have been prior discussion with the PDSA about Antis' final resting place; and he wrote to them for advice. It came by telegram: 'Advise putting old friend out of misery. Grave reserved.'[43]

In the early evening of 10 August 1953, Bozděch took Antis for their last short walk together. They had had thousands of evening walks during the years they were together; but this would be their last. He and his dog were driven to Inverness station, where they boarded the overnight train to London. It was a journey for reflection. The following morning, within about two hours of reaching London, they were at the Animal Sanatorium at Ilford in Essex. For Bozděch it was a 'heart breaking experience'; they had come a long way together over the years; now their journey together was at an end. Bozděch wondered if he could endure being there for the last part; but he answered that doubt very simply, by posing the thought that if their situations had been reversed, and he was approaching his death, Antis would have stayed with him until the end. And that final scene of the end of their journey together should be left to Bozděch.

> Gently placing his friend on the operating table, he laid his own head against that of his much loved pet and, with tears streaming down his face, murmured his last words of encouragement to the dog.
>
> To the end Antis had his dignity. As if knowing that his story was written, he lay quietly with his tired head in his master's

hands. Almost instantly, as the surgeon did his work, a drowsy feeling crept over Antis. All seemed over, then at the last moment, with his last remaining strength Antis slightly raised his head and gazed into the grief stricken face of his master. For a second Jan caught a startled look in the dimming eyes, then sighing gently, Antis was asleep.[44]

Antis has an imposing gravestone at the Animal Cemetery at Ilford. It is often difficult for an owner to find the appropriate expression to encapsulate adequately the qualities of a much loved dog: what is sincere for one person can be sentimentalism for another. At the top of the gravestone are the words, 'Antis D.M. Alsatian, died 11th August 1953, aged 14 years'. Below there are two parts to the inscription; the first is in English, and the second is in Czech. The first expresses a fond hope.

> There is an old belief
> That on some solemn shore,
> Beyond the sphere of grief,
> Dear friends shall meet once more.

The second brief part, in Czech, is a simple statement of truth: *VĚRNÝ AŽ DO SMRTI* (Loyal unto death).

However, in the acknowledged valour of Antis the unacknowledged worth of the man is reflected: he brought out the best in the dog; he respected him, and loved him. And in the last five years of the dog's life that love for each other was very important to Bozděch. He, like others who had fled Czechoslovakia, overnight lost all physical contact with family; and the inhumanity of a particular system of power, kept families apart and broke them up. Throughout those five years Antis was the faint link with his family, and a living presence on whom he bestowed love, and who greatly reciprocated. Whether or not he knew it, as he boarded the north train with Antis' collar in his valise, Bozděch was about to enter a period of profound grief. For him the death of Antis was more than the death of a wonderful dog: it signified the finality of all that he had lost.

CHAPTER ELEVEN

The Road Not Taken

But we who remember must bear witness: it was not only an epoch of terror, but also an epoch of lyricism, ruled hand in hand by the hangman and the poet.

Milan Kundera, *Life is Elsewhere*

So devoutly did the new regime in Czechoslovakia follow the precepts of Joseph Stalin, that not only the sins of the fathers, but also the sins of the grandfathers were to be visited upon their offspring. The first punitive action that the authorities took against Tatiana Bozděch and her son Jan was to evict them from their flat.[1] They had to move in with her parents. When news of this, carried by other escapees, reached Bozděch at Regensburg Refugee Camp, he felt reassured, assuming that the authorities would not harry her: had not her father impeccable credentials, having served as a Czech Legionnaire in the First World War, and later played a prominent part in the Prague Rising of May 1945? What Bozděch did not know then, however (not fully, even at the time of writing his manuscript), was the extent to which the regime was rewriting history.

Milan Kundera writes of one sad visual testimony to the cynical distortion of the past. On that February night in 1948, when Klement Gottwald, leader of the Communist Party, flanked by some colleagues, stood on the balcony in Prague to announce that they were now in power, it was bitterly cold; Gottwald was visibly feeling its effects; and his colleague Vladimír Clementis solicitously removed his own fur cap and placed it on Gottwald's head. The scene was permanently captured on film; the now smiling Gottwald, surrounded by comrades heralding in a new age. The photograph was reproduced in hundreds of thousands of copies, and appeared in school text books, posters and libraries. 'Four years later Clementis was charged with treason and hanged. The propaganda section immediately airbrushed him out of history and, obviously, out of all the photographs as well. Ever since, Gottwald has stood on that balcony alone. Where Clementis once stood, there is only bare palace wall. All that remains of Clementis is the cap on Gottwald's head.'[2]

To the embarrassment of the regime now in power, at the time Czechoslovakia was established, the Communist Party of the Soviet Union and the Third International had been stridently against its creation. The Second Congress of the Soviet Communist Party in 1924 had declared, 'The party cannot accept the bourgeois swindle about a Czechoslovak state-nation . . .' [3] That had to be undone: the process of screening off the Communist Party's early stance got underway seriously during the Second World War, and by 28 October 1948, the anniversary of the founding of the state, the Minister of Information in the Czechoslovak Government could declare to the Central Committee of the Party in Czechoslovakia, that the significance of the date depended on 'who writes the history.' He then expatiated, 'The truth is that without the Soviet October of 1917, there would be no Czechoslovak October of 1918.'[4]

After the war, Tatiana's father Col Zilka was to have been raised to the rank of general. As the paperwork was being processed in the Ministry, the communists seized power; and he did not get the promotion.[5] True to form, for one who never strayed far from the official line, Gen Svoboda, Minister of Defence, did not like former Legionnaires.[6] The Czech Legions that had served with the Allies in the First World War had been an important factor in the western powers recognising the need to recreate statehood for the Czech and Slovak peoples. But the Soviet interpretation of the Czech Legion in Russia was that it had been a tool of imperialism, intent on damaging the revolution, so, of course, after the communist coup of 1948, historians in Czechoslovakia reverted to Lenin's early view that 'the legionnaires were the hirelings of imperialism'.[7] Hence, a record of service in the Czech Legions was regarded as not in line with Party policy.

But there was another question mark against Col Zilka: he had had a leadership role in the Prague Rising during the final stage of the Second World War; he was aware how the Rising began and how it developed, and his non-political, military interpretation of it might not be consonant with the myth that was being created by the propaganda machine. What the Party had to reinforce to the populace at large – for its overall popularity after the war was not something the regime could take for granted – was that it had been the Soviet Union, supported by the Czechoslovak Communist Party, that had been responsible for the country's liberation from fascism, and now was the bulwark against renascent Nazism in West Germany.

The myth that the machine created about the Prague Rising passed into the history syllabus in schools, as Bozděch's son Jan later experienced. He was taught that the Uprising had been brought about by the working class, headed by the Communist Party. As an experienced Legionnaire, Col Zilka led groups of people in Žižkov in Prague in May 1945, and, in the privacy of the home, he gave Jan a very different picture.

> What happened in reality was that there was no Communist Party leading the Uprising: it was the people themselves. Whoever put a red ribbon on their arm, with RG – meaning the Red Guard – did not necessarily have to be a communist. These could also have been people who wanted to loot and ransack houses. The RG, which in Czech stands for 'Rudé Gardy', was nicknamed 'Rabující Gardy', meaning 'Ransacking Guards'. Another thing that my grandfather said was that the Prague Uprising was not led by any body, least of all the Communist Party: it was really an Uprising of the people, by the people.[8]

Thanks to the preservation of remarkable sound archives this interpretation, which, on the face of it, might seem slightly disingenuous (surely some structure had to shape the armed insurrection?) has been confirmed. Czechoslovak Radio issued the clarion call to take arms, and, from the command centre of the radio building, the radio waves were the medium of communication with the insurgents.

Fearful that the occupying forces would destroy the city of Prague before withdrawing, for some months Czech patriots in the radio station had been secretly preparing, moving equipment into the main broadcasting studio. Towards the end of April, the Germans reinforced defences around the building. Then the radio staff made their move. On the night of 4 May 1945, the broadcaster Zdenek Macal secreted himself in the building.

The 6 am news of 5th May startled listeners: Zdenek Macal was reading it in Czech in defiance of the occupying forces' diktat that Czech had to be assigned second place to German. The radio building was a bit of a rabbit warren; and staff, with some loyal Czechoslovak police turning a blind eye, began slipping in by the back, or from other floors. By the time the German director of the radio arrived with armed troops, the radio staff had barricaded themselves in the main broadcasting studio. Then at 12.33, over the airwaves came electrifying words.

> Calling all Czechs. Come to our help at once. Calling all Czechs. Calling all who call themselves Czechs. Come and defend Czech Radio. The SS are murdering Czech people here. Come and help us. You can still get in through the Balbinova Street entrance.[9]

Fierce fighting developed and spread across the city; it continued into the afternoon, and into the next day, but the German forces were unable to break into the radio building. With the Red Army in the east making its way towards Prague, and the American Army stationary (because of the three power agreement that the Soviets should liberate the country) on the country's western border, broadcasts, appealing for help, were made in Russian and English. A Scottish prisoner of war, who had escaped from captivity and joined the resistance before linking up with the insurgents, broadcast this message to the Americans and the British.

> Prague is in great danger. The Germans are attacking with tanks and planes. We are calling urgently our allies to help. Send immediately tanks and aircraft. Help us defend Prague. At present we are broadcasting from the broadcasting station, and outside there is a battle raging.[10]

The fighting round the radio station and throughout the city continued for four days. The advancing Soviet troops had only some minor mopping up to do: the insurgents had virtually liberated the city of Prague. Seventy-nine people were killed in the defence of the radio building, and over three thousand were killed liberating the city.

No, under the new dispensation of truth, a leader of resisters in Žižkov, and a former Czech Legionnaire, was not to be made a general. So Col Zilka, in the tradition of an apolitical army officer in a democracy, continued in his profession as a soldier. He and his wife had sufficient family concerns for they were now providing for their daughter Tatiana and her son Jan.

Bozděch's case came before the High Military Prosecutor in Prague on 6 May 1948, nine days after he fled. The Prosecutor's decision was that proceedings were to be initiated against Bozděch on three counts: the crime of plotting against the state, the crime of desertion and the crime of military treason. Included in the charges was the statement that he had been in contact with members of the British legation.[11] Indeed he had been in contact with the British Military Attaché and obtained an RT tape for the radio script he had written. In his absence, proceedings were suspended, but in the eyes of the state, he was guilty on all three counts.

His commanding officer, however, Vlastimil Chrast had been captured along with Gen Janoušek. Vlastimil was charged with 'high treason and contact with foreign powers. I think I was the foreign power', said his wife Pamela.[12]

> He had two trials. He had one . . . and I think it was a military trial. And he was given – I think he was given – twenty years. And Janoušek was given the death sentence. Then apparently, I don't know what happened, the prosecution intervened and called for a new trial. And of course I was hopeful then, but unfortunately that trial was in what they called the People's Court; and then they commuted Janoušek's death sentence to twenty years, and I think my husband got fifteen years.[13]

In terms of common humanity, it could be expected that a wife would be allowed to visit her husband in prison, and they would be permitted to correspond.

> Oh no. I wrote many letters. I never had a single letter from him, after he was taken. I wrote letters, I sent parcels; and I never knew whether he got them or he never got them. I was not allowed to write in English; I had to write in Czech, which,

of course, was very difficult for me because I didn't speak Czech very well – it's a very difficult language.[14]

Because of her husband, Tatiana Bozděch was made to suffer; there had to be vengeance – the authorities saw to that. When Jan was older, she told him that in 1948 the choice facing his father had been quite clear to her: he could have stayed, in which case he would be persecuted, or he could leave.[15] But as a result of his leaving, life for Tatiana for five or six years was difficult to the point of being insupportable. She was unable to remain in employment for more than two or three months at a time: as soon as her place of work was traced through the paperwork, her employers were made to dismiss her; but then the authorities would catch up with her again after she succeeded in finding a new job. For years she was put under pressure. But if she divorced her husband, she was told, life would become a bit easier for her from the political standpoint.

She now faced the kind of dilemma that her husband had had to confront in 1948: a choice that was really no choice. There was not going to be a change of regime through democratic processes because these no longer existed; neither would it be overthrown from within nor without – there was no hope of that happening. And her parents were now supporting her and her son. But how long could that go on? Her father was nearing retirement age for senior army officers. So with the same clarity of mind that she faced the reality of the situation in 1948, she now saw that there was no alternative.

However, due process of law had to be seen to have been gone through, even in a totalitarian state. But what were the grounds for divorce; and could one of the parties contest them? Desertion on the part of the husband might be claimed, but the point could be argued: he wanted the family reunited; she, however, was prevented by the authorities from following him of her own free will; and if he returned, he would be putting himself in jeopardy. Such legalistic niceties were irrelevant. In a socialist state the law was subordinated to the laws of the class struggle, as interpreted in the documents issued by the Communist Party.

Consequently, finely honed legal minds representing the wife and the husband fulfilled what was required, providing a formula by constructing a form of words, which, in its cynical twisting of semantics and disregard of the facts is breathtaking. The grounds for divorce were given as, 'the guilt of both parties'.[16] The effective date was retrospectively declared to have been 28 October 1948. It is very doubtful if Bozděch even knew that he had been divorced until years later; and he had no formal declaration of it until 1956.

Until recent time, not much was known in the west about the fate of former members of the Czechoslovak military who had fought with the western Allies, and who remained in their country after the communist coup. Their plight was to fall victim to the Stalinistic practice of imprisoning all who had served the capitalist powers during the war. No specific example can adequately encompass the inhumanity of their treatment, but two are recounted here. Arnošt Polak, a former member of No. 311 Squadron, and now Secretary of the Free Czechoslovak Air Force Association, who left the country before the communist coup, describes what happened to a friend who had served in the squadron.

> One of the chaps I flew with in the Irving crew, was a man called Jaroslav Hajek, whose nickname was Muču. We were very good friends; he left the forces in 1945, and as a result of the departure of the German population in the border areas, Czechoslovaks were allocated to the vacated areas, and he went to Karlovy Vary and he managed a shoe shop there happily, and he married the sister of another chap who flew with us in the Irving crew. Then in 1948 he was dispossessed and relieved from it – he was the manager. He was accused of treason, and he was tried and sentenced to 11 years in prison, and hard labour in the uranium mines. This destroyed his health. In 1960 he got amnestied, but lost all his rights as a citizen. On release he got a job as a lathe turner. He lasted a while but he died in 1994; his health was destroyed because of the conditions he had to work in. There were many, many others. He had done nothing. His only 'crime' was to have been a member of the RAF; and the communists trumped up fictitious charges.[17]

Not even service on the Russian front after a period in the west could expiate the guilt of those who served in the west, as Jan Bozděch explained.

> There were also people who worked in the east, with the eastern allies. There was the case of one airman, Feitel who

moved from England to Soviet Russia and served there, and then spent a year and a half in prison when he returned to Czechoslovakia after 1948. Apparently Mr Feitel said of his period in the Czechoslovak prisons that it was really degrading because they were locked up with the SS men whom they had been fighting against, and who were now laughing at them.[18]

The acclaimed Czech film, *Dark Blue World* (2001) tells the story of a small number of Czechoslovaks who served in RAF Fighter Command. Although its topic concerns the personnel in a Spitfire squadron during the war, the film's poignancy is heightened because time present is set in a communist prison after the coup; and the scenes of the airmen's wartime endeavours, losses and triumphs are contrastingly intercut with those of their current degradations. Incarcerated with a former member of the SS, they are treated brutally. The film also makes the point that though nominally sentenced to imprisonment, some of them, for political reasons, have been designated to die there; and situations are contrived by the prison authorities to ensure this happened.

The Czech writer, Iveta Irvingová, whose father served in No. 311 Squadron, was employed in the Defence Ministry. She worked in a section that dealt with veterans; and she took an interest in a project connected with the Normandy invasion. She was ordered to desist; and she was told by a senior officer in the Ministry, 'All Czechoslovak Army personnel who served some time in the west should not have been persecuted and prosecuted after 1948, they should have been hanged.'[19]

If the reasoning was that the 'guilty' airmen should be punished, and the wives of those who fled should be deprived of their rights, victimised and hounded, then, in due course, their children must be made to atone as well. Jan Bozděch was brought up by his grandparents, and in his very early years a new bonding was established and so he was sheltered from this background of oppression. Then in 1955, his grandfather retired from the army. Since 1948 he had been under a cloud with the regime because of his past actions – actions that in a free society would be described as patriotic service – and when he retired from the military, he was made to leave Prague. The family then moved to Červené Pečky near Kolín, where Jan lived until he was thirteen. During his time at primary school Jan really experienced no discrimination, until, that is, he was in 9th Grade – the transition level to the next sector of education. The school structure in the country was not founded on comprehensive lines: it was a differentiated, stratified system of vocational schools and secondary schools, and entry to it was controlled by the local education authority.

> I was applying to go to secondary school; my record of marks had always been excellent – except for music and behaviour, where I got a B. The Secretary of the local authority told me, 'Your family has had a negative stance towards our socialist regime. Your grandfather was a Legionnaire, your father was an airman who then emigrated, therefore you should prove that you have a positive stance towards the regime, so go and become a miner or a steel-worker or an agriculturalist.' I responded that I had always been interested in electrical engineering, and she replied, 'My Frantik (her son) is going to become a miner though.' But his school record was quite the opposite of mine, and I also added, 'Why should this idiot with such a record go, and what should he study?' And that was the first time that I got a bad mark for behaviour, because I was condescending to my class mates.[20]

Scholastic ability was not to be the criterion for Jan Bozděch, but family background; and he was not permitted to go to secondary school. Not at that time. However, with help from someone, he managed to get on to a three-year vocational course. At the end of which, he went to secondary school for two years; and he studied in the evenings. 'These were the worst two years of my life because there was so much to do.'[21] They may have been the worst two years of his life but Jan was an able student, and he was successful.

For years after he left Czechoslovakia, there was no contact between Bozděch and his family. Formal communication by letter in those years would have compounded the difficulties Tatiana faced. At that time, money could not be sent directly from the west to citizens of Czechoslovakia: it had to come via the Red Cross or the Czechoslovak Foreign Ministry.[22] Jan was about nine years old when his father, by now flying with Transport Command, began sending him postcards from countries outside the UK. Bozděch also sent him parcels, and because he was a young boy, Jan loved collecting stamps. The parcels, he can remember, were always packed by a 'Miss Jean', and among their contents was one particular delight that he still vividly recalls – the taste of Ovaltine. However, the family had to pay a hefty duty on these parcels, which had always been opened by customs officers.

In Soběkury, nothing could alleviate the sorrow that Bozděch's parents felt at the absence of their son for a second time. He would have known this, and for the first few years, he wrote letters to his father and signed them with a pseudonym, knowing that his father would recognise his handwriting.[23]

That the democratic republic the philosopher/President Tomaš Masaryk had ushered in thirty years earlier should come to this! Certainly President Beneš, in 1948, in the final months of his life, saw and feared for what lay ahead. He appealed to Communist Party leader Klement Gottwald that there should be no reprisals; and Gottwald promised that only the guilty would be punished.[24] Gottwald was little less cynical about keeping his promises than Stalin. And so a new dark age descended on the land. Five years later, at the end of March 1953, Stalin died; and just over a week afterwards, his disciple Klement Gottwald, in an ironic gesture of solidarity with the master into all eternity, followed suit. Although by 1956, the cult of the personality would be excoriated by Khrushchev, a climate of retribution had been set in those early Stalinist years, establishing a vicious culture of vengeance.

Had Bozděch remained in the country in 1948, would he have been pre-ordained to die in prison? Well he debated and discussed with colleagues for more than six weeks after Jan Masaryk's warning, and death, before taking action. As for his surviving prison? Probably not, he was to some extent a public personality because of the way his experiences with Antis in the RAF had been popularised in magazines such as *Rozlet*; his books, like all those about the Second World War, were now prohibited from being sold or distributed;[25] added to which, he had committed what in the Soviet bloc was the equivalent of the sin against the Holy Ghost – for which there was no forgiveness – by alluding to Stalin's pact with Hitler; and finally there were his political connections.

However, perhaps only those who remained can assess Bozděch's actions in fleeing. His son Jan, in adulthood, as we shall see later, followed in his father's and his grandfather's footsteps and made a career in the military. From that standpoint he reflects, 'In view of the fact that my father's life was in danger, then I can't really view it in any other way than positively.'[26]

His father, for his part though, deep down, for the remainder of his life was burdened: he felt that in putting himself beyond harm, he had brought suffering to his family.

Part IV

CHAPTER TWELVE

A Memoir

The struggle of man against power is the struggle of memory against forgetting.

Milan Kundera, *The Book of Laughter and Forgetting*

All hope of his family remaining a unit having long been abandoned, Bozděch reacted to the death of his dog by writing again. He was not the kind of writer who is driven by an inner compulsion to write: his books and radio script arose out of what had happened to his own country as a result of the rise of Nazism, and then the conflagration of the Second World War; and his main reasons for writing were to inform, and to honour comrades he had served with. However, the upheavals in central and eastern Europe had not subsided with the defeat of National Socialism; and the Soviet Union's expansionism also targeted Czechoslovakia – the only democracy to have fallen within Stalin's grip. So there was congruence with the early period; it was a different ideology but the same oppression: the end of an open society and the loss of personal freedom. This was the goad for writing again.

This time Bozděch chose Antis for his subject; his story was the part the dog played in their escape from Czechoslovakia. He began writing at RAF Dalcross, where he was to spend another two months after Antis died; and he completed the story after October 1953[1] when he was posted to No. 2 Advanced Flying Training School at South Cerney. He conceived the project – as his introduction to it makes plain – in the form of a newspaper or magazine article:

> Behind the brief paragraphs in which, a few months back, the press reported the death of Antis . . . lies a hitherto unrecorded story of canine courage, intelligence and fidelity.[2]

The story was of the 'leading role' that Antis had played in 'his master's dash to freedom with two fellow refugees from communist Czechoslovakia.' Bozděch gave the name Jan to the dog's master, and concluded his introduction, which – unlike the story itself – is written in journalistic style.

> Here is the story of their dash to the frontier as it was given the writer by Jan, still an exile in Britain. It is no ordinary story for Antis was no ordinary dog.[3]

Typed on foolscap, extending to about seven thousand five hundred words, it begins in the streets of Prague and ends as the three men and the dog cross the West German border. No antecedent information about Jan is given. The piece appears to have been designed as an end in itself, the final scene in a drama about a dog of war.

Bozděch sent it to the editor of the *Scottish Sunday Express*, who may have suggested to him (for there is no evidence that this episode was published in isolation) that instead he should write the whole story of his life with the dog. The second paragraph of Bozděch's introduction, for example, really invites this sort of response.

> It is not the story of Antis' war service with the RAF and French Air Force, though this in itself contained more thrills than many might find in a lifetime . . . Wounded by flak during the bombing of Hamburg, bombed and buried alive for three days in Liverpool, Antis survived all these horrors of war and more, to play a leading role in the greatest and most testing adventure of them all – his master's dash to freedom with two fellow refugees from communist Czechoslovakia.[4]

In any event, the paper's Editor warmed to the story; he saw the possibilities for its wider circulation, and he contacted the London HQ of the group.

Express newspapers were owned by Lord Beaverbrook, and at that time, the *Scottish Sunday Express*, like its sister papers in the group, was a broadsheet. The Editor's proposal was that the story should be serialised and run in three instalments, taking up a full eight-column page each week. He did not require HQ's authorisation for that however, but he did for international syndication of the story; and on 11 March 1954, he wrote to Bozděch to say that he had obtained a ruling on the Antis story, and was empowered to offer him fifty per cent of the net syndication profits for the exclusive newspaper and magazine rights. Pointing out that fifty per cent could amount to a significant sum, should the story (as he believed it would) have 'a world-wide appeal', he sent him an amended contract to sign.[5] Bozděch then set about writing the story of Antis within a framework of less than ten thousand words.

Opportunity was favourable. An instructor at an advanced flying training school, his weekly timetable was more regulated than it would have been on squadron duties; and by now he was a very experienced teacher, having performed the role during the war and for two years at Dalcross, so he had the leisure time to devote to his project. He had given material for the story of the dog – up until the end of the war – to the Prague publication *Rozlet* in 1945, and now he developed the story, writing first in Czech and then translating into English. Probably the bulk of the writing was completed while he was at the flying school.

However, his career in the air force was destined to move on. Throughout the six years he had served of his re-engagement his annual assessments (with one exception, when it was rated very good) were graded in the highest category, exemplary; and his skills proficiency was well above average. On 21 November 1954, he moved to No. 242 Operational Conversion Unit[6] at Dishforth where he undertook a four-month refresher course for signallers. While he was there he was promoted to Master Aircrew.[7] He continued with his project and all but completed it before being transferred to squadron duties.

On 27 March 1955, he was posted to RAF Lyneham, to No. 511 Squadron, which had been flying Hastings aircraft for some years on Transport Command's world routes. It may have been by chance – although more likely design – that Bozděch had not had to leave the UK between 1948 and 1953, the years when he had Antis, but now he was to travel extensively across the globe. After a month of training and familiarisation, he was on route, world wide, during May and June for almost two hundred hours' flying time.[8] However, overseas duties were not as intensive for him during the following two months, and he concluded the story of Antis, and sent it to the Features Editor of the *Scottish Sunday Express*.

The journalist who was allocated to the task was John Laurie. He entitled the story *The Mark of Courage*. It was to be serialised from 11 December 1955 and run on three consecutive Sundays (Scottish newspapers in the fifties, unlike their counterparts south of the border, were published on Christmas Day). On 3 December,[9] the Features Editor wrote to Bozděch, thanking him for his amendments to Laurie's draft, and confirmed that all the corrections had been made. He indicated that the paper had received clearance from the Air Ministry security branch; everything was set for publication, and advance reports suggested that 'it will make a resounding impact.' Bozděch had stipulated that he must have anonymity, and while the Features Editor respected this, he asked if he would mind having a photograph of himself published. When Bozděch returned to Lyneham after almost three weeks on route[10], he was able to catch up on his correspondence. And the Features Editor came back to him on 9 December, thanking him for the photograph, and, responding to Bozděch's observation that it would be odd to have his identity concealed while allowing his photograph to be published, assured him that it would not strike the reader as strange.[11] He also felt that the picture of him with Jan Masaryk would be excellent for the third instalment.

The start of the serialisation was billed as 'the true story of the Alsatian which became a legend in the Royal Air Force',[12] and it covered the period up until the end of 1940. Antis' master, the *Express* readers were told, was still serving in the RAF, and because he had family still in Czechoslovakia, he was simply being identified as Jan. The following week's episode continued with the remainder of the war years, and their arrival in Prague. Before it was published, however, on 15 December, Bozděch sent in one or two corrections to it and to the third instalment; and on 20 December, the Features Editor wrote to him to say that these had been incorporated, but he would have to change the description of the height of a hill from metres into feet, because their readers would not understand the Continental system. He pointed out, though, that anonymity had not fooled some of Bozděch's friends: one of whom had written a letter to the paper, which he enclosed;

and he indicated that the Syndication Service was showing signs of enthusiasm for the serial.[13]

In the final instalment, traces of the *Express*'s stance on Communism and the Soviet Union are apparent. 'Dog VC defies Red cordon of death' was the sub heading that introduced it, and underneath the photograph of Bozděch and Jan Masaryk the caption was headed 'the watcher', which referred to a picture of Joseph Stalin on the wall behind the pair. The reader was informed that Bozděch's persona Jan said, " 'Dr Masaryk was very worried. He told me to flee the country.' Three days later Mr Masaryk died in mysterious circumstances."[14] The telling of the last part of the story completely screened the personalities who aided Bozděch's escape or took part in it.

Collaboration between author and the newspaper's staff throughout was harmonious: he had no complaints about how they handled the story; they accepted the amendments he proposed to the drafts he was sent; and the Features Editor wrote, 'I did not realise that you are a full-blown author in your own right.' Then he went on to say how much he enjoyed putting the series through the process from writing to printing. And when he wrote, 'I think you will yet do well',[15] he was prescient.

Within the next few months, the syndication of *The Mark of Courage* led to its being published in: Australia, New Zealand, Sweden, France, Italy, Jamaica and Malaysia; and in terms of Bozděch's contract with *Express* Newspapers, he received a fifty per cent share of the royalties from these international sales. The story's publication in Italy, in the magazine *Opera Mundi* was to open up the prospect of a new development, for it caught the attention of a powerful figure in the movie industry.

However, at the close of 1955, Bozděch had the mixed feelings of satisfaction and disappointment that afflict the writer of a story that someone else then goes on to tell in part. Besides, a newspaper serialisation is ephemeral; he felt the story merited a book. And he set to work. From the way he went about the task, it is clear that he was very capable (it is understandable why he had been selected to work in the Air Ministry of the restored democratic republic of Czechoslovakia). Some of those who knew him well thought that mathematically he was very able. He had very good powers of recall, but the war years presented a challenge: dates, names of people and operational information had to be accurate. Although he obtained permission from the RAF to write, there would have been conditions attached; and formal approval for the project would not have brought with it access to operational record books of the period. He did not have his flying log books from the war years: he had had three log books covering his time in the pre-war Czechoslovak Air Force and the RAF, which he had to leave in Czechoslovakia when he escaped.[16] He worked from memory, from maps, from records – checking some points with former colleagues – and while there are minor inaccuracies during the war years, regarding dates and targets, his achievement is considerably authoritative.

Then there was the approach that he adopted to his material. This was not to be a fable. He wanted to weave the tale of an animal's prowess with historical fact, with the pathos of human suffering and sacrifice; and he determined to achieve it in an unsentimental way. At times he took the story teller's licence and made more of a story of the early part of his life with the dog, and developed scenes. He also revisited areas he had written about for a Czechoslovak readership in 1946 and 1947; and this produced some of his best writing. He translated his Czech manuscript into English himself; and while this gives rise to a slightly literal syntax at times, the overall impression is of strengths not weaknesses.

His methodology adds another dimension to the way he worked up the finished manuscript. He had a technological training; and he had some experience of the sound studios of Prague radio, and as a result he had a clear idea of what he wanted. He bought a high quality tape recorder, in Swindon, an expensive Philips machine for, what in 1956 was a considerable sum, £63; it had, or he acquired, a high quality microphone, and reading from his own English translation, choosing 3 ¾ speed, he dictated his manuscript. After a period of fifty years, the sound quality of Bozděch's remaining tapes is still remarkable: a senior sound engineer with the BBC found that they were in exceptional condition; and they had been well stored, for there was no sign of humidity – a problem associated with old tapes. Background noise of an aircraft taking off can be heard; and at one point, when a colleague came to his room, he simply let the tape run, and explained to him what he was doing. These features, unique to the oral/aural mode, add an authentic setting for his work.

During the early part of 1956, Bozděch spent fewer hours on route, and he was able to concentrate on writing in his spare time at Lyneham; but in June he had a lot more overseas commitments.

Then, from July his flying schedule eased up again; and during October it was confined to air tests, which took up only two and a half hours – until, that is, the last day of the month. For military plans had already been drawn up which required the deployment of No. 511 Squadron in a war zone; and at four in the afternoon of 31 October, operating as signaller in Hastings 476 piloted by Flt Lt Tierney, Bozděch flew to the staging post of Idris in Libya.[17]

Britain's world role and the government's interpretation of that role brought the RAF into its largest offensive since the Second World War. The Suez canal, in which Britain had had a stake with France, had been of strategic importance in two world wars. In 1952, the Egyptian monarchy was overthrown by a group of military officers, one of whom, Colonel Nasser, became President, and a much more nationalistic approach to the country's development followed. Britain retained good relations with Egypt though, and indeed was that country's main source for armaments until 1955, when it was replaced by Czechoslovakia. Over time, Britain's intelligence service produced a number of reports indicating that the Egyptian president was an agent of the Soviet Union – a view not shared by America's CIA.[18]

However, in July 1956, Egypt nationalised the Suez canal, closed it to Israeli shipping and blockaded the Gulf of Aqaba. The British government's response was that this illegal act must be overturned, by force if necessary. From an international perspective, however, the government was not on strong ground: the Suez Canal Company was an Egyptian company, and the Egyptian Government had indicated that the company's shareholders would be reimbursed at prevailing market prices. In great secrecy, known as the Protocol of Sèvres, Britain, France and Israel entered into collusion: Israel would invade the Sinai peninsula; then Britain and France, having issued an ultimatum to Egypt and Israel, would intervene militarily to separate the combatants and occupy the canal zone. On 29 October, according to timetable, Israel struck, and on 31 October, Britain and France intervened with force, bombing military targets.

On 1 November, Bozděch arrived in Nicosia.[19] Cyprus was two hundred and forty nautical miles from the Canal zone, and it became the main launch pad for the RAF. All the island's airfields became highly overcrowded with aircraft: there were 127 at Nicosia.[20] A bomber force, operating far from its own country, can generate the need for a great number of air transport sorties; and added to that a ground force had to be maintained. Transport Command therefore had a demanding role. On 3 November, Bozděch's Hastings flew over the Egyptian city of Alexandria, and dropped leaflets.[21] Two days later, they made a run over Gamil airfield in the Canal zone, and dropped paratroops and canisters.

In the face of international pressure a cease-fire was arranged. Militarily the campaign was successful, in that the Egyptian air force had been neutralised; politically, with a divided cabinet and the antipathy of most of the world, for a country that the previous decade had held the moral high ground for its stand against fascism, it was an inglorious episode.

It had repercussions too in the Soviet sphere of influence. A state of armed conflict between two European countries and Egypt brought into the open dissension between two pillars of NATO, Britain and America; this was interpreted by the Soviet Union as giving them a free hand to crush the Hungarian rising that was taking place at the same time. Unrest in Hungary had been building up for some time; Prime Minister Imre Nagy called for a multiparty political system, and on 1 November announced the country's withdrawal from the Warsaw Pact, declared the country's neutrality, and called on the United Nations and the western powers to protect its neutrality. Czechoslovak and Polish émigrés, normally inured to the Kremlin's hard line against deviationism among its satellite states, may, nonetheless, have briefly raised their hopes at what was happening in Hungary. If they did, they were soon disabused, for within three days the Soviet Union, taking advantage of the disarray in the western camp, invaded the country, surrounded Budapest and installed another puppet government.

Although a cease fire was in effect in the Suez canal zone, for the military personnel, however, some months were to pass before withdrawal took place. During that time Transport Command had a heavy schedule; it re-supplied the ground troops in the Canal zone; and it had a constant ferrying task, bringing spare engines and personnel to the theatre. For Bozděch, writing a book had been put on hold until he returned to Lyneham at the end of December.

He was well through the story by now, but dictating and writing were still being broken up by periods when he was sometimes weeks at a time on route. Then, on 2 May 1957, he was transferred to No. 99 Squadron of Transport Command, which was also based at Lyneham.[22]

His son Jan was now ten years of age, and around this time

Bozděch began writing to him, sending him postcards from countries he had stopped over in during long haul flights.[23] The regime in Czechoslovakia had relaxed some of its harsher practices, ever since Khrushchev stamped his authority on post-Stalinist policies – though victimisation of the families of those who had fled the country in 1948 still continued. Under Khrushchev the Soviet bloc became bent on influencing developments in third world countries. Some of the locations from which Bozděch sent those postcards to Jan came into that category, so the communication was less blatantly a signal from the capitalist west. In a letter to an English couple, Mr and Mrs Bird, whom he had first met during the war, he gives an example of the sort of opportunity that came the way of the aircrews.

> I am glad that the post cards sent from route pleased you. I would have liked to have sent you one from Goose Bay, Canada where we stopped for refuelling, but the girl at the paper kiosk must have fallen in love with a Yankee for she isn't very reliable these days. During the refuelling, when there is an hour or so to spare, we usually write a few post cards and, with the money for the postage stamps, leave them with the girl. Well it's quite easy to forget about things like that, and the young lady has certainly a good excuse for her forgetfulness since she is quite attractive and consequently very busy. Unfortunately Goose Bay is not the only place from where the post cards rarely reach their destination. I hope that the ones I sent from Nairobi (Kenya) and Bahrain (Persian Gulf) on 14 November arrived all right. I thought the pictures were rather lovely and that you would like them.[24]

For Jan, a young boy growing up in a closed society, the excitement of getting stamps from across the world was something that even in manhood he has not forgotten. Nor has he forgotten his acquired taste for Ovaltine from his boyhood – the Ovaltine came in parcels packed at No. 99 Squadron's base at Lyneham, but posted elsewhere.

In the same letter, Bozděch reveals the difficulties he had in trying to ensure that communications to his family got through without resulting in harm coming to the recipients; and he gives a fascinating glimpse of the regime's low-key attempts to lure him back into the country.

Please accept my sincere thanks and appreciation for your kind offer to send a Christmas present to my son. However, it won't be necessary to trouble you about this matter, for I have managed to send him a Christmas present from Hong Kong under a 'borrowed' sender's address. Nevertheless, I think it was very nice of you to think about the boy.

It may seem rather strange to you that I am experiencing such difficulty in trying to keep in touch with my home, or whatever is left of it. For ordinary people it is quite easy to write to Czechoslovakia whenever they wish, even from England. Unfortunately I am a marked man in communist Czechoslovakia and that is the reason why I have to use different senders' addresses. Otherwise the mail bearing my name would never reach its destination. In fact it would only endanger the safety of my relatives in Czechoslovakia, for being in communication with a deserter, reactionary, traitor etc, as the Czech communists furiously call the servicemen who have escaped from their paradise. It doesn't sound very nice, does it? Strangely enough a prominent Czech consul has asked me on several occasions to return 'home', offering me a most attractive job in Czechoslovakia and the full compensation for my 'lost years'.[25]

Bozděch's flying duties not only restricted the time he could devote to writing his book, they hindered him from exploring the possibilities for its being published. Fortunately, he had continuity for the typing of his manuscript, for his base was still at Lyneham, even after he had transferred squadrons; and from 1955 until 1958, a lady at Wooton Bassett typed the original script and three copies. However, he appears to have felt that his written English might not be good enough for publication, and so he commissioned a native English speaker, someone who was not a professional writer, to draft a version of his original. Although Bozděch's manuscript was not completed, on the prompting of his scribe, he tested the water, sending a few specimen chapters of his scribe's version, not his own manuscript, to a publisher. He was then away continuously on route for some time, mainly in the Far East, and the publisher had to write to him twice requesting some more chapters. Eventually, though, the proposal was rejected on the grounds that it was felt it could not be satisfactorily produced by the company. Bozděch discussed matters with a contact he had in the People's Dispensary for Sick Animals (PDSA), who gave him the name of a writer who worked for the BBC. Bozděch's approach to the individual was well received, but on hearing his ideas of much further research and rewriting being required, Bozděch decided not to go into partnership with him.

Instead he went to a firm of literary agents, and sent them his original manuscript. The literary agency's job was to advise him of his best commercial interests; and an agreement was arrived at whereby an established author, Anthony Richardson, would take Bozděch's manuscript (his scribe's version was ignored) and rewrite it; and George Harrap Publishers would bring out the resultant book. Royalties for the book were to be allocated with fifty per cent to Bozděch and fifty per cent to Richardson. However, the publisher's advance on royalties went to Bozděch, as the owner of the substantive material, and he then was to pay cheques to Richardson as sections of the text were written up. Richardson saw his scope as being able to create dialogue, build up a scene with more detail, and omit passages, if he thought it appropriate (for example, in the section dealing with the escape from Czechoslovakia, he omitted the passage in which Antis broke away from the escapees and began to chase the roe-deer). Bozděch, though, was to review and comment on the work as it progressed.

A fraught period followed: Bozděch had clear ideas on what was acceptable to him; there were rows galore. From quite early on, he must have had doubts about the wisdom of the arrangement he had entered into; and ironically (in the light of his reasoning for entering it in the first place) he was critical of Richardson's writing, for example, his patronising and stereotyping style in describing the French. The collaboration generated a great amount of correspondence. At times its tenor was acrimonious. Each of the three sections of the book was argued over, but none gave Bozděch more angst than Richardson's reworking of the third section.

> One can hardly separate the political aspects of the story (Part III) from the characters therein, and it does seem to me that distorting the facts can only serve to make the reader less sympathetic to the characters in the story and ultimately to the book as a whole. Furthermore, I would never approve written matter that is likely to endanger compatriots in Czechoslovakia . . .

I realise that it must be difficult, and possibly non-commercial for a writer and others to view this book as I do. Nevertheless, without wishing to sound melodramatic, one's integrity is a difficult thing with which to compromise. Because of this I have asked service authority for advice in any way they feel is right. Acting on their instructions, I am to have the MS Part III available for experts' examination, and also hold myself in readiness for an appointment sometime in the coming week.[26]

The partnership reached its nadir with Bozděch threatening to have his lawyers annul the contract, and the agency warning that he could be interpreted as being in breach of contract.

However, negotiation and rewriting continued. All the while, service life moved in its own imponderable way. On 14 July 1959, Bozděch was designated Telegraphist 1 and his rank became Warrant Officer.[27] This was not a promotion: Master Aircrew and Warrant Officer were at the same level.[28] At some point though (it is not clear when from his service record), he was recommended for a permanent commission.[29] Most likely he turned it down. As he was at the highest ranking non-commissioned level, his pay exceeded that of pilot officer, the lowest rung on the commissioned scale, and it was now not wartime, with an accelerated advance to flight lieutenant or squadron leader, so a commission for the sake of it was simply not worthwhile financially.

That he could have explored other options for bringing his book to production was suddenly and unhappily borne in on Bozděch. It happened quite late on in the partnership with Richardson, too late to change matters. Bozděch was at the stage of gathering photographs for the final production; and he had been advised by the secretary to the Editor of the *Scottish Sunday Express* that John Laurie, who had written the serial *The Mark of Courage*, was now on the staff of the *Daily Express* in London, and he might obtain the photographs that Bozděch wanted from the *Express* library. When he went to meet Laurie and explain what he wanted, Bozděch was unexpectedly thrown when Laurie told him that he felt it unfair that he had not been given the opportunity to complete the story of Antis in book form. Laurie was morally right, Bozděch felt; and the thought so distressed him that he completely forgot the purpose of his visit, and left without the photographs. However, he wrote to his agent on 6 January 1960 outlining what had happened, and he explained that although his duties abroad at the time had prevented his giving enough attention to the choice of a writer, that 'can hardly excuse my lack of thought in this respect. . . but it does suggest what a complicated mess I made of so straightforward a task.'[30] His agent quickly replied, reassuring him, of course, that he need not feel guilty, for a newspaper man would not necessarily have made a better choice of writer.

By March 1960, final agreement was reached on the text to be sent to the publisher; it was to be published under the title, *One Man and His Dog*. But even then Bozděch felt that the Antis book 'could have been better, much better', had it been written by a writer more sympathetic to animals. 'In spite of this I would make it clear that I do not think the book bad <u>as it now stands.</u>'[31] But he was still very unhappy with Richardson's depiction of how the communists came to power in Czechoslovakia. Responding to his agent's putting this down to Richardson's political ignorance, Bozděch retorted, 'his fictionalised tale of the events that brought about the communists' control of Czechoslovakia might well have been handed him by a member of that present regime.'[32]

It is interesting to compare and contrast Bozděch's manuscript, *Antis VC* with Richardson's *One Man and His Dog*. An important level in Bozděch's work is the way he wrote about the men he served with; and there are marked differences here between the two texts. Richardson added a lot of dialogue, replacing Bozděch's minimal use of direct speech. As a result, especially during the war years, some of the personalities come across very much as Anglo-Czechs. The integrity of the original is weakened.

Not only is the robustness of Bozděch's prose missing, so too is his insight and sureness of touch in depicting the bonding of comrades in war. Consider, for example, his tribute to his friend in No. 311 Squadron, Václav Štětka, whose peccadillo was always borrowing small amounts of money from his friends to pay for his convivial hours in the pubs in East Wretham, but who turned over a new leaf, and made a supreme effort to square all accounts on what turned out to be his last pay day – the day before his death over Germany: 'And so Štětka died, owing no man money and beloved by all who knew him.'[33] There is nothing comparable at any point in Richardson's version.

Nor do we find the sensitive, true representation of feeling that comes through in the original manuscript. Bozděch, returning from

Hackbridge kennels, where Antis, it seemed, was dying, entered a church. According to Richardson's rendering,

> It was a long time since Jan had prayed in a recognised place of worship and the accepted words had slipped his memory. He felt like an intruder, coming cap-in-hand to beg of a charity to which he had seldom subscribed. But he repeated again and again no formalized phrase but words from his untutored heart . . . 'Spare him a little longer . . . I am all on my own. . . Please, just a few more years. . . '[34]

Whereas Bozděch had written:

> He was not a religious man but, sick at heart, he approached the altar and sat down in one of the empty pews. His plaster-encased leg would not permit him to kneel but, staring at the cross before him, he bowed his head and tried to remember the prayers of his childhood. But the long forgotten words would not come. At last, abandoning his striving for the set forms, he opened his heart and implored the aid of that greatest of all Doctors. In the silence of the empty church he spoke to his God from the fullness of his heart, and his prayers were heard. It was as if strength had been given to him and he felt lighter and more confident as he emerged into the street some half an hour later.[35]

Moreover, Bozděch was able to convey empathy with Antis; and it might be expected that a reworking of his manuscript would endeavour to remain true to the feelings and emotions that he was able to project into the dog, particularly in scenes where the animal was in great distress. Not so; Richardson's stance was more detached and dispassionate; and indeed Antis emerges with a stiff upper lip. Where Bozděch described the condition of the dog, on the brink of death at Hackbridge kennels, and his own emotional response to the animal's plight in searing images, Richardson glossed the scene: 'His coat was lustreless and his eyes dim. But at the sound of his master's voice . . .'[36] Or, in another scene, describing his pet's trauma at East Wretham when his plane had been diverted to another airfield, and he had to be driven from hospital to be with him, Bozděch, with minimum detail, reveals his own feelings.

For a second Antis turned his tired eyes towards the bandaged face so close to his own; but Jan's voice vibrating with emotion sounded so strange that Antis did not recognise him. With a feeble sigh the dog closed his eyes once more. Suddenly as if galvanised by an electric shock, the weary body jerked back to life. Some scent, or some tone in that voice had struck a responsive chord.[37]

By contrast, Richardson passed over the scene, referring to the decision to contact the hospital, requesting the airman be brought for his dog, and then went on: 'Twelve hours later Jan and his dog were together in Norwich Hospital.'[38]

On the other hand, though, dealing with the escape from Czechoslovakia, Richardson expanded it into more of a story, transforming Bozděch's companion from Prague (to whom he had given the name Stefan) into a Major Novotny and creating a new character, Colonel Vacek. He introduced tension by having Col Vacek receive an urgent telephone call at one of their prearranged stopping places, and announce that he is compelled to return to Prague on a personal issue, and will try and rejoin them within twelve hours, but is heard of no more. However, Richardson and the publisher were understandably circumspect in referring to Jan Masaryk's death as murder: the final version was toned down, simply acknowledging that rumours were circulating about the death of Masaryk.

It is doubtful if an arrangement of the kind that Bozděch entered into – where another writer reworked his material – could satisfy him. The integrity of the original manuscript had been compromised for commercial reasons, and he felt this was no justification. He wrote to his agent, 'don't ever believe I meant to have it published just for the money.'[39] And he objected, with good reason, to the dedication, which the literary agent proposed for the book: the choice of words, 'To all the friends of Antis wherever they may be', pitched the work as a doggy story. Bozděch's deeper intention inscribed his manuscript to the wartime comrades with whom he had lost touch, but who, he hoped, would recognise him despite the fact his real name was withheld; 'Certainly they will remember Antis.' He may have pondered too whether the book would stand the test of time.

For Bozděch, it had been a long labour of love from early 1956; and now that the end was reached, and the story was with the publisher, another mile stone came by in his service career. It looked as though his flying days were over when, on 19 April 1960, he was transferred to the Southern Region Air Traffic Service Centre at RAF Uxbridge[40] to work in air traffic control. He had not been on route for some months while he was training at Compton Bassett, and he began to consider what he could do for his son and the family who had brought him up since infancy.

Sending money from the west to individuals in Czechoslovakia was not a simple matter: it had to be done by a circuitous route; and about this time Bozděch explored the method of transferring funds to the family to buy a television set.

> It was possible to get money but not directly: it went either through the Red Cross or through the Ministry of Foreign Affairs. The way we received the money for the television set it was not directly to us: my father had to transfer some money to the Tuzex, which was a shop that sold western goods basically, and you had to have special vouchers to shop there. So what happened was that we received the television set; we did not physically receive the money.[41]

That same year, the book was published. Sales went very well; Richardson had indeed written a popular account. The publisher's main interest in it all along, according to Bozděch's literary agent, was the story of the dog, and that was how the book was marketed. There was also its potential for film rights.

A genre of British war films developed and flourished in the decade that has just ended, a genre that has since become known in film studies as 'the-British-officer-class-at-war'. This is not altogether a caricature: in British films of this period about all three services, other ranks tended to fall into formulaic representation; in films about the RAF it was rare to come across characters who were sergeant pilots; and it is very difficult indeed to find a film of the period which even alluded to, far less gave representation to, the significant contribution made by the Polish squadrons and the Czechoslovak fighter squadrons and bomber squadron. What would the British film industry make of a story about a Czech airman and his dog? It did not have much opportunity to reflect on a suitable treatment: Hollywood saw the potential; and the book's film rights were bought by Twentieth Century Fox.

The large Hollywood studios tended to look for elements of the familiar that had worked well with audiences before, then rework them with a different take. So it was not by chance, as a glance at the personalities involved confirms, that it should have been Twentieth Century Fox that took up the film rights. Nor was it bought to be put on a shelf, simply to preclude other studios from obtaining ownership: it was at once developed into a project.

Darryl F. Zanuck, the co-founder of Twentieth Century Films, which later joined with Fox, was the powerful head of the studio. As a young man he had served in the US army during the First World War; some of his letters home had been published in *Stars and Stripes*, which determined him to become a writer; and in the Second World War he had the rank of lieutenant colonel and headed an army documentary film unit. But in his early years as a scriptwriter in Hollywood, he had written the screenplays for films about Rin Tin Tin, an Alsatian dog that had been found in Germany during the First World War and taken to the USA by an army captain. Scripts written by Zanuck were the basis of a very popular series of films. Here, however, was a well documented true story; behind it there was the original manuscript on which it was founded; and still serving in the RAF was the man who wrote it, and on whose experiences it was based.

In fact, Zanuck had seen the possibility of the story of Antis being made into a film almost four years before the book was published. With some impressive films to his credit, Zanuck, in the mid 1950s, had negotiated a special release agreement with the studio from his post as head of production that allowed him to become an independent producer; and he based himself in Paris. As a result of the syndication of the *Scottish Sunday Express*'s serialisation of *The Mark of Courage*, the story appeared in the Italian publication *Opera Mundi* in early 1956. Bozděch was with No. 511 Squadron at the time. He wrote, that in the spring of 1956,

After the story was published by the 'Opera Mundi', two representatives of Zanuck's film company, with Air Ministry authorisation, arrived at Lyneham Royal Air Force Station to discuss with me certain details. I was on route at the time, but they had considered it worth their while to wait four days for my return. They insisted on my word of honour that, when the book is eventually published, I would not deal with any other filming company without giving them a chance to consider the story.[42]

Now the film rights had been bought, and Zanuck's war epic for Twentieth Century Fox, *The Longest Day*, the account of the D-Day landings, was in the production stages; and this new project was one he was going to take forward. A common sequence in the studio system – even before approaching a director – was for a producer to bring a star on board. Often that method – in relation to the aura that an actor brought with him from previous roles – came up with an excellent choice. Such was the intended casting here: Zanuck offered the role of Bozděch to William Holden.

William Holden, who had served in the US Army Air Force during the Second World War, had been one of the most dependable of actors during the fifties. Although he had been associated with a number of romantic leads, he had won an Oscar for his performance as the sharp, enterprising aircrew Sergeant Sefton in Billy Wilder's *Stalag 17* (1953); he gave a fine performance, in another Second World War film, as the externally cynical but inwardly principled American in David Lean's *The Bridge on the River Kwai* (1957); and most recently, he had portrayed a sensitive, humane medical officer in John Ford's civil war film *The Horse Soldiers* (1959). Holden was interested in the project; and Zanuck arranged a meeting with himself, William Holden and Bozděch.

The Ritz Hotel London was the venue. Stationed at Uxbridge, Bozděch found it a convenient location, and had no difficulty in getting leave. This meeting, unlike the early discussions with the book's publishers, was of course in no sense a bargaining encounter; the deal had been done; Bozděch was simply being met and consulted, and sounded out about his preparedness to give advice during the production stage; and from the lead actor's point of view, it was an opportunity to observe some of the man's characteristics. It was a successful meeting; there was interest and enthusiasm. By this stage proposed casting had not been extended to anyone but the star – with one exception: the important role of Antis. Zanuck told them that an Alsatian dog, with appropriate training and the necessary photogenic qualities for the camera, had been found in Italy. The project was not yet 'green lit', where money for it was committed; but it looked promising; and the meeting concluded optimistically.

On the down side, however, Bozděch came across a problem in the book's first print in English; and it also appeared in the French translation, *Un Homme et Un Chien*, which had just been published by Les Presses de la Cité. In agreeing to Part III of the text, Bozděch had insisted that some wording, which he felt could identify his former Czechoslovak commanding officer, be excised, but the correction seemed to have been missed out in the final page proofs. He went to the publisher Harraps and then wrote to his agent.

> I feel it necessary to point out that this ex-RAF officer was only released from a communist prison in September 1960, after having served a twelve and a half year sentence for an offence against the communist regime. As you probably know, his English-born wife and child live and wait in London. In the circumstances, it appears to be quite clear what attitude the lady will adopt, should there be evidence that her husband has been inconvenienced in any way because of incrimination in our book.

He went on that he had been in touch with the Chief Editor of Harraps, who agreed on a form of words, which was approved by Mr Harrap, that in the reprint would give a different version of the part concerning the Czechoslovak officer and distort the sense of the original reference.

And he continued:

> I quite appreciate we may not undo the damage, or lessen the anxiety and distress this unfortunate family has been subjected to, but I am sure you will agree, we are obliged at least to try.[43]

As it turned out, there were no repercussions for Bozděch's former commanding officer, Vlastimil Chrast as far as Pamela could tell.[44] Although Vlastimil had been released from prison, he was still not allowed to communicate with Pamela or his son in the UK.

Scrutiny of the book, however, did indeed take place in certain offices in Czechoslovakia; and thought was given as to how best Bozděch might be damaged. No action was taken against his family – in propaganda terms that could be counter-productive, and possibly backfire, for the book was very popular and being translated into several languages. The strategy that was sanctioned turned out to be ill advised: it was decided to challenge him on the capitalist grounds of rights of ownership. One of the editorial staff of the Czechoslovak magazine *Rozlet* was (presumably) instructed to write to Bozděch, claiming that as some part of the Antis story had appeared in *Rozlet* between 1945-47, ownership of the material belonged to them. Bozděch clearly enjoyed the exchange. There seem to have been two letters from the magazine, and he dealt cursorily with the first, and this prompted a second. In his reply to it, he wrote part of it in Czech, quoting the words of his protagonist, but the rest of it he wrote in English; and he deftly turned the tables on his challenger, presenting himself as more sinned against than sinning. He framed his response in such a way as to discomfit his correspondent before higher echelons of the regime, charging him and his colleague with earlier profiteering.

> Perhaps I should add that over twenty magazines and news-papers have bought the story of Antis from me, and *Rozlet* was the only one which obtained the material without having to pay a penny for it, not even for the photographs. Undoubtedly you and Mr Kovarik himself must have done well; conse-quently your present attitude is ungrateful and could be described in stronger terms by a less mild man. . . .

It was a very controlled response, but he was unable to resist the sting in the tail with a postscript, which pointed up the sham of his correspondent's position, when, in truth, the sale or distribution of books about the Second World War was prohibited in Czecho-slovakia.

> PS I am glad to hear that you may read any material that interests you.[45]

Life in general assumed a pleasant flow for Bozděch around this time; and it followed a new direction. Although he had not been committed for some years, he had not formed a long-term rela-tionship, until, in 1961, through a friend, he met Maureen Parker at a dinner party. A relationship developed, and deepened; and six months later they married.

Shortly before the wedding though, Bozděch left the RAF. He had served almost continuously in the armed forces of three countries for almost thirty years. But no one takes up a career in the services in anticipation of making a lot of money; and he would have to face the exit door in 1967, at the age of fifty-five, with the less than rosy prospect of a lump sum and a modest pension.

However, he now had a windfall through the sale of the film rights. In the draft of his contract for the book, film rights were to be shared fifty-fifty, but, with good reason – because of the earlier approach by Zanuck's production company – Bozděch had argued that his position pre-dated the book's publication, so it was proposed that in the event of the film rights being bought as a result of earlier contact on his part, they would be shared, sixty per cent to him and forty per cent to Richardson.[46] His share of the book's film rights was a significant figure; he could now anticipate the end of his air force pay with more optimism; and so he took up the option of contracting[47] his service at the age of fifty.

It was also an appropriate time for him to leave the forces. His life had reached another of its turning points. He had worked for five years, in Czech and English, and brought to fruition his story of Antis and their life together; he had re-entered his past and written a work of integrity, affirming lasting values. And throughout the previous fourteen years he had not lived a family life. It was now time to leave the past and move on.

CHAPTER THIRTEEN

Gentleman of the Dusk

By making the most rational judgement of things, every man
may be, in time, master of every mechanic art.
Daniel Defoe, *Robinson Crusoe*

For a long time, Bozděch had felt that when he retired from the
RAF he would move to the area around Inverness, for his postings there held pleasant associations, and the countryside
reminded him of parts of western Bohemia. That was still what he
felt at the end of 1961, as he took steps to contract his period of
service. Maureen, however, suggested that they should move to
South Devon – a part of the world that she liked very much; so they
had a holiday there to help them decide. It was not a difficult decision: Bozděch was immediately attracted to the area; and they
bought a house in Salcombe.

Work of some sort was a priority for him: if they were to have
a family he would need to supplement his air force pension.
Thirty years' experience in the forces, most of it in technological
areas, where there was a wide range of staff development opportunities, encouraged flexibility of mind; and throughout his career
he had shown a determination to succeed at whatever he turned
his hand to.

First he applied for air traffic control work, with a preference for Exeter airport. Not content that his CV should show that he had recently acquired transferable skills from his work with the air force at Uxbridge he began to study. Reasoning that his application would be enhanced if he were able to offer two of the three international languages in which air traffic control is carried out (English, French and Russian), he began a distance-learning course in Russian, applying himself single mindedly. Eventually, however, it became apparent that nothing was going to come of the job application; ageism was probably a factor against him.

It was a friend who triggered the idea that set him off on the road of entrepreneur, suggesting to them that as they had remodelled and upgraded their own house, they had the skills to develop older properties as an enterprise. So Bozděch became a property developer, buying old cottages or houses and modernising them. In time it became a successful business. They worked as a team, both husband and wife putting in long hours. Bozděch was very focused, driving himself, barely taking time throughout the day to snatch something to eat. The property development business did well; and they were able to buy some land and built a new house in the pleasant hamlet of Ledstone. In time three children were born to the couple: Robert, Magdalena and Nina.

Small amounts of royalties augmented their income. The *Readers Digest* had featured *One Man and His Dog*; overseas editions of the book appeared in Sweden, Spain, Belgium, France, South Africa and Holland, and soon the list would include Switzerland and Japan. Then in the autumn of 1962, it was serialised in the BBC's radio programme, A Book at Bedtime.

Unfortunately, though, the proposed film about Bozděch and Antis failed to materialise. The vast epic movie *Cleopatra* had been a financial disaster for Twentieth Century Fox. In 1962, Darryl F. Zanuck was brought back from Paris to become Chief Executive of the studio, and set about restoring the company's fortunes. The success of his production *The Longest Day* (1962) helped to an extent, but some projects in their early stages were abandoned, among them, the story of the Czech airman and his Alsatian.

To an émigré, the events of 1968 in Czechoslovakia unfolded with astonishing speed. In January Antonin Novotny, who since 1953 held the post of First Secretary of the Central Committee, was ousted. He was replaced by Alexander Dubček. Dubček presented a marked contrast to the stereotypical glum-looking leaders of the past who exercised dictatorial power away from the public gaze. At the personal level Dubček attracted huge popularity; and his policies genuinely tapped into public aspirations. His leadership became connoted with the human face of socialism. A revival process of democratic procedures and structures started to come about; the press and television were allowed freedom of expression; debate and discussion were encouraged; and cross-border travel was easier. The Prague Spring was in bloom.

Evidence of a more open approach that allowed criticism of the recent past filtered through to the west. In March, Bozděch cut out a story by the *Daily Express* foreign service correspondent who reported on what had happened at the funeral of a member of the Czechoslovak squadrons of the RAF. The defiance implicit in the public and the clerical demeanour would have been unthinkable a decade earlier. But there was a particular poignancy in Bozděch's cutting out the article: it reported the funeral of his old friend, and best man, Gustav Copal, who had been with him in France and then in No. 311 Squadron. Gustav had been only forty-eight when he died. The paper's correspondent outlined Gustav's RAF service; and then went on to reveal that he had been pilloried by the regime after 1948. The priest conducting the funeral service implicitly condemned the great wrong that had been done to those former members of the RAF when he used in the oration words associated with the great Czech reformer Jan Hus.

> Kopal's death must serve to tell us that truth will always ultimately prevail. The nation will remember him.[1]

It was reported that one of the ground crew that had serviced Gustav's Wellington bomber, ex-sergeant J. Kollar had stood to attention by the coffin in his RAF uniform; and on the coffin there was a Union Jack and a Czech flag; and other former RAF men were in attendance. The spontaneity of such support, and its defiant expression from men who had hitherto been persecuted for having worn that same uniform in the west told of underlying depth of feeling.

Dubček came across as someone who believed in his ideals. But it was not the case that his leadership wanted Czechoslovakia to break off membership of the Warsaw Pact: in essentials it was committed to the Soviet bloc. One of the Secretariat of the Central

Committee, Zednek Mlynař expressed what he saw as the tradition Dubček came from.

> Dubček's practical attitude towards violent, dictatorial methods genuinely corresponded to the democratic and humanistic tradition shared by the nation: a Masarykian rejection of dictatorial violence and a longing for democratic reform.[2]

Relaxation of censorship had implications far beyond the realm of high politics: people were able to get access to previously proscribed books, such as those about the Second World War, and a new generation began to take an interest in that period.

After leaving secondary school, where he had to work exceedingly hard (he described them as the worst two years of his life) because of the enforced delay to his entering it, Jan Bozděch, like his father, and his grandfather, decided to join the military. He chose the army, and went to military vocational school, and after three years, became a professional army officer, in the radio communications field. It was only now, around the time of the Prague Spring that he was able to get hold of books about the Second World War, and find some context for the Czechoslovak units that had fought in the west. Until this time Jan had not read anything his father had published twenty years earlier.

> It was really only in 1967-68, when the regime was a bit more flexible, and there was a liberal period following, that I managed to get hold of some books about the period of the Second World War. That was when I thought about my father. I only read *Fighting with Fate*, because my cousin had told me of *Gentlemen of the Dusk* and I also read some of his short stories in magazines.[3]

More quickly than it flowered the Prague bloom was blighted. On 20 August, Soviet forces and their Warsaw Pact allies invaded the country. The passive, disciplined behaviour of the nation in the face of the invaders commanded wide admiration and respect in the west. Within months the reins of power were taken from Dubček and passed into the hands of Gustav Husak. Reforms were undone in the name of Normalisation; and a new period of repression began.

The failure of the Prague Spring was a bitter disappointment to many, in Czechoslovakia and abroad. It produced a new wave of exiles in the west, while those who had fled twenty years earlier became resigned again. Bozděch spent many hours in his study or in his garden. He did not socialise much. Certainly, he was very sociable about inviting friends to his house for a meal or for a holiday, but he was reluctant to go out as a family – except with members of the Czech community. However, he took no part in organised activities; and he was careful not to reveal any hostile stance towards the regime. It was just as well.

Not all policies set in train during the Prague Spring died out overnight: political and military rehabilitations of those persecuted under the Stalinist era continued. And Bozděch wrote to the Military Prosecutor's office in Prague, requesting that the criminal charges against him be reviewed. Now the criminal charge of desertion, which had been levelled against those of the military who escaped in 1948 – of which he was self-evidently guilty – had been the subject of a Presidential amnesty in 1960; but the criminal charges against him were more serious than could be covered by the amnesty concerning desertion: he had been charged with treason and with plotting against the state. In his letter to the Military Prosecutor, Bozděch simply stated that he had had to flee to save his life in 1948; and that he had never intended to commit crimes against the state, nor, indeed, had he ever committed such crimes. The letter, with its ramifications for investigation by the military and the Ministry of the Interior, made its way into the state's bureaucratic structure.

Meanwhile, in the tranquillity of South Devon, life for the entrepreneur and family man continued. In his business dealings he was regarded as straight as a die. In his family life he was devoted to his children – that was obvious; but he was difficult too. The major decisions had to be his; he had to be in command. Gradually, as she came to know more of his past – for he rarely spoke about it – Maureen realised that her husband probably had to function in that way: the determination that had driven him to survive so many blows meant that he could not let go; he had to be in control. He was also a maverick, she felt; he would have been successful no matter where his lot was cast. But there was a sensitive side to him. Once, after some hours in his study, he told Maureen that he had started to write a children's story; it was about a dog that went to heaven. Like his earlier writing, it was in Czech. There were several pages of a manuscript, but he never finished it. Maureen, at the time, felt that perhaps it would have been too sad.

Growing up with some knowledge of their father's life with Antis, it was inevitable that the Bozděch children should want a dog. But their father ruled it out completely; there could be no question of their having a dog. He never spoke about the war, and he gave them no reason for his adamant refusal. Aware that he was an indulgent father, and fond of animals, with the clear logic of children, they knew that it was not a matter of principle with him that there should be no animals in the house, and so they persisted – why not? Because he had been very much alone, Maureen felt that her husband must have keenly felt the death of Antis; and so she explained to the children that their father, 'promised Antis, he swore that he'd never have another dog. And you can understand: it was an amazing animal.' That was something they could understand, even if they did not altogether accept.

Normalisation in Czechoslovakia had now been in place for two years, and political rehabilitations had ceased; but not in the military, and on 1 June 1971, there came an official response to Bozděch's request that his case be reviewed. Lt Col Dr Ladislav Zázvůrek, Senior Prosecutor of the High Military Prosecutor's Office in Příbram, promulgated Resolution Vn 1414/70 formally discontinuing criminal proceedings against former Captain Václav Robert Bozděch,

for the crime of desertion according to Articles 183, 197 No. 5 of the Military Criminal Code,

because criminal proceedings are inadmissible (Article 11 (1a) of the Criminal Code).

II. On the basis of Article 172 (1c) of the Criminal Code, I hereby discontinue criminal proceedings of the accused

for the crime of plotting against the Republic according to Article 2 of Act No. 50/1923 and for the crime of military treason according to Article 6 (2) of Act No. 50/1923

because it has not been proven that the crime was committed by the accused.[4]

The Senior Military Prosecutor then went on to give the justification, and in doing so turned the spotlight on how the totalitarian
judicial system worked in 1948, when people could be subjected to
criminal prosecution on the basis of a mere suspicion. He
recapitulated that on the decision of the former High Military
Prosecutor in Prague on 6 May 1948, proceedings were initiated
against Bozděch for,

1. the crime of plotting against the Republic according to
   Article 2 of Act No. 50/1923 Collection, because he and
   another person made contact with representatives of the
   English Legation [sic] in Prague in order to cooperate in
   organizing illegal absconding of persons with anti-state
   intentions across the border of the Czechoslovak Republic,
   and, on the basis of an agreement with them, was preparing to flee the country in order to establish contact with
   anti-state elements conducting activity against the Czechoslovak Republic;
2. the crime of desertion according to Articles 183 and 197 No.
   5 of the Military Criminal Code, because he, at the end of
   April 1948, fled the Czechoslovak Republic, with the intention to evade his military service duty for good,
3. the crime of military treason according to Article 6 (2) of Act
   No. 50/1923 Collection, because having crossed the border
   he reported to intelligence authorities of a foreign power
   and disclosed to them everything he knew about the
   Czechoslovak army in his capacity as an officer, namely
   things of a confidential nature.[5]

On the basis of a review of the case, the Senior Military Prosecutor
established that Capt Bozděch did commit the crime of desertion.
However, this crime was subject to amnesty by the President of the
Republic from 9 May 1960, and criminal proceedings were inadmissible. And as far as other crimes were concerned, the suspicion
against the accused was not sufficiently justified. First, the
Prosecutor went on to specify how the crime of plotting against the
state used to be defined: a crime committed by a person who had
conspired with another person in order to plot against the Republic,
or had 'come into direct or indirect contact with a foreign power or
foreign officials, namely military or financial officials, or who had
committed other acts to achieve these ends'. Then he gave his find-

ings; and he revealed that the Ministry of the Interior had carried out an investigation into Bozděch's activities since leaving Czechoslovakia.

> From the evidence which forms part of the file, it is not possible to prove and justify this suspicion properly. No such facts were found nor evidence obtained which would indicate that the above crimes had really been committed by the accused. The former High Military Prosecutor based his decision on an assumption which had not been thoroughly substantiated and which was based on the so-called theory of notoriety according to which every soldier who at that critical time fled the country would enter the service of the enemies of the state and, in conjunction with the foreign power he would commit the worst crimes against the Republic to the effect of the Act on the Protection of the Republic.
>
> However, in the given case no specific evidence was found which would support this criminal activity. Neither has it been found that the accused had committed criminal acts against the Republic upon his leaving the country, as follows from the ČSSR (Czechoslovak Socialist Republic) Interior Ministry report No. IM-056/20/70.
>
> Therefore, the criminal proceedings against the accused have to this effect been discontinued according to Article 172 (1c) of the Criminal Code.[6]

Cleared of criminal charges against the state, rehabilitated by the Czechoslovak military, secure with his British passport – although, as it is clear from letters to his sister Pavla[7], he intended keeping his Czechoslovakian citizenship – he could reasonably expect to have a request for a visa to visit his homeland approved.

Fortune's wheel turned again though. He had been a man of great stamina and in robust health, but Bozděch suffered a slight stroke; and he temporarily lost the power of one hand. However, with his characteristic determination, he persevered and regained the use of the hand. His letters of the period show no deterioration in the neatness of his handwriting.

A particularly sensitive matter for members of the military, both in the east and the west, during the cold war, was contact with family or friends in the putatively hostile camp. Bozděch was now a civilian, and no longer constrained in this respect, but he was still on the same see-saw with his son Jan, an army officer in a country of the Soviet bloc. For some time Jan had not been victimised because of his family background, but contact with his father was not advisable in the interests of his career. Nevertheless, in August 1973, when Jan was about to be married, his father sent him a congratulations card along with some sterling notes. As an army officer, Jan had to report the contact with abroad, and hand over both the card and the money. 'So it was only then that I was reproached for having problems due to political reasons.'[8]

One method that Bozděch adopted to contact his son was to use an intermediary, a Czechoslovak citizen who was allowed to travel to the west and who therefore was able to meet émigrés. Such a person was Dr Melnik, who visited Bozděch at his home in South Devon.

> Dr Melnik was asked by my father to go and contact me, and he managed to do so in the late summer of 1973. Dr Melnik talked to me about one possibility why my father's visa was refused. Apparently there was some kind of a regulation that those airmen, or army personnel, who emigrated from Czechoslovakia were indebted to the Czechoslovak state for their education and their military training. And apparently some people who paid the Czechoslovak state a few pounds – it wasn't much – could get a visa and travel to Czechoslovakia. But my father said, 'I'm not going to pay them anything because they have stolen enough from me.' That was apparently the reason his visa was turned down. I'm not certain whether this is the truth, but this is what I was told by Dr Melnik. But he gave me the names of three officers who had also emigrated and who had paid their debt, and who were allowed to come and visit Czechoslovakia.[9]

However, the only evidence there is that Bozděch applied for a visa, and had it refused, was not as early as Dr Melnik's visit to Jan: it appears over a year later. On 27 September 1974, Bozděch wrote to the Visa Department of the Czechoslovak Embassy in London requesting a Czechoslovak tourist visa for twenty-one days. He included all that was required for a visa: application forms, passport and photographs and a cheque for £2; and very importantly, he sent a photocopy of Dr Konrad's letter concerning his rehabilitation. He concluded his letter,

> I think perhaps I should add that I left Czechoslovakia on 30 April 1948 without travel documents.
> I became a British subject by naturalisation on 29 June 1951.[10]

His request for a tourist visa was refused. On 21 October 1974, Bozděch then wrote a letter appealing to the Czechoslovakian Ambassador to the Court of St James.

The Ambassador
Embassy of the Czechoslovak Socialist Republic
28 Kensington Gardens
London
W8

Dear Mr Ambassador

The reason I am taking the liberty of writing to you directly is my wish to put on record the fact that despite a decision reached by the 'Higher Military Procuracy' in Příbram in June 1971, confirming my full and complete rehabilitation, on 17 October 1974 your visa department courteously informed me that the Czechoslovakian authorities did not give them their permission to grant me a Czechoslovakian visa.

In view of the circumstances and for the reason that I have never been politically engaged against the Czechoslovakian Socialist Regime, it would appear that the Czechoslovakian authorities reinitiated resentment of those who served with the Allies during the Second World War, and who dared to express publicly their painful experiences which forced them to leave their Motherland in 1948.

Whatever may be the true position as regards the reason upon which the Czechoslovakian authorities established their decision, I shall be grateful if you will kindly give this letter consideration.

For your perusal I enclose a Photostat copy of Dr Konrad's letter which contains the precise wording as the declaration by the 'Higher Military Procuracy' in Příbram. As far as I understand the original document could be obtained only by a personal presentation.

Might I in conclusion add that my primary object in applying for a Czechoslovakian visa was to visit my two elderly sisters and the graves of my parents.

Yours sincerely

R V Bozděch [11]

There is no reference either to any earlier request for a visa having being turned down, or that a prior condition for applying was to have paid the tax or levy. Now that seems odd, for Bozděch was normally punctilious in referring to precise records. Then there is the final sentence of his letter, stating that his 'primary object' in applying for a Czechoslovakian visa was, 'to visit my two elderly sisters and the graves of my parents.' That seems a heart-felt statement from an émigré; and it is difficult to believe that he would have been prepared to let a small sum of money (if that is indeed what it was) be the principle which prevented him achieving it. Moreover, he thought that the reason he had been turned down was on political grounds for what he had written, but he confronted any alternative, 'whatever may be the true position'; so he challenged the authorities to give an explanation.

Even thirty years after the Second World War, sensitivity at the highest levels in the Warsaw Pact countries to the role the Soviet Union had played between 1939-1941 was acute. For example, the year before Bozděch's visa application was turned down, Prince Philip made the first visit by a member of the British Royal Family to the Soviet Union. He was carefully briefed by the Foreign Office to avoid taboo subjects including Stalin and the early part of the Second World War. All went well until one particular reception. If the newspapers are to be believed, Prince Philip is prone to making indiscreet remarks; but on this particular occasion he won the unstinting admiration of a senior British official, whose report back is in the National Archives.

At this point Philip put the knife in and twisted it exquisitely asking Mazur [his host] whether he appreciated the significance of the anniversary that had just passed, September 3. Lunkov [the Russian ambassador in London] smartly answered that the second world war had begun on that date, whereupon Prince Philip remarked that it had for us, but not for them, and that we futilely thought we were fighting for the freedom of Poland.[12]

The hand of royalty's exquisite twisting of the knife might be briefly endured during a state visit, but the Soviet bloc authorities would not tolerate embarrassment from émigrés, and the issue of visas to them was closely policed. Certainly some of Bozděch's compatriots got permission to return on a tourist visa, but it was clear to him that even although he had been rehabilitated by the military – barring some earth-shaking change within its political system – he would never be allowed to see his homeland again.

Spurred on by a letter from a young researcher, he turned his attention to his old squadron, No. 311 Squadron. In 1974, Jack Rennison was serving in the RAF in Germany; he was the second generation of his family to wear the grey blue uniform of the junior service: his father, Flt Sgt Jack Rennison had been one of a number of the British personnel who had served in the squadron's ground crews during the war, and his son, thirty years later, set out to write a history of the squadron. On 26 November 1974, he wrote to Bozděch. His father, he said, had given him a lot of background about the squadron, and 'the inspiring story of yourself and Antis was well known to me'.[13] What came as a request to Bozděch to identify personnel from some photographs and an enquiry about the squadron's Liberator bombers after their return to Czechoslovakia turned into a detailed series of correspondence that went on over six months, and involved his friend Franta Sadil. Franta was four years older than Bozděch, and an experienced airman; he had served as a wireless operator in the Czechoslovak Air Force before the war, and he continued in that role in No. 311 Squadron.

Bozděch's reply was delayed, however. He explained that 'after having suffered a second minor stroke' his efficiency had been affected. Nonetheless, he had already been in touch with his friend and they were both 'intensely interested in your work'. He then went on to give detailed information about some of the final sorties of the Liberators over the coast of Norway as late as early June 1945, and he reported that the Czechoslovak Air Force was allowed to use them until New Year 1946, when they were returned – he thought – to the US air authority.

Over the next few months Bozděch read from the Czechoslovak Air Force War Archives. He went into highly detailed exposition of fact; he wrote a short account of one air crash; and he was able to add anecdotal information about some of the personalities – such as Sqn Ldr Pickard, who for a time was Officer in Charge of Operational Flying with No. 311 Squadron and who made a practice of 'taking out the freshmen for their first operational mission'.[14] It was at this point too that he referred to the help he himself received from the British Air Attaché in Prague in May 1947 when he was dramatising his script on Pickard's last mission, which was then broadcast on Czechoslovak radio.

Within the family though, Bozděch rarely spoke about the past, but Christmas can be a nostalgic time. His daughters, Magdalena and Nina had been taking recorder lessons at school; and at Christmas, he would ring up Franta Sadil and hold the receiver while his daughters played *Silent Night* on the recorder down the phone line. He used to tell them about how Christmas was celebrated in Bohemia in his boyhood. They were allowed to open a present on Christmas Eve, but there was more of a communal celebration than children were used to in Britain: a large papier mâché model was filled with sweetmeats, and the children of the little community, armed with sticks, would hammer on this model, which was suspended off the ground, until it split open and disgorged its goodies.

School days had their memories for him, and one tale of a punishment he received stayed with his children. Corporal punishment was an accepted part of sound educational theory and practice at the time; and he had committed some misdemeanour in class, for which he was called out to the floor to be caned on the palm of the hand. The teacher made him hold out his hand, and held his own hand under the pupil's, thereby increasing the impact of wood on flesh; and very quickly, as the cane was descending, Bozděch pulled back his hand and, to the delight of the class, the teacher caned himself. This of course escalated the degree of punishment that had to be meted out. It was winter, and the ground was freezing; and Bozděch was made to kneel on dried peas in the school play-ground.

He was not a religious man. He told Maureen that when he was young he had had a row with the priest over something, and never again attended church services. However, he had no objections to his children being baptised into the Church of England.

Normally he was silent about his adult life, although there was one intriguing area from his postwar days in Czechoslovakia that he did speak about. He had assembled a large collection of photographs; in several of these he appears in the company of Jan Masaryk, and there is a photograph of the body of Jan Masaryk lying in state. In his manuscript *Antis V.C.*, as we have seen, Bozděch claimed that Masaryk had been murdered on 9 March 1948 (the night before his body was found in the courtyard of the Ministry building). Among his papers and photographs, Bozděch kept a two-page article from *The People* newspaper of Sunday 15 February 1970, which was taken from a book by an American writer Claire Sterling, entitled *The Masaryk Case*.

There had been no public inquiry in Czechoslovakia in 1948 into the death of Masaryk. However, during the liberal climate of the Prague Spring, an inquiry was set up, but by the time it reported, it was 1969, and the Russian tanks were stationed in the country. That inquiry conceded that the cause of death could have been an accident. Claire Sterling had set out during the days of the Prague Spring to research into Jan Masaryk's death; she interviewed officials in Prague, both during the period when it was not an offence for people to speak openly, and afterwards when there was a danger in so doing. She went beyond that, however, and collected material in the UK from émigrés, and she interviewed a leading forensic expert in London, Professor Francis Camps.

Purely on the basis of details about Masaryk's body, Professor Camps made observations that were to prove prescient, and would be confirmed thirty-four years later in Prague at the first independent forensic inquiry into the death. The facts were that the body had been found some twelve feet out from the wall beneath a small bathroom window; it was soiled. For a man of Masaryk's weight, to have projected himself forward from a small window sufficient to land twelve feet away would have required tremendous force. Furthermore, Professor Camps stated emphatically that in his experience, 'people who commit suicide do not lose control of their bowels.'[15] However, he went on that he had known of one form of violent death that caused such a physiological reaction: 'in the final stages of suffocation'.

At the anecdotal level, the researcher spoke with the wife of Masaryk's steward, Václav Topinka, who had seen the body, and had noticed a small puncture in the skin behind one ear, covered with congealed blood. Was it, Claire Sterling posed, an indication of lethal injection or bullet wound? Death by shooting had also been Bozděch's interpretation of how Masaryk met his death.

The article was of interest to Bozděch, who spoke to his family about it. But to young people, conflicting theories about a political murder were of little interest. Nor was their father's reluctance to talk about the past a matter they thought in the least unusual. The future was ahead of them, and Robert, approaching school leaving age, was turning his thoughts to a career in the military, following in his father's footsteps.

As it had been in adulthood that Jan Bozděch, a young army officer in Czechoslovakia, began to think about his father, so it was that as an adult, when she had her own family, Magdalena Bozděch came to have greater insight into her father.

> I think that all the time we were growing up he was punishing himself, in a way, probably because he had left his family; and he thought that, in some way, he couldn't enjoy himself, or us – act like a normal family would be – because of the circumstances. I'm sure he felt guilty.[16]

He was by now sixty-seven years of age; but he never really retired from his business; and he had weathered two slight strokes. However, it was not the central nervous system that was to fail him.

By the time the cancer presented, it had advanced too far to be treated. He had gone into a clinic for an exploratory operation, and was diagnosed with cancer of the pancreas. He returned home.

Knowing that their three children would soon face a grief that would be very hard on them, Maureen thought that they should have another life presence in the house, and she suggested to them that they should get a puppy. Her father was quite ill by this time; and Magdalena brought the puppy to him.

> I remember bringing him this little Jack Russell cross; and he looked at it, and he was so angry that we'd brought this dog in. And I said to him, 'I know you didn't want us to have a dog, but it's not Antis, it's our dog, it's not your dog.' So he lived with it, ignoring it.[17]

He would not pat the dog, talk to it, or pay it any attention. Or almost none: 'I did see Dad, when we were eating our Sunday lunch – and after he had been telling us not to feed the dog at the table – he was giving him titbits.'[18] Given that he himself now faced the fading of the light, his stance at this time after all those years underlines the strength of feeling he still had for the memory of Antis.

Bozděch died on 27 February 1980. A local newspaper carried an obituary, which included a photograph of him, taken when he was in the Defence Ministry in Prague, in the uniform of a captain in the Czechoslovak Air Force.

At one point, on a matter of principle to him, something on which he was not prepared to compromise, he had written: 'I may have lost many things in my life, but I haven't lost self-respect, and I'm not going to let that happen.' There was no danger of that happening. He had endured setbacks and loss, yet held on to his sense of the integrity of self; and he carried the consequences of his actions internally, and in typical Czech fashion, with a quiet demeanour, based on inner strength; perhaps motivated by the belief that, in the long term, truth would prevail.

CHAPTER FOURTEEN

Distant Landfall

Of course, the most moving event of the week was the appearance, and the speech, of President Havel of Czechoslovakia before a joint session of both houses of Congress. Time and again, cries of 'Bravo' went up, and five times he was accorded something that happens to a Presidential address only once, and at the end of it: namely a standing ovation.

Alistair Cooke, 'Presidential Ghosts' 23 February 1990

Within a decade of Bozděch's death, the social system he had escaped from to avoid being persecuted by it had collapsed. Democracy was restored to a hard-line communist state; restitution was made to those who had suffered, or had fled, for having served their country in the west; and in his case, Bozděch was posthumously promoted to the rank of colonel in the Czechoslovak Air Force.

But events unfolded slowly, both at the personal and the policy levels. Within weeks of her husband's death, Maureen learned that she was not entitled to a widow's pension from the RAF. The reason was that they had married after Bozděch had left the service; if the marriage had taken place while he was serving, his widow would have received a proportion of her husband's pension. These were the rules; if there was hardship, Maureen was told, she could approach the Royal Air Force Benevolent Fund.

This was not just a quirk of the capitalist system; in the Czechoslovak Socialist Republic the rules in this sort of case were broadly the same.[1]

Within a month of his father's death, Robert Bozděch was in the British army; he joined the Royal Tank Regiment; and for a four-year period, both of Bozděch's sons, by his two marriages, were soldiers, serving in the armies of the Warsaw Pact and NATO respectively.

In Czechoslovakia, subtle policy changes were taking place in the military echelons; and the machinations of those Jan Bozděch called 'the old culprits', those who held his family background against him in the 1970s, were overturned: 'in the early 1980s nobody criticised me, or had anything against me because of my father.'[2] Then in 1983, Jan took the same career path that his father had taken thirty-seven years earlier: he was posted to army headquarters at the Ministry of Defence. Given the persecution that he had experienced from the end of his primary school days onwards, this was a considerable achievement. He, however, offered a comment on that system, one that is not often attributed to it these days.

> Now I will say something that you may not like too much; but, as opposed to the current regime, the communists sometimes knew how to appreciate a person if there was work behind him or her – so they knew how to appreciate a specialist.[3]

True though that may be, there was also an elegant pattern to the way that Jan's military career concluded.

The same year that Jan Bozděch was promoted into army headquarters in Prague, in London, his father's famous 'dog of war' was being featured in an exhibition at the Imperial War Museum. Thirty years after his death, Antis' Dickin Medal, along with the certificate and photographs of the dog went on display. Two members of staff from the Imperial War Museum went to South Devon to collect the materials. The theme of the exhibition was Animals in War, which had an accompanying book of the same name by Jilly Cooper. The exhibition proved to be a popular event that ran for six months, and was repeated twenty years later.

Seismic shifts started to take place in the earth's political plates. In 1985 in the Soviet Union, Mikhail Gorbachev was appointed First Secretary of the Central Committee. A reformer, he introduced a radical programme of restructuring the economy, allowing more openness of information and pursuing détente with the west. There were profound implications for the satellite countries when Gorbachev made it plain that, unlike Brezhnev, he no longer considered that the Soviet Union was the fount of all wisdom for communism. The pace for change was set in Poland by the union Solidarity. To be sure, Czechoslovakia was still a hard-line communist state; intellectuals were still being imprisoned for demanding freedom of expression. Nonetheless, it was they who made the running; among their number was the much imprisoned playwright Václav Havel. Then in April 1989, Alexander Dubček gave an extended interview on Hungarian television, reflecting on the policies of the Prague Spring, defending them, and condemning the way it had been crushed. A few months later the Polish senate denounced the Warsaw Pact invasion of Czechoslovakia in 1968, and apologised for Poland's part in it.

In November 1989, a group called Civic Forum, representing a broad spectrum of anti-communist opinion came into being and brought moral pressure for change. Events followed quickly; and the deputies of the Federal Assembly unanimously elected Václav Havel as President of Czechoslovakia. Within weeks, in February 1990, he was addressing a joint session of both Houses of Congress in the United States. Two sentences from his speech in Washington sum up the dazzling speed of the Velvet Revolution.

> When they arrested me on October 27, I was living in a country ruled by the most conservative Communist government in Europe, and our society slumbered beneath the pall of a totalitarian system. Today, less than four months later, I am speaking to you as the representative of a country which has complete freedom of speech, which is preparing for free elections, and which seeks to establish a prosperous market economy and its own foreign policy.[4]

Havel's impact that day in Washington was described by Alistair Cooke in his *Letter from America*.

> At one go, the first time we ever heard him, he provided the sort of rare satisfaction that must have come to people listening, for the first time, to Abraham Lincoln or Winston Churchill.[5]

In his first New Year's day address to the nation, Václav Havel reminded his countrymen and women of the price that so many had had to pay, in the long term, to help bring about their new freedom.

Many citizens perished in jails in the 1950s, many were executed, thousands of human lives were destroyed, hundreds of thousands of talented people were forced to leave the country. Those who defended the honour of our nations during the Second World War, those who rebelled against totalitarian rule and those who simply managed to remain themselves and think freely, were all persecuted. We should not forget any of those who paid for our present freedom in one way or another. Independent courts should impartially consider the possible guilt of those who were responsible for the persecutions, so that the truth of our recent past might be fully revealed.[6]

The restoration of honour and restitution for those who had served in the west, and who had been dismissed and persecuted, or had fled followed a logical formula that took into account their previous rank and reasonable career expectations. In Bozděch's case, he was posthumously advanced to the rank of colonel.

In the United Kingdom in 1994, the impending sale of Antis' Dickin Medal was written up in the newspapers. 'Dog of war "VC" to be auctioned by Sotheby's'[7] read the *Daily Telegraph* headline. There was a photograph of Field Marshal the Earl Wavell presenting the Dickin Medal to Antis forty-five years earlier, another of the medal and of Maureen. She had decided to sell the medal and give the proceeds to her three children. The following week, the *Daily Mail* produced a two-page spread, announcing the imminent auction, and summarising the story of Bozděch and Antis, along with photographs of the dog, the medal and bomb damaged Liverpool, speculating that the medal would go for over fifteen thousand pounds.[8] At the auction though, Antis' medal was sold for over eighteen thousand pounds. Its purchaser was not only delighted by his acquisition, he became interested in the story, and later succeeded in buying the film rights of the book from Twentieth Century Fox when, in 2001, Fox 'quitclaimed' those rights to Born Free Films Ltd.[9]

It was at the personal level, though, that news of the event made greatest impact. Tom Oddie, who had been a colleague and friend of Bozděch when they served in No. 8 Air Gunnery school fifty years earlier, read about it and on 24 May 1994 wrote to Maureen. He keenly felt regret, as he put it, that he had not persisted with the Air Ministry when they stonewalled his enquiries about Bozděch's return to the UK. However, Tom had been meticulous in keeping his wartime papers; and he was able to send Maureen correspondence that the two had exchanged, and the formal letter of 1 December 1944, from the Czechoslovak Inspectorate awarding him the Czechoslovak Air Force Observer's Badge. He attributed the award of the honour to Bozděch (whom he had always called Bob), 'it was thanks to Bob that I was presented with the Czech wings'.[10]

From a younger generation who had served in the RAF in the postwar years, there came a letter from a Justice of the Peace, who as a young national serviceman had been stationed at RAF Lyneham in the mid fifties, recalling the impression Bozděch had made on these young men.

> He was a charming man, who took the time to speak to young-sters like myself, despite the difference of rank, age and seniority, which was most refreshing to someone far from home and lonely. . . I always remembered his kindness, and his patience, and all of the young airmen held him in great respect. He was, to me, a most remarkable person.[11]

In Prague the advent of the fortieth anniversary of the end of the Second World War in Europe created a demand for more information about that era. The situation was comparable to the mid forties, after the Occupation: few in the Czech lands in the past forty years had any opportunity to read about the part their compatriots had played in the defeat of Nazi Germany; and to mark the anniversary, the publishing house Toužimský & Moravec intended to republish Bozděch's *Fighting with Fate (Souboj s osudem)* 'as a memory of the author'.[12] This book was the tribute that Bozděch had made to the Czech pilot Frankie Truhlář who had twice survived plane crashes at the cost of horrific burns to his face. On 31 May 1995, the publishers wrote to Maureen to ask her agreement to republish or to let them know her conditions. They owned the text of the story in Czech, and they pointed out that the editor's revision would be small and only amount to updating some language usage from the 1940s to the present day.

In her reply Maureen wrote,

My husband told me of the tragic life story of Frankie Truhlář and I am more than pleased to hear that Truhlář's family and fellow countrymen can at last know his story . . . My only condition if the book *Souboj s osudem* is published is that my husband's son by his first marriage in Czechoslovakia should receive royalties. His name is Jan Bozděch, and when I last heard of him, he was serving with the Czech Air Force and living in Prague.[13]

The book was duly published, preceded by another of Bozděch's books, *Bombers Attack*.

In an open society, sooner or later, it was inevitable that the enigma of Jan Masaryk's death should be re-examined. It had long been suspected that Masaryk had been murdered by the KGB on Stalin's authorisation. The inquiry that began during the Prague Spring was overtaken by the Warsaw Pact countries' invasion, and so was not an impartial investigation. Much of its evidence was anecdotal, and contradictory, focusing on the state of mind that Masaryk may, or may not, have been in at the time. It was only when a forensic scientist, Professor Jiři Straus, investigated the case, purely from the forensic evidence, and concluded that a man of Masaryk's weight and level of fitness could not have landed so far from the building if he had jumped, that there was compelling reason for the case to be re-examined. As a result of these findings, the file was reopened and, in early 2004, the Czech police concluded that Jan Masaryk had been murdered. The Office for the Documentation and Investigation of the Crimes of Communism, adjourned the case, 'because the Russian authorities refuse to provide materials which could help identify the killers.'[14]

The state that Jan Masaryk's father, the philosopher-President Tomaš Masaryk led into being in 1918 – that 'far away country' that Neville Chamberlain expediently described it in 1938, or the bridge between East and West that Edvard Beneš valiantly envisaged it in the 1940s – separated in the Velvet Divorce into the Czech and Slovak Republics, and at the dawn of the twenty-first century, both became members of the European Union.

What place has the Czech Republic accorded in its history to the generation who fought in the west during the Second World War, and whose contribution was traduced for decades by a totalitarian regime? Long before he became President, Edvard Beneš gave his assessment of the Czech Legions who fought in the First World War in these terms:

> On the whole our troops may be taken as representing the chief features of the Czech national character. They exhibited its vitality, its perseverance, its common-sense methods of handling a situation, but at the same time its tendencies towards contentiousness and undue sensitiveness.[15]

That evaluation is likely to be every bit as appropriate for the succeeding generation. They are now known about in their own country; a literature has emerged about their deeds, which included honourable mention of Antis, in a book entitled *Alsatian Antis: Heroic RAF Flyer* (*Vlčák Ant: Hrdinný Letec RAF*) by Iveta Irvingová, daughter of a former pilot in No. 311 (Czechoslovak) Squadron.

Justice was not done, however, to all who had been persecuted by the regime for having served in the west, and some were forgotten, as Arnošt Polak discovered. He found out that his friend from No. 311 Squadron days, Jaroslav (Muču) Hajek, whose health had been broken by enforced hard labour in the uranium mines, to the extent that it brought on his early death, had for some obscure reason been overlooked:

> I discovered on the tenth anniversary of his death that whilst many less deserving chaps were treated as heroes, his fate was totally forgotten. Through my connection with the Czech Airmen's Association I started an action that culminated in the placing of a commemorative plaque on his house in Moravia, with all the appropriate ceremonials, in the presence of the Head of the Czech Air Force, and a large number of local dignitaries. It ended with a sumptuous banquet in the local pub. So finally justice was done.[16]

But what happened to the prosecutors, the judges and the jailers? Pamela, wife of Vlastimil Chrast (Bozděch's CO in the Defence Ministry), who was pilloried and imprisoned for over twelve years, comments, 'Nobody has ever been held to account for these things, the imprisonment of those who served in the west during the war – nobody.'[17]

Exiled former members of the Air Force, who escaped the onset of totalitarianism and settled in the west, were invited by the State to official ceremonies. They were flown to Prague and symbolically honoured. Some did not live to make it back to base.

When Homer's Odysseus returned from his years of journeying to his homeland, disguised as a beggar, he was recognised only by his faithful dog Argos. When Bozděch made his escape that April morning of 1948, he took his loyal Alsatian with him; and although he was to travel far on the world routes of Transport Command, he was never allowed to return to his homeland to be reunited with the remnant of his family; but in October 2004,[18] in the old city of Prague, his son Jan and his daughter Magdalena from the UK, met for the first time.

Notes

Chapter One
1 Bozděch papers.
2 Archiv Ministerstva vnitra Česke Republiky (Archive of Czech Ministry of Home Affairs).
3 V.R. Bozděch, *Gentlemeni Soumraku (Gentlemen of the Dusk)* (Prague, Mladá Fronta, 1947).
4 V.R. Bozděch, *Souboj s osudem (Fighting with Fate)* (Prague, Toužimský a Moravec, 1947).
5 Bozděch manuscript.
6 Pamela Schutzmann interview.
7 Bozděch papers.
8 Ibid.

Chapter Two
1 W.V. Wallace, *Czechoslovakia* (Boulder, Colorado, Westview Press, 1976), p. 53.
2 Ibid., p. 117.
3 E. Beneš, *My War Memoirs* (London, George Allen & Unwin Ltd., 1928), p. 429.
4 Ibid., p. 416.
5 Maria Dowling, *Czechoslovakia* (London, Arnold, 2002), p. 15.
6 Archiv Ministerstva vnitra Česke Republiky (Archive of Czech Ministry of Home Affairs).
7 Iveta Irvingová, *Vlčák Ant: Hrdinný Letec RAF (Alsatian Antis: Heroic RAF Flyer)* (Prague, Otakar II, 2000), p. 293.
8 J. Korbel, *The Communist Subversion of Czechoslovakia 1938-1948: The Failure of Coexistence* (Princeton, New Jersey, Princeton University Press, 1959), p. 18.
9 Josef V. Polišenský, *History of Czechoslovakia in Outline* (Prague, Bohemia International, 1991 edn.), p. 115.
10 Vojenský historický archiv (Army Historical Archive).
11 Ibid.
12 Zdeněk Hurt, *Czechs in the RAF* (Walton on Thames, Red Kite, 2004), p. 6.
13 Alexander Werth, *The Twilight of France: 1933-1940* (London, Hamish Hamilton 1942), p. 149.
14 Jewish Virtual Library, http:// www. Jewishvirtuallibrary. Org/jsource/ Holocaust/ IMTCzech html.
15 Alexander Werth, *The Twilight of France*, p. 159.
16 Wallace, *Czechoslovakia*, p. 201.

17   N. Henderson, *Failure of a Mission: Berlin 1937-1939* (London, Hodder and Stoughton Ltd, 1940), p. 136.

18   William Shirer, *Berlin Diary: The Journal of a Foreign Correspondent 1934–1941* (New York, Tess Press, 2004 edn.), p. 100.

19   Ibid., p. 101.

20   Ibid., p. 106.

21   William Shirer, *The Rise and Fall of the Third Reich: A History of Nazi Germany* (New York, Nationwide Book Service, by arrangement with Secker and Warburg, 1980 edn.), p. 389.

22   Ibid., p. 401.

23   Ibid., pp. 423-4.

24   Ibid., p. 411.

25   Zdeněk Hurt, *Czechs in the RAF*, p. 6.

26   Radio broadcast on 27 September, reported in *The Times*, 28 September 1938.

27   *Hansard*, 5 October 1938, cols. 360-367.

28   Zdeněk Hurt, *Czechs in the RAF*, p. 6.

29   Iveta Irvingová, p. 293.

30   Ibid., p. 294.

31   Ibid., p. 294.

32   Zdeněk Hurt, *Czechs in the RAF*, p. 6.

33   V.R. Bozděch, *Gentlemeni Soumraku* (*Gentlemen of the Dusk*), introductory section, unpaginated.

Chapter Three

1   C. Mercer, *Legion of Strangers* (New York, Holt, Rinehart and Winston, 1964), p. 36.

2   Ibid., p. 36.

3   Ibid., pp. 38-9.

4   M.A. Liškutín, 'The Czechoslovak Air Force in War' in L.W. White (ed.) *On All Fronts* (New York, Columbia University Press, 1991), p. 127.

5   Z. Kordina, 'Those Months in France', in L.W. White (ed.) *On All Fronts* (New York, Columbia University Press, 1991), p. 25.

6   Vojenský historický archiv (Army Historical Archive).

7   *Sunday Mail*, October 4, 1942.

8   *Rozlet*, No. 8/1945.

9   Bozděch manuscript.

10   Archiv Ministerstva vnitra Česke Republiky (Archive of Czech Ministry of Home Affairs).

11   Bozděch manuscript.

12   Ibid.

13   Richard Beith collection.

14   Archiv Ministerstva vnitra Česke Republiky (Archive of Czech Ministry of Home Affairs).

15   Bozděch manuscript.

16   Ibid.

17   Ibid.

18   Ibid.

19　Z. Kordina, 'The 1940 Evacuation of Czechoslovak Forces from France', in L. W. White (ed.) *On All Fronts* (New York, Columbia University Press, 1991), p. 71.

20　Ibid., p. 69.

21　Bozděch manuscript.

22　Z. Kordina, 'The 1940 Evacuation of Czechoslovak Forces from France', p. 72.

23　Ibid., p. 73.

24　Vojenský historický archiv (Army Historical Archive).

25　Ibid.

26　Ibid.

27　Ibid.

28　Bozděch manuscript.

29　Ibid.

30　Bozděch manuscript.

31　Ibid.

Chapter Four

1　Alan Brown, Ph D Thesis, p. 36.

2　Bozděch manuscript.

3　J. Němec, 'The Crisis of the Czechoslovak Army in England in the Second Half of 1940', in L.W. White (ed.) *On All Fronts* (New York, Columbia University Press, 1991), pp. 86-7.

4　R.H.B. Lockhart, *Jan Masaryk: A Personal Memoir* (London, Putnam, 1956), p. 27.

5　Bozděch manuscript.

6　Liškutin, 'The Czechoslovak Air Force in War', p. 128.

7　Bozděch manuscript.

8　RAF Personnel Management Agency.

9　V.R. Bozděch, *Gentlemeni Soumraku (Gentlemen of the Dusk)*, unpaginated.

10　Lockhart, *Jan Masaryk: A Personal Memoir*, pp. 29-30.

11　Bozděch manuscript.

12　Ibid.

13　Ibid.

14　Ibid.

15　Vojenský historický archiv (Army Historical Archive).

16　Archiv Ministerstva vnitra Česke Republiky (Archive of Czech Ministry of Home Affairs).

17　Bozděch manuscript.

18　Ibid.

19　RAF Personnel Management Agency.

Chapter Five

1　Bozděch manuscript.

2　H. Němec, 'Remembering the 311th (Czechoslovak) Squadron, Royal Air Force', in L.W. White (ed.) *On All Fronts* (New York, Columbia University Press, 1991), p. 112.

3　Ibid., p. 112.

4　Lambert, A., 'Setting the Scene, 1917-42', in *Royal Air Force Historical Society* (incorporating the Proceedings of the Bomber Command Association's 60th Anniversary Symposium) Journal 31, p. 91.

5   Air Ministry, *Bomber Command Continues: Account of the Rising Offensive against Germany July 1941-June 1942*, p. 17.
6   Bozděch papers.
7   Historical Journal of Film, Radio and Television.
8   Bozděch manuscript.
9   Bozděch papers.
10 PRO AIR 27/1686.
11 Ibid.
12 Ibid.
13 Ibid.
14 Vojenský historický archiv (Army Historical Archive).
15 Bozděch manuscript.
16 Film, *Target for Tonight*.
17 PRO AIR 27/ 1686.
18 Ibid.
19 J. Gellner, 'A Stint with the 311th (Czechoslovak) Squadron, Royal Air Force', in L.W. White (ed.) *On All Fronts* (New York, Columbia University Press, 1991), p. 103.
20 PRO AIR 27/1686.
21 Bozděch tapes.
22 Bozděch manuscript.
23 Ibid.
24 Ibid.
25 PRO AIR 27/1686.
26 Bozděch tapes.
27 V.R. Bozděch, *Gentlemeni Soumraku (Gentlemen of the Dusk)*, pp. 26-7.
28 PRO AIR 27/1686.
29 Gellner, 'A Stint with the 311th (Czechoslovak) Squadron, Royal Air Force', pp. 104-5.
30 PRO AIR 27/1686.
31 V.R. Bozděch, *Gentlemeni Soumraku (Gentlemen of the Dusk)*, p. 27.
32 Grinker, R. R. & Spiegel, J. P., *Men Under Stress* (Philadelphia, Blakiston, 1945), p. 34.
33 Bozděch, *Gentlemeni Soumraku (Gentlemen of the Dusk)*, p. 26.
34 B. Lockart, *Jan Masaryk: A Personal Memoir*, p. 36.
35 Vojenský historický archiv (Army Historical Archive).
36 Bozděch manuscript.
37 Gellner, 'A Stint with the 311th (Czechoslovak) Squadron, Royal Air Force', p. 106.
38 Bozděch manuscript.
39 Ibid.
40 PRO AIR 27/1686.
41 Bozděch manuscript.
42 Ibid.
43 PRO AIR 27/1686.
44 Ibid.

45 Ibid.
46 Vojenský historický archiv (Army Historical Archive).
47 Royal Air Force Personnel Agency.
48 PRO AIR 27/1686.
49 Gellner, 'A Stint with the 311th (Czechoslovak) Squadron, Royal Air Force', p. 105.

Chapter Six

1 Bozděch manuscript.
2 Ibid.
3 Ibid.
4 Vojenský historický archiv (Army Historical Archive).
5 Bozděch manuscript.
6 *South Wales Echo*, Tuesday 3 March 1942.
7 Ibid.
8 Ibid.
9 Bozděch manuscript.
10 Vojenský historický archiv (Army Historical Archive).
11 Tom Oddie interview.
12 Ibid.
13 Arnošt Polak interview.
14 Ibid.
15 *Sunday Mail*, October 4, 1942.
16 *Ross-Shire Journal*, October 9, 1942 and the *North Star* October 10, 1942.
17 *Sunday Mail*, November 8, 1942.
18 Vojenský historický archiv (Army Historical Archive).
19 Tom Oddie interview.
20 Ibid.
21 Bozděch manuscript.
22 M. Ash, *This Noble Harbour: A History of the Cromarty Firth* (Edinburgh, Cromarty Firth Port Authority in association with John Donald Publishers Ltd., 1991), p. 96.
23 Tom Oddie interview.
24 Arnošt Polak interview.
25 Bozděch papers.
26 Ibid.
27 Ibid.
28 Tom Oddie interview.
29 Vojenský historický archiv (Army Historical Archive).
30 Ibid.

Chapter Seven

1 Vojenský historický archiv (Army Historical Archive).
2 J. Gellner, 'A Stint with the 311th (Czechoslovak) Squadron, Royal Air Force', p. 106.
3 C. J. M. Goulter, *A Forgotten Offensive: Royal Air Force Coastal Command's Anti-Shipping Campaign, 1940-1945* (London, Frank Cass, 1995), p. 235.
4 PRO AIR 27/1690.

5   Arnošt Polak interview.
6   Bozděch manuscript.
7   Ibid.
8   Ibid.
9   PRO AIR 27/1690.
10   Pavel Vančata collection.
11   Arnošt Polak interview.
12   Ibid.
13   Bunty Fialka interview.
14   Lockhart, *Jan Masaryk: A Personal Memoir*, p. 43.
15   Churchill, W.S., *The Second World War: Volume VI Triumph and Tragedy* (London, Penguin, 2005 edn.), p. 442.
16   Ibid., p. 422.
17   PRO AIR 27/1690.
18   H. Ripka, *Le Coup de Prague* (Paris, Plon 1949), p. 29, quoted in Korbel *The Communist Subversion of Czechoslovakia* p. 129.
19   Bozděch papers.
20   Claire Sterling, *The Masaryk Case* (London, Harper Row, 1969), pp. 17–8.
21   Ibid., p. 18.
22   Alan Brown, Ph D thesis.
23   Ibid., p. 151.
24   PRO CAB 121/360: COS Committee report, 11.6.45, quoted in Brown, p. 156.
25   PRO AIR 2/6947, quoted in Brown, p. 159.
26   Bozděch tapes.
27   Vojenský historický archiv (Army Historical Archive).
28   Aberdeenshire Air Training Corps document, undated.
29   PRO AIR 27/1690.
30   Bozděch papers.

Chapter Eight

1   Bozděch manuscript.
2   PRO AIR 2/6947 quoted in Brown, p. 153.
3   Archiv Ministerstva vnitra Česke Republiky (Archive of Czech Ministry of Home Affairs).
4   A. Brown, Ph D thesis.
5   Arnošt Polak interview.
6   Pamela Schutzmann interview.
7   Iveta Irvingová, p. 294.
8   Bozděch papers.
9   E. Muir, *An Autobiography* (Edinburgh, Cannongate 1993), p. 254.
10   J. Korbel, *The Communist Subversion of Czechoslovakia*, p. 155.
11   Arnošt Polak interview.
12   Bozděch manuscript.
13   Tom Oddie interview.
14   National Library Prague.
15   V.R. Bozděch, *Gentlemeni Soumraku (Gentlemen of the Dusk)*.
16   Ibid., unpaginated.
17   Ibid.

18 Ibid.
19 Ibid., p.16; original, Hansard, 13 May 1940, col. 1502.
20 Ibid., p. 26.
21 Ibid., pp. 26-7.
22 Ibid., pp. 26-7.
23 J. Korbel, *The Communist Subversion of Czechoslovakia*, p. 42.
24 Ibid., pp. 43-4.
25 Václav R. Bozděch, *Souboj s osudem* (*Fighting with Fate*).
26 E.R. Mayhew, *The Reconstruction of Warriors: Archibald McIndoe, the Royal Air Force and the Guinea Pig Club* (London, Greenhill Books, 2004), p. 78.
27 Bozděch papers.
28 I. Herben in *Le Figaro*, 12 August 1948, quoted in Korbel, *The Communist Subversion of Czechoslovakia*, p. 183.
29 B. Lockhart, *Jan Masaryk*, pp. 51-2.
30 Z. Zeman, *The Masaryks: The Making of Czechoslovakia* (London, Weidenfeld and Nicolson, 1976), p. 212.
31 Bozděch manuscript.
32 Ibid.
33 Pamela Schutzmann interview.
34 B. Lockhart, *Jan Masaryk*, pp. 74-5.
35 Bozděch manuscript.
36 Korbel, *The Communist Subversion of Czechoslovakia*, p. 7.
37 Muir, *An Autobiography*, p. 268.
38 Bozděch manuscript.
39 Pamela Schutzmann interview.
40 Archiv Ministerstva vnitra Česke Republiky (Archive of Czech Ministry of Home Affairs).
41 Pamela Schutzmann interview.
42 Ibid.
43 Ibid.
44 Ibid.

Chapter Nine
1   Bozděch manuscript.
2   Bozděch papers.
3   Ibid.
4   Ibid.
5   Ibid.
6   Ibid.
7   Bozděch manuscript.
8   Bozděch papers.
9   J. Korbel, *The Communist Subversion of Czechoslovakia*, p. 162
10 Bozděch papers.
11 Ibid.
12 Ibid.
13 PRO AIR 2/10739, in Brown p. 170.
14 Bozděch tapes.
15 Ibid.

16 Ibid.
17 Ibid.
18 Bozděch papers.
19 M. Kerner, 'General Ludvik Svoboda: Czechoslovak Patriot or Communist Collaborator', in White, L.W. (ed.) *On All Fronts: Czechs and Slovaks in World War II* (East European Monographs, No. CCCXIX, Boulder: distributed by Columbia University Press, New York, 1991), p. 232.
20 Ibid., p. 237.
21 Bozděch tapes.
22 RAF Personnel Management Agency.
23 Bozděch tapes.
24 RAF Personnel Management Agency.
25 Bozděch tapes.

Chapter Ten
1 RAF Personnel Management Agency.
2 Bozděch tapes.
3 RAF Personnel Management Agency.
4 Air Historical Branch, (RAF) Ministry of Defence.
5 Bozděch tapes.
6 Ibid.
7 RAF Personnel Management Agency.
8 Bozděch tapes.
9 Ibid.
10 Ibid.
11 RAF Personnel Management Agency.
12 Bozděch tapes.
13 Ibid.
14 Bozděch manuscript.
15 Bozděch tapes.
16 Ibid.
17 Bozděch manuscript.
18 Ibid.
19 Air Historical Branch, (RAF) Ministry of Defence.
20 Bozděch manuscript.
21 Bozděch papers.
22 *Sunday Express*, 30 January 1949.
23 Pamela Schutzmann interview.
24 D. Fraser, *Knight's Cross: A Life of Field Marshal Erwin Rommel* (London, HarperCollins, 1994), p. 275.
25 *The Animal Magazine: the Official Journal of the People's Dispensary for Sick Animals* (April 1949).
26 Bozděch manuscript.
27 Tom Oddie interview.
28 Bozděch papers.
29 Ibid.
30 RAF Personnel Management Agency.
31 Bozděch manuscript.

32 RAF Personnel Management Agency.

33 Ibid.

34 Ibid.

35 Ibid.

36 Bozděch papers.

37 RAF Personnel Management Agency.

38 Bozděch manuscript.

39 Bozděch, *Gentlemeni Soumraku (Gentlemen of the Dusk)*, p. 107.

40 Ibid., 107.

41 Bozděch manuscript.

42 Ibid.

43 Ibid.

44 Ibid.

Chapter Eleven

1 Jan Bozděch interview.

2 M. Kundera, *The Book of Laughter and Forgetting* (Hammondsworth, Middlesex, Penguin Books, 1986), p. 3.

3 J. Korbel, *The Communist Subversion of Czechoslovakia*, p. 27.

4 Ibid., p. 17.

5 Jan Bozděch interview.

6 Ibid.

7 J.F.N. Bradley, *The Czechoslovak Legion in Russia, 1914-1920* (Boulder, East European Monographs, Distributed by Columbia University Press, New York, 1991), p. 1.

8 Jan Bozděch interview.

9 David Vaughan, 'The Battle of the Airways: the extraordinary story of Czechoslovak Radio and the 1945 Prague Uprising'. Radio Prague, http: //www. Radio.cz/en/ article 40469.

10 Ibid.

11 Bozděch papers.

12 Pamela Schutzmann interview.

13 Ibid.

14 Bozděch papers.

15 Jan Bozděch interview.

16 Bozděch papers.

17 Arnošt Polak interview.

18 Jan Bozděch interview.

19 Iveta Irvingová interview.

20 Jan Bozděch interview.

21 Ibid.

22 Ibid.

23 Jři Malik interview.

24 J. Korbel, *The Communist Subversion of Czechoslovakia*, p. 6.

25 D. Sayer, *The Coasts of Bohemia: A Czech History* (Princeton, New Jersey, Princeton University Press, 1998), p. 259.

26 Jan Bozděch interview.

Chapter Twelve

1 RAF Personnel Management Agency.
2 Bozděch papers.
3 Ibid.
4 Ibid.
5 Ibid.
6 RAF Personnel Management Agency.
7 Ibid.
8 Bozděch Flying Log Book.
9 Bozděch papers.
10 Bozděch Flying Log Book.
11 Bozděch papers.
12 *Scottish Sunday Express*, 11 December 1955.
13 Bozděch papers.
14 *Scottish Sunday Express*, 25 December 1955.
15 Bozděch papers.
16 Bozděch Flying Log Book.
17 Ibid.
18 K. Kyle, 'Setting the Scene', in *The Proceedings of the Royal Air Force Historical Society* No. 3 (January 1988), p. 10.
19 RAF Personnel Management Agency.
20 D. Smallwood, 'The Planners' Perspective', in *The Proceedings of the Royal Air Force Historical Society* No. 3 (January 1988), p. 30.
21 Bozděch Flying Log Book.
22 RAF Personnel Management Agency.
23 Jan Bozděch interview.
24 Bozděch papers.
25 Ibid.
26 Ibid.
27 Ibid.
28 RAF Historical Branch.
29 RAF Personnel Management Agency.
30 Bozděch papers.
31 Ibid.
32 Ibid.
33 Bozděch manuscript.
34 A. Richardson, *One Man and His Dog* (London, George Harrap, 1960), p. 245.
35 Bozděch manuscript.
36 Richardson, *One Man and His Dog*, pp. 244-5.
37 Bozděch manuscript.
38 Richardson, *One Man and His Dog*, p. 162.
39 Bozděch papers.
40 RAF Personnel Management Agency.
41 Jan Bozděch interview.
42 Bozděch papers.
43 Ibid.
44 Pamela Schutzmann interview.
45 Bozděch papers.

46 Ibid.
47 RAF Personnel Management Agency.

Chapter Thirteen
1   *Daily Express*, March 21, 1968.
2   Mlynař, Z., *Night Frost in Prague: The End of Humane Socialism* (London: C. Hurst & Co, 1980), pp. 122-3.
3   Jan Bozděch interview.
4   Bozděch papers.
5   Ibid.
6   Ibid.
7   Jiři Malik interview.
8   Jan Bozděch interview.
9   Ibid.
10 Bozděch papers.
11 Ibid.
12 *The Guardian*, April 26, 2004.
13 Bozděch papers.
14 Ibid.
15 *The People*, Sunday 15 February, 1970.
16 Magdalena Jarvis interview.
17 Ibid.
18 Ibid.

Chapter Fourteen
1   Iveta Irvingová interview.
2   Jan Bozděch interview.
3   Ibid.
4   Václav Havel, *Towards a Civil Society: Selected Speeches and Writings 1990-1994* (Prague, Lidové Noviny Publishing House Ltd., 1995), p. 31.
5   Alistair Cooke, *Letter from America 1946-2004* (London, Allen Lane, 2004), p. 334.
6   Havel, *Towards a Civil Society*, p. 16.
7   *Daily Telegraph*, Tuesday 3 May 1994.
8   *Daily Mail*, 9 May, 1994.
9   Fox Research Library.
10 Bozděch papers.
11 Ibid.
12 Ibid.
13 Ibid.
14 Rob Cameron, 'Police close case on 1948 death of Jan Masaryk – murder, not suicide'. Radio Prague, http:// www. radio.cz/en/article/ 49113.
15 Edvard Beneš, *My War Memoirs*, p. 372.
16 Arnošt Polak interview.
17 Pamela Schutzmann interview.
18 Magdalena Jarvis interview.

Bibliography

Air Ministry. *Bomber Command Continues: The Air Ministry Account of the Rising Offensive against Germany July 1941-June 1942*. London: HMSO, 1942.

The Animal Magazine: the Official Journal of the People's Dispensary for Sick Animals (April 1949).

Archiv Ministerstva vnitra Česke Republiky (Archive of Czech Ministry of Home Affairs).

Ash, Marinell. *This Noble Harbour: A History of the Cromarty Firth* (eds. Macaulay, J. & Mackay, A. M.) Edinburgh: Cromarty Firth Port Authority in association with John Donald Publishers Ltd., 1991.

Bates, H. E. *Fair Stood the Wind for France*. London: Longman Group Ltd., 1971 edn.

Beneš, Edvard. *My War Memoirs*. London: George Allen & Unwin Ltd., 1928.

Bozděch, V. R. *Bombardéry Utoei (Bombers Attack)*. Prague: Magnet Press, 1993 edn.

——, *Gentlemeni Soumraku (Gentlemen of the Dusk)*. Prague: Mladá Fronta, 1947.

——, *Nepřítel v dohledu (Enemy in Sight)*. Prague: Toužimský a Moravec, 1947.

——, *Souboj s osudem (Fighting with Fate)*. Prague: Toužimský a Moravec, 1995 edn.

——, Manuscript.

——, Papers.

——, Tapes.

Bradley, J. N. *The Czechoslovak Legion in Russia, 1914-1920*. Boulder: East European Monographs, Distributed by Columbia University Press, New York, 1991.

Brown, A. *Airmen in Exile: The Allied Air Forces in the Second World War*. Stroud: Sutton Publishing, 2000.

——, Ph D thesis, www.ssci.freeserve.co.uk/airmen.

Bulgakov, Mikhail. *The Heart of a Dog*. London: The Harvill Press, 1999.

Cameron, Rob. 'Police close case on 1948 death of Jan Masaryk – murder, not suicide'. Radio Prague, http:// www. radio.cz/en/article/ 49113.

Churchill, W. S. *The Second World War: Volume VI Triumph and Tragedy.* London: Penguin, 2005 edn.

Cooke, Alistair. *Letter from America 1946-2004.* London: Allen Lane, 2004.

Coren, Stanley. *How Dogs Think: What the World Looks Like to Them and Why They Act the Way They Do.* New York: Free Press, 2004.

Dowling, Maria. *Czechoslovakia.* London: Arnold, 2002.

Fox Research Library.

Fraser, D. *Knight's Cross: A Life of Erwin Rommel.* London: HarperCollins, 1994.

Gellner, J. 'A Stint with the 311th (Czechoslovak) Squadron, Royal Air Force'. In *On All Fronts: Czechs and Slovaks in World War II*, edited by White, L. W., East European Monographs, No. CCCXIX, 103-107, Boulder: distributed by Columbia University Press, New York, 1991.

Goulter, C. J. M. *A Forgotten Offensive: Royal Air Force Coastal Command's Anti-Shipping Campaign, 1940-1945.* London: Frank Cass, 1995.

Grinker, R. R. & Spiegel, J. P. *Men Under Stress.* Philadelphia: Blakiston, 1945.

Hansard, 5 October 1938, cols. 360-367.

Havel, Václav. *Towards a Civil Society: Selected Speeches and Writings 1990-1994.* Prague: Lidové Noviny Publishing House Ltd., 1995.

Henderson, N. *Failure of a Mission: Berlin 1937-1939.* London: Hodder and Stoughton Ltd., 1940.

Hurt, Zdeněk. *Czechs in the RAF.* Walton on Thames: Red Kite, 2004.

Irvingová, Iveta. *Vlčák Ant: Hrdinný Letec RAF (Alsatian Antis: Heroic RAF Flyer).* Prague: Otakar II, 2000.

Jewish Virtual Library, http:// www. Jewishvirtuallibrary. Org/jsource/ Holocaust/ IMTCzech html.

Kerner, M. 'General Ludvik Svoboda: Czechoslovak Patriot or Communist Collaborator'. In *On All Fronts: Czechs and Slovaks in World War II*, edited by White, L. W. East European Monographs, No. CCCXIX, 231- 244, Boulder: distributed by Columbia University Press, New York, 1991.

Kobak, A. *Joe's War: My Father Decoded.* London: Virago Press, 2004.

Korbel, Josef. *The Communist Subversion of Czechoslovakia 1938-1948: The Failure of Coexistence.* Princeton, New Jersey: Princeton University Press, 1959.

Kundera, Milan. *Life is Elsewhere.* London: Faber and Faber, 1986.

——, *The Book of Laughter and Forgetting.* Hammondsworth, Middlesex: Penguin Books, 1986.

Kusin, V.V. *From Dubček to Charter 77: A Study of 'Normalisation' in Czechoslovakia 1968-1978.* Edinburgh: Q Press Ltd., 1978.

Lambert, Andrew. 'Setting the Scene, 1917-42', in *Royal Air Force Historical*

Society (incorporating the Proceedings of the Bomber Command Association's 60th Anniversary Symposium) Journal 31 (2004): 85-96.

Liškutín, M. A. 'The Czechoslovak Air Force in War'. In *On All Fronts: Czechs and Slovaks in World War II*, edited by White, L. W. East European Monographs, No. CCCXIX, 125-142, Boulder: distributed by Columbia University Press, New York, 1991.

Lockhart, R. H. B. *Jan Masaryk: A Personal Memoir*. London: Putnam, 1956 edn.

Mamatey, V. S. and Luža, R. eds. *A History of the Czechoslovak Republic 1918-1948*. Princeton, New Jersey: Princeton University Press, 1973.

Mayhew, E. R. *The Reconstruction of Warriors: Archibald McIndoe, the Royal Air Force and the Guinea Pig Club*. London: Greenhill Books, 2004.

Mercer, C. *Legion of Strangers*. New York: Holt, Rinehart and Winston, 1964.

Mlynář, Z. *Night Frost in Prague: The End of Humane Socialism*. London: C. Hurst & Co., 1980.

Muir, Edwin. *An Autobiography*. Edinburgh: Cannongate, 1993 edn.

National Archives (PRO) AIR 27/1686.

National Archives (PRO) AIR 27/1690.

Němec, H. 'Remembering the 311th (Czechoslovak) Squadron, within the RAF Bomber Command (August 1940-June 1942)'. In *On All Fronts: Czechs and Slovaks in World War II*, edited by White, L. W. East European Monographs, No. CCCXIX, 109-123, Boulder: distributed by Columbia University Press, New York, 1991.

Polišenský, Josef, V. *History of Czechoslovakia in Outline*. Prague: Bohemia International, 1991 edn.

Richardson, Anthony. *One Man and His Dog*. London: George Harrap, 1960.

Ripka, H. *Le Coup de Prague*, Paris: Plon, 1949.

Sayer, D. *The Coasts of Bohemia: A Czech History*. Princeton, New Jersey: Princeton University Press, 1998.

Shirer, William L. *Berlin Diary: The Journal of a Foreign Correspondent 1934-1941*. New York: Tess Press, 2004 edn.

——, *The Rise and Fall of the Third Reich: A History of Nazi Germany*. New York: Nationwide Book Service, by arrangement with Secker and Warburg 1980 edn.

Sterling, Claire. *The Masaryk Case*. London: Harper Row, 1969.

Vančata, Pavel. *Klikař Roger (Lucky Boy Roger)*. Prague: Nakladatelství Ostrov, 2004.

Vaughan, David. 'The Battle of the Airways: the extraordinary story of Czechoslovak Radio and the 1945 Prague Uprising'. Radio Prague, http:// www. Radio.cz/en/ article 40469.

Vojenský historický archiv (Army Historical Archive).

Wallace, W. V. *Czechoslovakia*. Boulder, Colorado: Westview Press, 1976.

Werth, A. *The Twilight of France: 1933-1940*. London: Hamish Hamilton, 1942.

White, L. W. ed. *On All Fronts: Czechs and Slovaks in World War II*. East European Monographs, No. CCCXIX, Boulder: distributed by Columbia University Press, New York, 1991.

Zeman, Z. *The Masaryks: The Making of Czechoslovakia*. London: Weidenfeld and Nicolson, 1976.

Index

Agde, 25, 28–29
Air Ambulance Unit, 134
Air Transport Auxiliary, 49
Albrecht, Joska, 26, 38
Alexandria, 168
Algeria, 23–24, 30
Amiens, 76, 103–104
Animal Cemetery Ilford, 6, 147
Animal Sanatorium, 146–147
Animals in War (book by Jilly Cooper), 199
Antis,
  becomes Bozděch's dog in France, 5, 25
  flies with him on short flights, 27
  taken with him after Fall of France, 29–32
  brought into UK evading quarantine, 32
  takes part in search and rescue during
    blitz, 40–42
  trapped for days in a bomb crater, 43–44
  stows away on Wellington bomber to be
    with Bozděch, 53
  fitted with oxygen mask flies on
    operational sorties, viii, 4, 54
  wounded by enemy fire, 4, 61–64,
  his fate decided by a court for having
    chased sheep, 68
  has ideal life for a dog at RAF Evanton,
    66–75
  becomes mascot of 311 Squadron for
    second time, 79–88
  after war brought by Bozděch to Prague,
    91
  officially recognised as a military dog,
    93–94
  accompanies him when he escapes in
    1948, viii, 110–131
  in quarantine in UK suffers separation
    distress, 134–138
  awarded the Dickin Medal, 139–141
  final years on RAF stations, 143–146
  buried at the Animal Cemetery Ilford,
    146–147
  memorabilia of his wartime service
    displayed at Imperial War Museum,
    199

  his Dickin Medal auctioned by Sotheby's,
    201–202
Appapa (transport ship), 30
Aqaba, Gulf of, 167
Ardennes, 26
Armstrong Whitworth Whitley, 69
Austin Seven, 82
Australia, 129, 165
Austria, 13, 15–16, 96
Austro-Hungarian Empire, 4, 9–12
Avro Anson, 70

Bahrain, 169
Bajer, Jaromír, 81–82
Battle of Britain, viii, 39
Bavaria, 113
BBC, 3, 39, 64, 82, 93, 166, 171, 183
Beaverbrook, Lord, 163
Belgium, 28, 183
Belgrade, 94
Beinn a Bhuird, 86–87
Ben Wyvis, 66
Beneš, Edvard, President (of
    Czechoslovakia), 5, 9–10, 13, 16–20, 22,
    28, 35–36, 38–39, 47, 56–57, 60, 78–80,
    83, 87, 96, 98–99, 104–107, 128, 157,
    203–204
Beneš, WO, 84
Benešová, Hana (wife of the President), 5,
    103
Beránek, Jaroslav, vii–ix
Berchtesgaden, 17
Berlin, 51, 65
Béziers, 29
Blackburn Botha, 69, 72
Bloch MB–200, 14
Blois, 28–29
Bohemia, 9, 11–12, 15, 19–21, 66, 113, 182,
    194
Bombers Attack (*Bombardery Utoei*) (book by
    VR Bozděch), 97, 203
Bordeaux, 28
Boulton Paul Defiant (aircraft), 38, 40

Bozděch, Jan (son of VR and Tatiana), ix, 104, 108, 148, 150, 152, 154–157, 185, 190, 199, 203, 205
Bozděch, Jiři (father of VR), 11, 92–93, 157
Bozděch, Magdalena (daughter of VR and Maureen), ix, 183, 194, 196, 205
Bozděch, Maureen (née Parker, wife of VR), 7, 180–181, 183, 186–187, 194–196, 198–199, 202–203
Bozděch, Nina (daughter of VR and Maureen), 183, 194
Bozděch, Robert (son of VR and Maureen), 183, 196, 199
Bozděch, Václav, Robert (VR),
  his early training, 12–14
  makes career in CAF, 14
  flees country after entry of German troops, 4, 20–22
  joins French Foreign Legion, 4–5, 23–25
  transfers to French Air Force, 5, 25–31
  acquires Antis, 5, 25
  serves as air gunner in battle of France, 5, 27
  escapes after Fall of France, 5, 28–32
  smuggles Antis into UK, 5, 32
  posted to No. 312 Fighter Squadron, 38–44
  transfers to No. 311 Bomber Squadron, 45–65
  takes Antis on operational sorties, 54–64
  does a stint with Training Command, 66–77
  second tour of duty with No. 311 Squadron, 79–88
  returns to homeland after the war, taking Antis, 91
  posted to the Defence Ministry, 94
  marries and has a son, 95–97
  writes about the air war, 5, 97–104
  Jan Masaryk is godfather to his son, 104
  flees country taking Antis after communist coup, 6, 110
  spends two months in refugee camps in Germany, 122–129
  rejoins RAF, 130
  while he is hospitalised his dog loses will to live, 134
  transferred to be nearer Antis, 134–135
  avoids personal publicity when Antis decorated with Dickin Medal, 139–141
  RAF postings ensure the pair are not separated again, 142–146
  takes Antis on their last journey together, 146–147
  in Czechoslovakia his wife forced to divorce him, 153–154
  decides to write the story of Antis, 161
  has a short version published in newspaper, 164–165
  works on extending story to book length, 165–171
  serving in Transport Command tries to keep in contact with his family, 168–170
  serves in Suez campaign, 167–168
  book based on his MS published, 8, 176
  film rights bought by Twentieth Century Fox, 176–178
  meets film producer Darryl F Zanuck, 178
  leaves RAF, remarries and raises a family, 180–181
  becomes successful entrepreneur, 183–196
  rehabilitated by Military Prosecutor in Czechoslovakia, 187–189
  refused visitor's visa to Czechoslovakia, 190–192
  after fall of communism posthumously promoted to rank of Col in CAF, 7, 198, 201
Bozděchová, Anna (sister of VR), 11
Bozděchová, Magdalena (mother of VR), 5, 92–93, 157
Bozděchová, Maria (sister of VR), 11, 93, 191–192
Bozděchová, Pavla (sister of VR), 11, 93, 189, 191–192
Bozděchová, Tatiana (née Zilka, wife of VR, 1946–48), 94, 104, 108–110, 115, 133, 142, 148, 152–154, 156
Bremen, 50, 54, 61, 128
Brest, 50, 52, 57, 61, 65
Bristol Beaufort, 74
Britain, 11, 15–16, 39
British Air Ministry, 6, 37, 51, 71, 75–76, 122, 129–131, 133, 138, 164, 202
British Council, 37, 95–96, 107
British Embassy, Prague, 104, 109, 152, 188, 194
British Home Office, 143
British Ministry of Agriculture, 130
British Movietone News, 64
Brno, 108
Browning Mk 2, 69
Budapest, 168
Busina, Capt Emil, 30

Calais, 21, 27, 50
Camps, Prof Francis, 195
Canada, 52, 169
  Royal Canadian Air Force, 52
Čap, Mírek, 39–40
Čapka, Josef, 50, 52, 56, 63
Carlé, Erwin, 24

Casablanca, 30
Cauzaux, 26
Cecelia 1598 C (Wellington bomber), 50–64
Červené Pečky, 155–156
Česka Kubice, 113
Chamberlain, Neville, 17–19, 203
Charles University, 107
Chartres, 25
Chateauroux, 25, 27
Chatterton, Ken, 75
Cherbourg, 58
Chicago, 20; International Civil Aviation
    Conference of, 78
Cholmondeley, vii–viii, 35–36
Chrast, Pamela (Schutzmann), 95, 108–110,
    125–127, 139, 152–153, 179, 204
Chrast, Vivian (son of Pamela and Vlasta),
    109, 127, 179
Chrast, Col Vlastimil (Vlasta) (Wg Cdr), 95,
    108–110, 125–127, 152–153, 179, 204
Churchill, Winston, ix, 19, 26, 39, 83–84, 86,
    100, 200
Churchill, Winston (grandson of wartime
    prime minister), ix
Cidonia (transport ship), 30
Civic Forum, 200
Civil Defence, 41
Clacton, 64
Clementis, Vladimir, 149
Cnoc Fyrish, 66, 73
Cologne (Köln), 53, 61, 65
Communist Party of Czechoslovakia viii,
    96–97, 102, 104–105, 119–120, 128,
    149–150, 153, 183; of Soviet Union, 13,
    149, 199–200
Cooke, Alistair, 200
Cooper, Jilly, 199
Copal, Gustav, 38, 50, 94–95, 184
Cowbridge, 68
Cromarty Firth, 66, 73
Cupak, Vladimir, 67–68
Cyprus, 167–168
Czech Legions, 10, 13, 36–37, 88, 148–149,
    152, 204
Czech People's Party, 9
Czech Republic, 3, 7, 203–204
    Archive of Ministry of Home Affairs, 7
    Military Archive, 7
    Office for Documentation of Crimes of
        Communism, 203
Czechoslovak Air Force (CAF), pre-war, 14,
    23–24, Tomas Masaryk 1st Air
    Regiment, 14; incorporated into RAF,
    36–93; postwar, 85–86, 93–110, 193,
    198, 201
Czechoslovak Air Force Association Free,
    70, 154
Czechoslovak Airlines, 78, 93–94

Czechoslovak Army Brigade, vii, 36, 87
Czechoslovak Embassy London, 7, 190–192
Czechoslovak Inspectorate, 37, 74–76, 92,
    95, 139, 202
Czechoslovak Medal for Valour, 5, 51, 65
Czechoslovak Ministries
    Agriculture, 119–120
    Defence, 5–6, 94–111, 165, 199
    Food, 128
    Foreign Affairs, 5, 105–106, 156, 176
    Interior, 97, 105, 187–189
Czechoslovak National Assembly, 105, 120
Czechoslovak National Committee, 35
Czechoslovak National Council, 9, 84–85
Czechoslovak National Land Fund,
    119–120
Czechoslovak Provisional Government in
    Exile, 36, 39, 56, 60
Czechoslovak Radio, 17, 84, 150–151, 166,
    194
Czechoslovak War Cross, 5, 52, 61
Czechoslovakia, 9, 11, 13, 15, 18–20, 39,
    60–61, 78, 83, 87, 94, 112, 148–158,
    161–162, 167, 170–173, 176, 179,
    183–184, 198–201

Daily Express, 172, 184
Daily Mail, 201
Daily Telegraph, 201
Dakota aircraft, 6, 142
Danube river, 123
Danzig, 13
Dark Blue World (film directed by
    Jan Sverák), 155
Darmstadt, 124
Davenport, Marcia, 106
Decastello, Lt, 21
Delbos, Yvon, 14–15
Dickin Medal ('the Animal Victoria Cross'),
    ix, 3–4, 61, 139–141, 143, 199, 201
Dieburg, 124–129, 139
Dingwall, 70–72
Distinguished Flying Cross (DFC), 57
Dornier 217, 43–44
Dornoch Firth, 79
Drtina, Prokop, 80, 105
Dubček, Alexander, 183–185, 200
Duff Cooper, Sheila, 96
Dunkirk, 27, 50, 52
Dusseldorf, 53

Earls Court London, 140–141
Eden, Anthony, 60–61
Egypt, 167–168
Eisenhower, Gen Dwight, 83–84
Elgin, 87
Enemy in Sight (Nepřitel v Dohledu) (book by
    VR Bozděch), 97

Essen, 58, 61
European Union, 203
Exeter, 183

Fialka, Bunty (wife of Karel), 82
Fialka, Karel, 82
Fieldfare, HMS (Royal Naval Air Station), 66
Fighting with Fate (Souboj s Osudem) (book by VR Bozděch), 97, 102–103, 185, 202–203
France, vii, 9, 11, 13, 15–16, 18, 21–30, 35, 74, 99, 165, 167, 183
Frankfurt Am Main, 94, 130, 132
František, Sgt Josef, viii
French Air Force (l'Armée de l'air), 25, 142 112 Bataillon; BC 11/8, 27
French Foreign Legion, 23–25, 28, 30, 142
French Resistance movement, 58,103–104
Furth Im Wald, 113, 121

Gamil airfield, 168
Gellner, Jan, 52, 57–58, 62, 65
Gentlemen of the Dusk (Gentlemeni Soumraku) (book by VR Bozděch), 8, 58–60, 62, 97–98, 144, 185
George Harrap Publishers, 171
German Sudeten Party, 16
Germany, 11–13, 16–20, 23–24, 60, 78, 85; West Germany, 6, 112–113, 150, 162
Gestapo, 5, 20–21, 42, 76, 91–92, 94, 103
Gib-el-Dersa (Egyptian ship), 30
Gibraltar, 30–31, 74
Gneisenau (German battle cruiser), 65
Godesberg, 18
Goose Bay, 169
Gorbachev, Mikhail (1st Secretary Central Committee), 199–200
Gottwald, Klement, 96, 102, 104–105, 148–149, 157
Gruden, Sgt, 50, 56–57
Guinea Pig Club, 102

Hacha, Emile (successor President to Beneš 1938–9), 19
Hackbridge kennels, 133–138, 174
Hague, 94, 130–131
Hajek, Jaroslav, 154, 204
Hamburg, 61, 128
Hamm, 53–54, 101
Hanover, 61, 128
Harwich, 130–131
Hastings 476, Handley Page, 163, 167–168
Havel, Václav (President of Czechoslovakia 1989–92; Czech Republic 1993–2003), 200–201
Henderson, Nevile, 16–17
Henlein, Conrad, 16, 18

High Military Prosecutor: Prague, 6, 152, 186; Příbram, 187–189, 191–192
Hitler, Adolf, Chancellor and Fuehrer, 13, 15–17, 19–20, 57, 102
Hlobil, Capt, 30
Holden, William, 178
Holland, 55, 130, 183
Hollywood, 64, 176
Holub, Václav, 128
Hong Kong, 170
Hospitals: Innsworth, 134; Norwich, 175 Military Rehabilitation Units; Chessington, 135–138 Collaton Cross, 134–135
House of Commons, 18–19, 60–61
Hrubý, Karel, 21, 92
Hughes, Corp, 131, 133
Hungary, 96, 168 Hungarian Rising the, 168
Hus, Jan, 184
Husak, Gustav, 185

Idris, 167
Imperial War Museum, 199
Indian Army, 87
International Refugee Organisation (IRO), 122, 124
Inverness, 66, 69, 146, 182
Irvingová, Iveta, 155, 204
Israel, 167
Italy, 9, 165

Jagger, Dean, 144
Jamaica, 165
Janoušek, Gen Karel, (Air Vice Marshal), 37, 50, 56, 76, 78, 80, 85–86, 91–92, 95, 108, 125–126, 138–139, 152
Japan, 183
Jicha, Václav, 42–43
Jodl, Gen Alfred, 15
Joseph, Emperor Franz, 9

Kacíř, PO, 50, 56
Kaplan, František, vii
Karlovy Vary (Karlsbad), 83, 154
Kent, Duke of, 57
Kerner, Miroslav, 128
Khrushchev, Nikita (1st Secretary Soviet Communist Party), 157, 169
Kiel, 61, 65
Klatovy, 92
Kolin, 155
Kollar, Sgt J, 184
Konrad, Dr, 191
Korda, Václav, 52, 57
Kordina, Zdenek, 28
Krakov, 21
Kraliček, Franta, 113

Kundera, Milan, 148–149
Kust, Václav, 21
Kyjov, 92

Lančik, PO, 50, 56–57
Laurie, John, 164–165, 172–173
League of Nations, 13
Ledstone, 183
Lenin, Nikolai, 149
Les Presses de la Cité, 178–179
Liberator B24, 79–91, 193
Libya, 167
Lincoln, Abraham, 200
Liškutín, Mira, 25, 36
Liverpool, 35, 39–40, 42, 87, 201
Lockhart, Bruce, 35–36, 39, 60, 105–106
Lockheed company, 40, 43
London, 9, 17–18, 26, 28, 94, 146
Luftwaffe, 27–28, 79–80

Macal, Zdenek, 151
MacRobert, Lady, 49
McIndoe, Archibald, 92–93, 102
Malaysia, 165
Male Bronowice, 21
Malik, Jiři, 157, 189
Mannheim, 52, 61–64
Mark of Courage The (newspaper
    serialisation by John Laurie), 164–165,
    177
Maron, 25
Marshall Plan, 104
Marsom, Gp Capt John, 76
Masaryk, Jan, 5, 7, 19, 39, 56, 60, 79, 83, 95,
    104–106, 108, 157, 165, 175, 195–196, 203
Masaryk, Tomaš Garrigue (founder and 1st
    President of Czechoslovakia), 9–11, 13,
    96, 105, 131, 157, 203
Masaryk Case The (book by Claire Sterling),
    195–196
Melnik, Dr, 190
Menšik, Josef, 74, 144–145
Meonia (merchant ship), 30
Merklin, 11, 21
Merseyside, 31–32, 42–43
Messerschmitt ME 109, 121
Military Institute, Prague, ix
Mlynař, Zdenek, 184–185
Montpellier, 29
Moravia, 5, 9, 12, 15, 20–21, 42, 92
Moray Firth, 143
Morocco, 30
Moscow, 79, 102, 104
Mosquito bomber, 103
Moulins, 29
Muir, Edwin, 95–96
Munich, vii, 19–20, 60–61, 96
Munro, Sir Hector, 73

Munster, 61

NAAFI (Navy, Army and Air Force
    Institute), 43–44, 64–65
Nagy, Imre, 168
Nairobi, 169
Náprstek, Col (CAF), 108
Nasser, Col Gamal Abdel, 167
NATO (North Atlantic Treaty
    Organisation), 168, 199
Němec, Herbert, 47–48
Neuralia (transport ship), 31–32
Nevers, 29
New Zealand, 165
Nichols, Sir Philip, 83
Nicosia, 167–168
Nîmes, 29
Normandy, 77, 79
North Star (weekly newspaper), 71
Northmoor (former collier), 31
Norway, 79–80, 193
Norwich, 54
Novar estate, 73
Novotny, Antonin, 183
Nuremberg, 17–18

Ocelka, Wg Cdr Josef, 50–51, 57, 64
Oddie, Tom, 69–76, 97, 141, 202
One Man and His Dog (book by Anthony
    Richardson), 173, 183
Opera Mundi (magazine), 165, 177
Oran, 23, 30
Orkney Islands, 80
Ostrava, 21
Oxford aircraft, 80, 87

Palace Hotel Prague, 93–94
Paris, 9, 26–28, 94
Patton, Gen George, 5, 84–85, 96, 105, 151
Pau, 25
People (newspaper), 195
People's Dispensary for Sick Animals,
    (PDSA), ix, 138–141, 146–147, 170–171
Pétain, Marshal Henri Philippe, 28
Philip, Prince, 192–193
Philips electrical company, 166
Pickard, Gp Capt Charles, 49, 51, 64–65, 68,
    76, 103–104, 194
Pilsen, 12, 83–84, 92, 96
Plymouth, 134
Polak, Lt Col Arnošt, 70, 72, 80–82, 94, 97,
    154, 204
Poland, vii, 13, 20–21, 25, 35, 112, 193, 200
Port-Vendres, 30
Prague, 5–6, 8–9, 14, 19–20, 35, 62, 83–85,
    87, 91–92, 95–96, 104–105, 111, 148–152,
    162, 202, 205
Prague Rising the, 84–85, 94, 148, 150–152

Prague Spring the, 183–185, 195, 200, 203
Preštice, 11, 125
Prinz Eugen (German battle cruiser), 50, 52, 57–58, 61
Protocol of Sèvres, 167

Readers Digest, 183
Red Army, 5, 78, 83–85, 87, 94, 96, 151
Red Cross, 71, 156, 176
Red Guard, 150
Regensburg, 122–124, 148
Rennison, Flt Sgt, 87, 193
Rennison, Jack (son of ex-Flt Sgt Rennison), 193–194
Reynaud, Paul, 28
Ribbentrop, Joachim von, 16–17
Richardson, Anthony, 171–176, 181
Richter, Maj, 126–127
Ripka, Hubert, 84
Ritz Hotel the, 178
Robertson, Robert, vii
Rommel, Field Marshal Erwin, 140
Rora Head, 80
Ross-Shire Journal, 71
Royal Air Force (RAF), vii-ix, 4–6, 39, 92
    Bomber Command, 3–4, 6, 45–65, 70, 79, 140
    Coastal Command, 79–87
    Fighter Command, 38–44
    Training Command 66–77, 87–88
        No. 2 Advanced Flying Training School, 161–162
        No. 8 Advanced Flying Training School, 143–146
        No. 7 Air Gunnery School, 69
        No. 8 Air Gunnery School, 66–74, 97, 202
        No. 240 Operational Conversion Unit, 142
        No. 242 Operational Conversion Unit, 163
        No. 1 Radio School, 76–77
        No. 4 Radio School, 139–142
        No. 14 Radio School, 86, 123
    Transport Command, 6, 156–157, 205
    Squadrons
        No. 27, 142
        No. 511, 6, 163–168
        No. 99, 168–175
        No. 311 (Czechoslovak), viii, 3, 6, 8, 38, 45–65, 76, 79–92, 95, 97–103, 140, 142, 154, 173, 184, 193–194, 204
        No. 312 (Czechoslovak), 38–44, 74
    Stations
        Cardington, 132–134, 139
        Chelveston, 67
        Coltishall, 54
        Compton Bassett, 176

Cosford, 36–38, 40
Cranwell, 76–77
Dalcross, 72, 143–146, 161, 163
Dishforth, 163
Duxford, 38–39, 57, 98
East Wretham, 6, 48–65, 101, 142, 173–175
Evanton, 66–74, 79–80, 143–145
Honington, 45–48
Innsworth, 134–138
Lyneham, 6, 163–175, 177, 202
Manston, 87–88
Millerton, 4
Netheravon, 142
North Luffenham, 142
Pembray, 75
South Cerney, 161–162
Speke, 39–44
St. Athan, 67–68, 86, 123
Swanton Morley, 74, 139–142
Tain, 79–88
Upper Heyford, 142
Uxbridge, 176–183
Wiesbaden, 130
Wilmslow, 67
    Air Historical Branch (RAF), 7
Royal Air Force Benevolent Fund, 198–199
Royal Air Force Personnel Management Agency, 7
Royal Air Force Volunteer Reserve, 37
Royal Tank Regiment, 199
Rozlet, 25, 92, 95, 157, 163, 179–180
Runciman, Lord, 17–18
Rundstedt, Gen Gerd von, 27
Russia, 9, 13, 203
Ruzyn, 91, 93–94

Sadil, Franta, 193–194
Salcombe, 182
Scharnhorst (German battle cruiser), 65
Schejbal, Wg Cdr, 57
Scottish Sunday Express, 162–165, 172, 177
Šejbl, FO, 50, 56
Sète, 30
Shirer, William, 17
Siddall, Gordon, 75
Sidi-bel-Abbès, 23–25
Silmudre, Yvette, 26
Škoda company, 14
Slvia, R, 74
Slovak Republic, 203
Slovakia, 20
Smrkovský, Josef, 84–85
Soběkury, 11–12, 21, 74, 92–93, 142, 157
Sokol movement, 12
Sotheby's, 3, 201
South Africa, 183
South Devon, 6, 182–197, 199

South Wales Echo (evening newspaper), 68
Soviet bloc, 112, 157, 169, 184–185, 190, 192–193
Soviet Union, 13, 16, 18, 54, 57, 60, 85–87, 95–96, 100–101, 104, 128, 150, 165, 167, 192–193, 199–200
Spain, 74, 183
Spaleny, 113
Speaking to my Country (collection of radio broadcasts by Jan Masaryk), 95
Spitfire, 86, 91, 103
SS (Schutzstaffel), 155
Stalin, Joseph, 13, 79, 87, 96, 102, 106, 148, 157, 161, 165, 203
  Stalinist, 4, 154, 169, 186
Stavanger, 85
Sterling, Claire, 195–196
Štětka, Václav, 32, 38–40, 42–43, 45–46, 48, 51, 173
Straubing, USAF base, 122
Straus, Prof Jiři, 203
Stromovka Park, 95, 115
Suez Canal, 6, 167–168
Sunday Express, 138–139
Sunday Mail, 71
Surrey, 133
Svatobořice, 92
Svoboda, Gen Ludvík, 95, 128, 149
Sweden, 165, 183
Swindon, 166
Switzerland, 183

Target for Tonight (film directed by Harry Watt), 51, 64–65
Thetford, 48, 138
Tierney, Flt Lt, 167
Topinka, Václav, 195
Toulouse, 28
Tours, 28
Toužimský & Moravec, 202–203

Truhlář, František (Frankie), 93, 102–103, 202–203
Truman, Harry, President (of USA), 83
Tuzex, 176
Twelve O'Clock High (film directed by Henry King), 144–145
Twentieth Century Fox, 3–4, 6, 176–178, 201

U-boat, 79–80, 84, 85
United States, 9, 11, 52, 78, 95, 168
United States Army Air Force (USAAF) (later USAF), 122
United States Zone of Occupation, 113, 121
Ursula 1516 U (Wellington bomber), 52, 65

Velvet Divorce the, 203
Velvet Revolution the, 200
Versailles, 13
Vicherek, Gen A, (CAF), 28, 91, 95, 98
Vienna, 96
Vlatava river, 83, 95

WAAF (Women's Auxiliary Air Force), 37
Warsaw Pact, 168, 184–185, 192, 199–200, 203
Washington, 11, 200–201
Watt, Harry, 51
Wavell, Field Marshal the Earl, 4, 140–141, 143, 201
Wehrmacht, 26–28
Wellington bomber, 26, 48–65
Wooton Bassett, 170
WRNS (Women's Royal Naval Service), 82

Zanuck, Darryl, F, 3–4, 6, 145, 177–178, 181, 183
Zázvůrek, Ladislav, 187–189
Zilka, Col, 94, 127–128, 149–150, 152–153
Žižkov, 150, 152